The Urge to Fly

The Urge to Fly

FROM STICK-AND-STRING TO JET AGE

Don Robertson

Foreword by Jeffrey Quill

Quiller Press
London

First published in 1996 by
Quiller Press Limited
46 Lillie Road
London SW6 1TN

Designed by Jo Lee
Printed and bound in Great Britain by
Biddles Ltd, Guildford and King's Lynn

CONTENTS

Dedicated to my wife, Ella,
who endured so much throughout
our 46 years of marriage

FOREWORD

by Jeffrey Quill

O nly 80 years after the Wright brothers made the first controlled, powered flight at Kitty Hawk, non-stop flights between London and California by aeroplanes carrying more than 300 passengers are commonplace. Military aeroplanes fly regularly at twice the speed of sound and Concorde provides a daily and luxurious passenger service across the Atlantic at this speed.

The aeroplane has introduced a completely new dimension into transport and hence into modern life and international affairs. Journeys which once took weeks or months are now completed in a day or little more. People have become mobile to an extent undreamed of at the turn of this century and, amazingly, this has all been achieved in little more than the natural lifetime of a man.

Yet there were times when, to those involved in aviation, progress often seemed slow and laborious; every inch of the way seemed a struggle against all manner of problems and frustrations – technical, operational, financial, political and human. Particularly did this apply during the early part of Don Robertson's flying life.

He learned to fly privately in 1928 and then went to Canada where he found employment in a company operating aeroplanes into the far North. It was the aeroplane which opened up those vast inhospitable snow-bound regions, carrying supplies and mail to areas hitherto accessible only by sledge and dog team. Northern Canada was, of all places, a 'natural' for aviation and this account of early pioneering commercial flights makes a fascinating and unusual tale.

Technically and operationally, World War II provided a massive stimulus to aviation. The acute urgency and background of prolonged crisis meant that problems had to be solved more or less regardless of expense and human effort.

The second part of the book describes Robertson's activities as a Fleet Air Arm pilot at sea and then as a test pilot, first at Vickers-Supermarine, where he was a most valued colleague of mine, and later at the Aeroplane and Armament Experimental Establishment at Boscombe Down. Here he was engaged in the testing of new and high performance fighter aircraft for the Royal Air Force and Royal Navy as well as armament testing. This culminated in the testing of some of the very early jet fighters so his extensive flying experience took him from the 'stick and string' days of the twenties to the dawn of the jet age.

Don Robertson was particularly well fitted both by training and temperament to be a test pilot and to be closely involved in the often abstruse and frustrating problems which beset the development of new aircraft. He was a practical engineer who loved engines and all things mechanical and who instinctively knew that before you can presume to test something you must first thoroughly understand what it has to do, how it does it, and why.

The book will awake many memories with those who flew as Don Robertson did, during the great formative years of aviation, and it cannot fail to be of great interest to those who study the amazing history of the aeroplane.

Jeffrey K Quill, OBE, AFC, FRAeS

PREFACE

O ne day in 1975 as I opened the drawer of my desk, my first Log Book fell out. To my surprise, on turning the first pages containing details of my early flying days at Brooklands and in Canada, it brought memories flooding back of dates, places, people and with every flight meticulously recorded in my pilot's Log Book, it is probably the most carefully kept record of any diary. All my other records such as photographs and cuttings had been lost in the London blitz during the second world war. It is said that when one reaches old age, the memory returns to one's childhood and this was certainly the case when I decided to write my first book.

Having lived a very active life up to that time my memories were almost entirely of the Second War years when I had been fortunate enough to meet many expatriates in the aviation world and fly a succession of new and interesting aircraft. In the armed services one is not aware who decides one's destiny but with a philosophy of doing whatever I was told without question, a stream of interesting jobs came my way for which I am eternally grateful.

Since being grounded through poor sight and high blood pressure in 1971, I had concentrated on multi-hull sailing, power boat racing and building and operating hovercraft all of which took me away from a quiet home life. However in retirement in the Isle of Wight my thoughts have returned to memories now largely of people, not of things, and I have found peace of mind. The war was, of course, a tremendous forcing ground for the development of aircraft and many books on the subject have been published. Our efforts in the late 1920s and early 1930s to establish Civil Aviation may look pathetic to the present generations but a relatively short period of time had passed since the Wright brothers had made their first controlled flight. At the time there were some who had the vision and determination to do the pioneering and I am proud to be associated with some of these men and their vision of the future Air Transportation scene as opposed to military progress in this field. Historical records are lacking of those early years and with this book I have tried to remedy that.

ACKNOWLEDGEMENTS

I should like to thank all those friends who have helped me with this book, especially Jeffrey Quill for teaching me all about test flying and for checking the Spitfire portion of the book for accuracy. I owe my thanks also to Bee MacKinnon for help on technical details of handling notes for pilots of many wartime aircraft, Buster Hallett (Captain N G Hallett RN DSC) for advice on the Naval background and Richard Muspratt (Squadron Leader) for reminiscences of test work which we carried out together at Boscombe Down.

On a visit to Canada after a period of 50 odd years I met Stan McMillon, who had recently retired after 24,000 hours flying in the North, and Tim Sims from the Wright Whirlwind Engine Company who as engineer had made the first mail flight to the Arctic coast with Wop May in 1929. They have encouraged me to continue with this work.

I have been fortunate in obtaining the assistance of Susan Darby, an editor and writer, who has re-written and re-positioned parts of the text which were out of chronological order and thereby re-directed my thoughts and memories to many long forgotten episodes from the past. Without her help and inspiration I could not have completed the book.

Richard Riding who is the editor of the magazine, *Aeroplane Monthly*, has kindly allowed me to use many original photographs from his very extensive library reaching back to the very early days of flying. Also to Charles E Brown of *Flight magazine*.

From Canadian records I am indebted to various authorities in Ottawa, Edmonton and Calgary for their permission to use their records and photographs, some of which I had taken myself.

Some early family photographs have been included to illustrate the text which describes my early interest in motorcycles and cars.

PART 1

The Urge to Fly

CHAPTER 1

A Camel on the Beach

I was playing on the broad, flat beach at Hunstanton in Norfolk, England when I heard an odd noise approaching from the sea, the sound of an engine spluttering and eventually stopping altogether. My heart began to beat faster. It was the summer of 1917 and I was nine years old.

My eyes searched the coastline which, to a small boy, seemed to stretch to the ends of the earth when suddenly, to my intense excitement, I saw the aeroplane as it appeared through the broken cloud, gliding straight towards me. The propeller was stationary and the only sound was the wind whistling in the flying-wires; it made a perfect landing, splashing through the pools of water left by the receding tide and coming to a stop only a hundred yards away. I dropped everything and ran over to see, arriving first but hesitant about going too close.

My heart was pounding as the pilot jumped down from the cockpit and walked round to the front to look at his engine, which I now saw was dripping oil. I stared up at his face, spotted with oil and half-hidden by goggles and a leather helmet which had a patch of fur on the forehead and rolls of leather protecting each ear; a long double-breasted brown leather overcoat came down below his knees giving him an air of authority. In my eyes he was a real hero to be able to fly such a thrilling machine.

It was a single-seater biplane, very rakish and with a big propeller but before I knew what was happening a small crowd had gathered and the pilot was issuing quick instructions. With a man on either side lifting the tail, we all pushed on the wings, wheeling the aeroplane backwards up the beach above the high-tide mark to the safety of dry sand.

I remember the powerful-looking engine, partly enclosed under a shining metal cowling, but above all, I remember the thrill of actually touching it and noticing how lightly built the silver wings were. Before the local policeman arrived to guard it, I managed to peer into the cockpit with its small hinged windscreen and saw the two cocking handles and the oiled breaches of guns gleaming in the sun

There was a strange smell, not only the dope, but something sickly and sweet; I plucked up the courage to ask the pilot what it was. That was how I first learned that the rotary engine of the Sopwith Camel used castor oil!

The next morning I could not wait to return to the beach so, rising early, I dressed hurriedly and ran to the beach before breakfast. I stared at the empty piece of sand with the lines of the aeroplane's wheels, the only visible evidence that it had been there. My disappointment was intense but as I gazed up at the sky the seed of ambition and determination to become a pilot had been sown within me.

That summer of 1917 was a memorable one. I was staying with my mother and my two elder brothers, Jack, 14 years old and, David, 13, in a large Victorian boarding house during the summer holidays. On several occasions we were dragged from our beds in the middle of the night and told to crouch in the cupboard under the stairs while we listened to the Zeppelins passing overhead. There was plenty of warning as they were slow fliers, their engines being heard some way off as they came in from the direction of the North Sea. No bombs were dropped on us and it was assumed that they had been using the Wash as a good navigational fix on the way to London.

Our real home was an old coaching inn on the Oxford Road in the heart of Beaconsfield, Buckinghamshire, which we rented. One evening, following our return from Hunstanton, I was in my bedroom when my mother called me. She was standing outside watching an air-raid taking place over London, the sky lit up by searchlights and pierced by anti-aircraft gun flashes. As we stood watching, one searchlight beam which had been swinging to and fro suddenly picked up a reflection from the hull of a Zeppelin. Immediately the other searchlights homed in, picking it out brilliantly against the night as a perfect target. Shortly afterwards I saw a burst of flame from the top of the Zeppelin. The fire spread rapidly forward, the nose dipped and as the craft gathered speed, diving towards the ground, the flames enveloped the whole nose, leaving the sight of the bare skeleton framework of the hull etched in my memory. As the Zeppelin disappeared behind the trees in the distance it seemed unbelievable that such an enormous craft could disintegrate totally in a few seconds. That vision has remained clearly in my memory to this day and although the instant destruction of such a large craft was spectacular I do not remember, as a child, even contemplating the fate of its occupants.

Never a close family, it had become more fragmented in 1915 when my father was wounded while making a solo reconnaissance in France. A Staff Officer in the Royal Engineers, my father had been attached to the staff of Lord Plumer who was in command of the 2nd Army deployed at the northern end of the front. While carrying out the reconnaissance my father was hit by a sniper's bullet which penetrated and shattered his thigh. It took him 24 hours to crawl back to the road where he was found lying in great pain and discomfort. He was brought back to London where he spent six weeks in the Sister Agnes Home, now the King Edward VII hospital close to Hyde Park Corner. The bones in my father's leg did not knit so the surgeon decided to insert a steel strip attaching it to the bones with wooden screws.

This was one of the first cases where metal has been left in a human body and it was to remain there for the next 35 years, until his death in 1952.

My mother decided that her place was in London with my father and I was sent, at the age of eight, to Norfolk House Preparatory School where my brother, David, had been before moving on to Rugby.

I hardly knew my father and although I was very fond of my mother I did not spend much of my childhood with her. I was born in 1908 and I seemed destined never to be as bright or intelligent as my brothers. Shortly after my birth the family moved to Kingston, Ontario where my father was a Royal Engineers Instructor at the Canadian Military College. By 1912 the entire family had relocated to Quebec City for a year and although we returned to England a year later in 1913, renting the house in Beaconsfield, it was not many months before my father was sent to fight in France.

I never came to terms with being at school, hating it from day one at Norfolk House right through my years at Rugby until I finally left abruptly due to lack of finance when my father was prematurely invalided out of the army. I do not think I would have been accepted into Rugby if it had not been for my brother, David, who was very clever; Jack had gained a scholarship to Winchester College.

I was lonely at school, not interested in learning and found the teachers uninspiring. My time was spent in drawing motor bike designs, reading books on racing cars and aircraft fighting in France. I was a shy and nervous boy and this lack of confidence made me more determined to achieve my ambition to enter the world of aviation.

My mother, having settled in London to look after my father, made arrangements for my brothers and myself to spend our school holidays with my grandmother in Earl Soham in Suffolk. She had an enormous garage which had been built to house her son's Austin racing car and her Minerva. One day a neighbour called Mr Lamotte came to the house and asked my grandmother if he could keep his car in the garage.

Mr Lamotte had arrived in the village about two years before with a huge white Mercedes in which he went off every day, reputedly to motor all over the country. My grandmother did not make a decision straight away as with a foreign name and a German car, there had been much gossip among the local population who suspected him of being a spy. He had responded however with an action for slander which put an end to the talk. In any event Mr Lamotte, probably in order to influence my grandmother in making the decision of the garage in his favour, invited me to go for a drive with him, which was a tremendous treat.

We went to Orford on the River Alde, to the starting box of the local sailing club, which overlooked a tongue of land and was within sight of the North Sea. This strip happened to be government property and was used for various aeroplane trials by the Aeroplane and Armament Experimental Station at Martlesham, which later moved to Boscombe Down.

The Mercedes, typical of the mark, had outside exhaust pipes and chain drive to the back wheels with a four seater touring body. I was thrilled with it all, especially when on our return journey we touched 60 miles an hour, no mean speed in those days. Mr Lamotte was given the use of the garage but not before an aunt who still treated him with a certain amount of suspicion, removed the powerful headlight from the Austin and put it in the attic to prevent him from using it to signal to German submarines off the East Coast. I have often wondered what became of Mr Lamotte.

My most vivid memories from my childhood were invariably involved in different forms of travel, whether by land, sea or air. I remember one afternoon at school while we were playing football, some large balloons, of the type used for artillery observation, passed overhead. They were evidently on some kind of a training exercise, probably launched from the aerodrome at Northolt.

We stopped playing, tilted our heads upwards to watch them flying freely in a light south-easterly wind when, to our delight and excitement we spotted a straggler trailing a long rope with a kind of anchor hanging down almost to ground level. It was obviously going to land but it missed our playing field and drifted into the farmer's field next door on the other side of a line of trees. Our game of football forgotten, we all rushed over through the trees and scrambled over the fence. The basket carried two men and when the anchor snagged on something, the whole outfit had pivoted downwards and hit the ground with a resounding thump, throwing the men out as the basket tipped over. The gas bag was still about half full and, now lightened, it was threatening to take off with the empty basket when the men shouted to us to hold the rope. A crowd of boys rushed forward to secure it and the bag gradually deflated.

It was a chaotic scene with ropes, fabric and people intermingling with each other. The crew had us running about like a lot of ants, pulling away the netting which enclosed the gas bag, unrigging gear from the basket and getting hold of a horse-drawn wagon. Considering our inexperience, it was astonishing how quickly we had it all folded, stacked and loaded onto the wagon; although they had landed at about three o'clock, they were away before dark. Looking back on the incident I feel sure they must have spotted a lot of schoolboys and decided to take advantage of many hands making light work. Since that day I have always wanted to go up in a balloon or airship but unfortunately I have not had the opportunity.

During the summer of 1916 my brothers and I were sent to stay with my father's aunt, Mrs Middlemore, instead of going to our grandmother's. Mrs Middlemore owned an island in the Orkneys called Hoy which partially enclosed a large, deep water inlet called Scapa Flow, and was the naval base for the Home Fleet.

Although I was only eight years old, I realised there was a great deal going on and Mrs Middlemore always seemed to be entertaining naval officers from the fleet. The three of us had a great time exploring the island and helping a bit around the house. As there was no village on this very bleak, windswept island, we were forced to make our own entertainment.

We were greatly excited when a senior officer told Jack he could borrow a trawler to take us all for a picnic. We set off to spend the day in a small bay a few miles away where there was a shelving beach. I remember there was an old winch for pulling up fishing boats with a wire cable; very tempting to a small boy who liked to balance on things. On the way home I was allowed to go down into the engine-room which was very hot and smelly but all the works were fully exposed which greatly impressed me.

From a very early age I had been interested in mechanical things. Someone had given me a model steamboat, a destroyer, which was my pride and joy. I soon found out that if I spilt the methylated spirit into the bilge when I was filling the burner and screwed up the safety valve a bit, it would go faster.

In 1918, when I was still boarding at Norfolk House Preparatory School, the pupils were summoned into the main classroom where the headmaster told us that the Germans had asked for an armistice and that the war was at last over. We were given a half day holiday and we spent the rest of the day playing in the nearby woods.

My father spent a year in Italy as Liaison Officer to the Italian Army (Italy having been our ally during the First World War) but after his return to England in 1919, he was still convalescing from his wound. Jack had left school and was at Sandhurst training to be an officer but during his holidays he joined the rest of the family at a house we had taken in Downderry, a village on the Cornish coast near Plymouth.

He brought with him an old 1914 model Bradbury motorcycle with a belt drive but no gearbox or clutch, making starting up a question of pushing and taking a running jump. My brothers and I used to go off together, two on the carrier, and ride around the hilly country which was quite a challenge, especially the hairpin bends. Being the youngest, my perch was right at the back and on hills I had to jump off when the engine began labouring, leaving David to do the same when they came to a hairpin bend. This was highly dangerous but the aim was to get as far up the hill as possible before jumping off and was great fun.

The Bradbury was much too valuable an asset for me to be allowed to ride on my own but shortly afterwards David bought a Levis, single speed, belt-drive motorcycle. This machine was regarded with disdain by some as it was only a two-stroke and lacked the he-man touch of the Bradbury but it gave me my first experience of being in sole control. I used to ride it along an unmade road which was totally illegal because I was only eleven years old but there were no policemen about and I had been truly bitten by the urge to travel fast.

Despite the fact that school exams were not my strong point I managed to pass into Rugby – more due to David's reputation rather than my own academic merits.

When I arrived at Rugby David was already in the sixth form while I was in the lowest form called Shell. Being located in the centre of England, Rugby had a good mixture of boys from all over the United Kingdom and did not, like Eton or Harrow, draw from only one social strata. I went to a relatively new 'house' called Hawkesworth which I cannot say I enjoyed very much as I did not make any real friends, nor did I form any good relationship with any of the teachers. I could see no point in learning Latin and my thoughts, instead of being concentrated on academic subjects, were full of all things mechanical, my favourite place being the metal workshop in the science department. My time spent at Rugby was a very lonely one with my parents absent abroad and David leaving the school the year after I had arrived. The Housemaster lived behind a green baize door within Hawkesworth House and, although he knew I had no family in close proximity, he never invited me into his home.

As is usual in most public schools in England, sport played an important part in one's standing among friends and, although I played rugby and cricket, my entrance into the team was not an auspicious one. During my first term I was put down to play at one of the outlying fields but unfortunately I went to the wrong pitch, disgracing myself and letting down my team. That evening the captain of the dormitory made me bend over the foot of the bed and gave me a beating with a gym shoe. It did not hurt very much but it left me with a feeling of resentment as well as insecurity.

I was quite a good runner, however, winning the half mile race for the under thirteens and I did manage to get my running colours. The big long distance race was the Crick, about twelve miles, but I was not eligible as it was for the over fifteens. It was probably just as well because, although I had the determination and endurance, I had no idea of training and used to starve myself before running to prevent myself getting too fat!

One day an aeroplane supposedly made a forced landing on one of the playing fields but this was somewhat doubtful as the owner was a local playboy by the name of Le Champion. He was constantly driving around in a noisy sports car and although my interest was in the aeroplane, I jumped at the chance of riding in the car when he asked me if I would like to. It was a pre-war racing car made by the French armament firm, Schneider, and fitted with some elementary mudguards to comply with the highway regulations.

I rode in the mechanic's seat, working the air pump which pressurised the rear fuel tank to feed the fuel to the engine. The huge exhaust pipe ran past my elbow and straight out of the back, which had the big round fuel tank across, between the rear wheels and two spare tyres strapped to it. We set off down the London Road at speed, a great thrill. Thankfully no-one spotted me and I got away with it but had I been caught the result would certainly have been painful or might even have meant expulsion.

After the war, in 1919, my father was fortunate enough to land a wonderful, and not too exacting, job as Military Attaché in Stockholm. This post covered Norway, Denmark, Finland and the Baltic States and was a highlight in my parents' lives as it was well paid and involved a great deal of entertaining. Each summer I went out for my holiday with them, getting plenty of sailing in the archipelago to the east of Stockholm, with its many islands and sheltered waters.

Every year the Royal Navy showed the flag by making a cruise around the Baltic and part of the Embassy's job was to entertain them. My father did his share and during the final year of my parents stay there, 1923, my brother David and I were invited to return to England in a naval ship. The date of departure from Gothenburg more or less fitted in to my return to Rugby so this was a thrilling opportunity not to be missed.

The departure was delayed a couple of hours while we waited for Prince George who was serving in one of the destroyers and had, I believe, met a particularly attractive Swedish girl. We were given a berth in the cruiser HMS *Danae* with a midshipman detailed off to look after us. I was fifteen years old and the experience of being on board an actual warship at sea and seeing this brief picture of life in the navy with its ancient traditions, left a lasting impression on me. Instead of returning to England as we had expected, we went to Invergordon, north of Inverness, and as we were entering the Moray Firth a sailor was seen to fall overboard from a destroyer up ahead. We immediately took action and a search was started but there was no sign of the man; after an hour or so another ship was ordered to continue the search but sadly without result.

We had missed the daily train to the south and were resigned to being late back to Rugby. The Headmaster, Dr Vaughan, had only recently taken over the position but he was already known to be a great disciplinarian and when I received a message to appear in his study a day or two later, I was very frightened as I had never met him. He was a very large, fat man and I was so nervous I could hardly speak, no doubt making a very poor impression, but all I received was a lecture about responsibility and obligations to the school.

We had a very up-to-date science school and I remember one day the teacher giving us a demonstration of the effectiveness of modern fire extinguishers. He put a basin of water in the middle of the classroom, poured a bottle of petrol into it and set it alight. There was a big burst of flame and smoke as he walked over to the extinguisher, broke the seal and directed the squirting liquid on to the fire. Unfortunately this action spread the flaming petrol all over the floor and tiers of seats opposite, causing some damage. Everyone managed to get out but this incident only confirmed my opinion that this teacher was not terribly intelligent. After that, in order to shorten our exposure to him, we used to screw up the pendulum of the master electric clock, thus shortening his lesson period very slightly.

War wounds caused my father's premature retirement from the army in 1923 and the subsequent drop in income necessitated my leaving Rugby. I was not too sorry about this as I had hated my time there but of course it meant I had left school with absolutely no qualifications. With the help of my father, I continued my education through correspondence courses and I began taking French lessons once a week. We had been lent a terrace house in Aldeburgh on the east coast by my godmother, a musical friend of my mother's, but in 1925 my parents decided to take a villa in the south of France at Hendaye Plage, where the cost of living was cheaper. David had joined a family firm, Wedd Jefferson, as a Jobber in the Stock Exchange and Jack was with the Gordon Highlanders.

The correspondence course had culminated in me taking a City and Guilds examination and it was while I was waiting for the results that I drove my parents to Hendaye. During my stay there I worked in a garage for a few weeks and tried to learn French but in actual fact I only learned the technical terms of car mechanics.

Soon after our arrival I saw an advertisement for a flying display at Biarritz, about twenty miles away, so I persuaded my father to drive me there. The grass airfield was narrow and flat with tall trees at each end and a celebrated French army pilot, Captain Robin, was to give an exhibition of stunt flying in a parasol monoplane with strut-braced wings.

In taking off he kept the wheels on the ground until just short of a line of trees, when he pulled up into a vertical climb. At the top he executed a neat stalled turn, diving vertically and flattening out only just in time to roll his wheels along the ground to the opposite end of the field, when again he pulled up vertically and followed with a stall turn and dive. This he repeated for the third time, having ended each climb with a little more height in hand.

He followed this with a very polished display of more conventional manoeuvres such as loops, rolls and a spin, finishing with a circuit of the airfield in a continuous series of rolls – a feat I now know to be particularly difficult. As he passed over our heads in a final dive and zoom, about five feet of the starboard wing broke off and fell away. He had sufficient speed to be able to continue for some distance with only two-thirds of the wing but as his speed decreased, so the wing went down and he disappeared behind some trees in a right-hand turn.

Like a fool, and with many others, I ran over to see what had happened only to be met in a gateway by a group of men carrying the very badly injured Robin on a short length of wooden fencing. One lesson I did learn from seeing this accident was never to be curious about aeroplane accidents. The incident did not diminish my determination to make flying my career however.

On my return to England, despite being under age, I applied for a short service commission in the Royal Air Force but, following my medical examination board at Hampstead, I was turned down as my eye-sight did not meet the required standard. I was extremely disappointed but my parents were very relieved as the First World War was still vivid in their memories, when a pilot's life expectancy was, on average, six weeks; training had been minimal and there were no parachutes.

After a series of rooming houses, my parents bought a house near Eggesford on the border of Exmoor. Located on the side of a steep hill, it was very isolated and the water supply was dependent on a ram pump located in a small stream which gave constant trouble. At the time my father was quite unable to drive our Austin 12 so, although I was only seventeen, I did all the driving, fetching doctors and medicines and so on with occasional trips to the station at Exeter to pick up visitors.

While at school I had further developed my great interest in motorcycles, originally sparked off by my brother Jack's early machines. I followed avidly all the accounts of the TT races and read about the development of new types of engines. Overhead valves, aluminium pistons, sleeve and rotary valves were being tested at this time on motorcycles, which in those days had a much better performance than any motor car. My own first motorbike was a Royal Enfield, a 1914 model V twin with overhead inlet valves and two speeds. I fitted 'drop' handlebars and footrests to make it more sporty and more like the TT racing bikes; it would do about 50 miles an hour. Later, David lent me his AJS, a famous make named after A J Stephens (a triple winner of the TT) and a much more sophisticated machine. I had a string of old motorbikes which included one of the famous Indian models, a V twin with a single belt drive and a hand clutch, an ABC which had a two cylinder horizontally opposed engine across the frame with a built in gear box, years before its time, and a Rudge, a single cylinder 4-valve, 4-speed bike.

I still remember the tremendous thrill when I bought my first new bike, financed by my share of David's win in the stock exchange sweep that year. It was an OEC Temple produced by the makers of motorbikes which had set a world speed record.

In 1925, as an alternative to the RAF and very much a second choice, my father persuaded me to take a three year apprenticeship course in engineering with Armstrong Siddeley Motors at Coventry.

CHAPTER 2

A Training of Sorts

In 1925 when I began my three-year apprenticeship with Armstrong Siddeley, the company was making cars, aeroplane engines, tanks and, at the subsidiary company of Armstrong Whitworth, aircraft. It was a progressive company in many fields of engineering, pioneering the self-changing gearbox, the supercharging of aeroplane engines and the all metal construction of aircraft.

Arrangements had been made for me to live at the Vicarage of Holy Trinity Church in Coventry, situated about three miles from the factory, which meant I could ride my bicycle to and fro to work. (Unfortunately the church was to be completely flattened during the blitz of Coventry in World War II which saw most of the city destroyed.) My hours of work were quite long, 47 ½ hours a week, including Saturday mornings, for which I was paid the handsome sum of thirteen shillings. By the time I was in the third year of my apprenticeship my pay had risen to 30 shillings a week (£1.50).

I spent the first six months in the machine shops where I learned to use a lathe, drilling machines, milling machines and heat treatment, followed by six months in the car assembly section and six months on aeroplane engine assembly. There were about twenty apprentices and it was not long before we had learned how to speak the language of engineers and how to make simple parts such as back axle shafts, push rods and bearing housings. We were allowed a half day, once a week, to study at the Coventry Technical College where the standard of education was appallingly low with teachers who no doubt had qualifications, but were indifferent to the imparting of information to their students. Even at Rugby the application of mathematics and science to engineering had not been explained to me and it was very many years before I realised how much I had missed.

When I had completed half my apprenticeship, my enthusiasm for engines was so obvious that I was sent to the Experimental Aircraft Engine Department. The two fitters there were called Alf and Charlie, both of whom, in their youth, had hand built some of the early cars. In those days skilled men such as these made the whole car – frame, petrol tank, radiator and of course the engine; they even filed the cams for the engine's valves before keying them to the camshaft. They were born mechanics with tremendous practical knowledge and were the backbone of our engineering industry before mass-production took over.

Soon after I was transferred, we were charged with stripping down Sir Alan Cobham's Jaguar engine which he had just used in his seaplane to fly to Singapore and Australia; a great privilege for an apprentice.

The first superchargers were high-speed centrifugal fans driven by three equally spaced step-up gears from the crankshaft, the gears incorporating slipping clutches to cushion the loads during acceleration. The wedge shaped friction pads frequently melted from slipping and molten metal, like bronze wire, filled the casing. I know because my job was to rub the new clutch pads in with grinding paste. The Jaguar was the first supercharged high-altitude engine to achieve regular production, thus giving the RAF's Siskin superior climb performance over any rival fighter.

In the experimental shop we built an entirely new and bigger air-cooled radial, called the Leopard, rated at 800hp, a tremendous power at that time. I was bicycling to work one morning having stayed at the factory very late the previous night servicing the engine on the test bed, when I heard the Leopard start up. A large part of Coventry could hear the noise but where I was, a mile from the plant, the sound was shattering.

On arrival, the foreman and the shop mechanics, which included me, were summoned by the Chief Tester who said that the engine had seized up. We were instructed to saw it apart to find the cause and when we had, it was obvious what had happened; someone had forgotten to turn on the main oilcock because there was no oil in the pipes. Blame for this very expensive mistake had to be laid at the door of the test shop crew who were responsible for the running and tests but the report to the authorities did not show this. It stated that it was due to an air leak through a fine hair crack in an induction pipe which caused a weak mixture and, consequently, a burnt piston. This reason was eventually accepted by the authorities and all further development was stopped, the project being abandoned. The cover-up left me feeling disillusioned with those in control and that, together with the General Strike in 1926, made me decide that, on completion of my apprenticeship, I would go abroad.

As an apprentice I was not directly concerned with the General Strike but, when the time came to walk out, the older men, in spite of being urged by hot-heads, were reluctant to go, spending a lot of time cleaning their machines and looking over their shoulders for reassurance from their immediate neighbours. They were fully aware of the danger to their jobs but it takes moral courage to stand up among one's fellow men and raise objections; most of us do not have that sort of courage. Finally, at about 11.00am, the chairman, Mr Siddeley, accompanied by the works manager and secretary, came round to every department and made a brief speech explaining that the company could not carry on with a partial labour force. The whole factory complex was shut down for a week and of the 8000 men who had been employed, only about half were given their jobs back. The slump continued until the start of re-armament in the middle thirties.

During the First World War there had been a great deal of labour trouble in the shipbuilding yards, particularly among the communists in the Glasgow area, and a large number of men had been persuaded by higher wages to move south to Coventry in order to make shells. Since that time Coventry and the car makers there have had a strong communist streak and have consistently suffered from labour troubles.

The last year of my apprenticeship was spent in the Armstrong Whitworth Aeroplane Drawing Office which was very interesting. The Atlas, an all-metal day bomber for the Royal Air Force, and the Argosy, a three-engined airliner for Imperial Airways, were being designed and built. Apart from some indifferent draughtsmanship, my only contribution was to design the fuel filter for the Atlas, inspiration coming from Bovril's bottle design. At that time Bovril was using a circular clamp to hold the lid on the top of the bottle so I adapted this idea to fasten the filter element to the base. It was hardly an original idea but it did go into production.

During my years in Coventry, a distant relative of mine, 'Binks' Riley, came to live at the same digs and we became great friends. He was an apprentice with Riley cars but he was not related to them, and when his training was finished he took a Riley car to the States, driving it from one coast to the other; it must have been one of the first British cars to be seen there. Afterwards he bought a filling station on Long Island and was one of the first people to sell Ethyl, the leaded petrol which in a high compression engine gave a big increase of power with less fuel. Leaded petrol is frowned upon now but we would not have won the Schneider Trophy outright in 1931 or indeed the Battle of Britain without it.

Before the General Strike Armstrong Siddeley were producing between 300 and 400 cars a week, made on a batch production method in very large machine shops.

All the lathes, milling machines, grinders and so on were driven by belts from overhead shafting, making it impossible to see the far side through the forest of belting; like a scene from the dark satanic mills of the industrial revolution. In spite of the age of the machinery, parts for the aeroplane engines and aircraft were being made alongside parts of cars. The advances in machine tools made since then have transformed the engineering world by introducing automatic and electrically controlled tools. The Americans, whose early labour force was largely made up of unskilled immigrants, were necessarily, and still are, the operators of these new mass-production tools, whereas we had tended to rely on our very skilled artisans.

Another fundamental change which has taken place since then has been in the elimination from cars of a separate chassis. In 1925, Coventry's streets were full of skeleton chassis being driven by testers sitting perched up on makeshift soap boxes. Armstrong Siddeley were the exception to the rule as they made their own bodies using a wooden frame over which was stretched a tough fabric. I think the salesmen must have had to stress the elimination of squeaks and rattles while playing down the durability factor.

My own interest had originally been focused on cars which seemed to me to have a very big future but the glamour of working on aeroplane engines and aircraft was too strong a draw. It was fortunate as the motor industry soon proved to be unreliable with slump following boom as one manufacturer or another caught the mood of a fickle market leaving its competitors without orders. In the case of Armstrong Siddeley, the time from which they had been unable to produce enough cars to meet the demand until they could virtually sell none was only a couple of months. Armstrong Siddeley were well placed to benefit from the spin-off from research and development expenditure on aeroplane engines as aluminium pistons and white-metal bearings were just coming into use for car engines, improving efficiency and relieving the new car buyer of a large part of the irksome job of 'running in'.

All cars fitted with the new-fangled front wheel brakes carried a red triangle warning plate on the back – a kind of status symbol. As the production of cars increased so did the percentage of unskilled drivers, with the consequence that the shortcomings of the crash type gearboxes and jerky clutches of the day became very evident. Although driving licences were mandatory there were no driving tests and the age limit for motorcycles was fourteen years and sixteen years for cars. Although the company had pioneered the installation of fluid flywheels and self-changing epicyclic gearboxes with some success, these features had to be shelved under the pressure of increased costs. Ultimately, it was the Americans who came up with the practical and cheap answer, a synchronising device which prevented the driver clashing the gear teeth, although it had been invented by an Englishman. Unable to interest any of the manufacturers in England, he had taken it to Detroit and sold an exclusive licence to General Motors who still use it to this day.

Part of my work in the Drawing Office entailed me making frequent visits to the aerodrome at Baginton where the Atlas and Argosy were being built. There had been relatively few developments in aerodynamics since World War I and design was focused on improving the structure. Wood gave way to metal and rubber shock-absorbing cord to coil springs in the undercarriage. Looking back, it is interesting to see how the design of new vehicles is influenced by the old; the first cars were called horseless carriages and they looked it, the carriages of early trains copied the stage coach and aeroplanes were, at that time, still under the influence of the original 'stick and string' conception. Specially shaped sheet steel and tube construction merely replaced the wooden spars, frames and longerons.

The bi-plane layout was relatively efficient up to about 100mph, but any suggestion of reducing drag by building a monoplane was taboo; some scientist had ordained that no monoplane structure could be made strong enough and the Air Ministry were therefore not in the market for them.

The only effort made to improve aerodynamic efficiency was the building of a special experimental aircraft incorporating a bi-plane wing with adjustable root fittings. These allowed the same wing to be re-rigged with a bigger gap and more stagger and sweepback. It was quite the most awful monstrosity but was one way of measuring the effects on drag before the days of full-scale wind tunnels.

For those of my generation it is hard to accept the new words used in aviation today; aileron, fuselage and nacelle all reflect the early French influence. In the thirties, the newly formed Air Registration Board, advisers on civil aviation to the Air Ministry, laid down that a propeller should become an airscrew, a fuselage an airframe and much later, in deference to our American allies, an aerodrome became an airfield. Inevitably the language of the industry gradually changed but even now I wince on hearing the word 'plane', worse still 'airplane', although I sometimes use the word aircraft instead of aeroplane myself. Developments in the field of propulsion have by stages gone from propeller through pure jet, turbojet, bypass jet, turboprop, ducted propellers taking us almost back to where we started. The latest term to be coined however, namely the RB 211, is in my opinion, a poor effort to describe this great Rolls-Royce high technology engine with its huge inbuilt ducted impeller.

My apprenticeship with Armstrong Siddeley was completed in 1928 and, with some knowledge of aircraft engineering behind me, I had thought I would be able to find work in commercial aviation – but this was not to be. I had been saving every penny I could and with that plus some I borrowed as well as the proceeds from the sale of a car I went to Brooklands motor-racing circuit to learn to fly privately. The lessons were £4.10s an hour, a tremendous sum but I only took five hours dual and three solo before getting my licence so the total cost amounted to £36. The country was still in the aftermath of the Great War and anyone connected with civil aviation was considered either scatter-brained or a playboy.

Brooklands was a very famous motor racing circuit about twenty minutes by train from London. It was joined by a footbridge to Byfleet where the aeroplanes were housed in the Hawker sheds which had been built for the First World War. The group of us, living in a bungalow near the sheds, were a mixed crowd of aviators, racing drivers, actors and rich sportsmen whose main past time seemed to be drinking, starting early in the day and finishing long after the pubs closed. There were no regular hours but life moved fast with an atmosphere of devil-may-care prevailing among the older experienced pilots who had flown in the war. With the average life expectancy of pilots who had flown over France being only a few weeks, it was not surprising that drinking habits acquired then had left their mark.

While in Coventry I had not been interested in the usual pub crawl beer drinking, simply because it was too expensive and every penny counted. At Brooklands, however, I had to drink spirits to be in the swing and to keep up with my friends. Certainly flying in an open cockpit with the wind in one's face and the cold, noise and anxieties of it all did produce a fierce thirst.

On my first flight Colonel Henderson, who owned the school of flying, took off and then, at 200 feet, handed the Avro 504 over to me with the remark, 'keep her straight.' Later, after telling me to make a turn, he allowed me to get into a tighter and tighter spiral dive until I found, purely by chance whilst in a panic, that, by putting on top or opposite rudder, I was able to get myself out of a frightening situation. It was a crude lesson but one I never forgot.

When I reflect on those early flying days I can see how crude the aeroplanes were and how very new flying was. There was always a sense of danger lurking in the back of one's mind and during my three week course, one of the students, Miss Welby, spun in and was killed. Both Colonel Henderson and an instructor called Davenport had fatal accidents shortly afterwards.

We were, after all, only one generation after the Wright brothers, too short a time for man to have absorbed and overcome all the thousands of new problems presented by actually flying. Nevertheless, even with the knowledge available then, the whole approach was far too casual.

On weekends we used to fly over to a field by the river at Runnymede, taking up joyriders at 5s a head. My job was to sell tickets but it was well worth it as I was getting two cross-country flights free.

The Avro 504 was a good trainer, relatively safe while its controls accentuated such effects as a sensitive rudder and aileron drag; not having any fixed fin area, it had a lack of directional stability and made correct use of the rudder vital. The flying school's motley collection of aeroplanes had various engines including two V-8s, the RAF 90 and the Renault 80 driving a large four-bladed propeller through reduction gears and also a 10 cylinder Anzani radial. This Anzani engine must have been one of the first air-cooled radials to be built, a classic conception to be followed by a very long line of highly successful engines. The Anzani, however, was very weak in detail design with automatic inlet valve, single ignition and an exhaust manifold which looked like a plumber's dream. The worst feature was the inadequate length of the cooling fins, obvious to the pilot soon after leaving the ground when the power gradually faded as the engine began to overheat. It is interesting to visit the aeronautical section of the Science Museum in South Kensington, London, to study and compare the Anzani with a Bristol Centaurus. It is wondrous what man can achieve in a period of 25 years if he puts his mind to it.

Immediately following my first lesson with Colonel Henderson, he handed me over to another instructor, Duncan Davis, who was a much better teacher. After only 5½ hours flying time, I was sent up solo and I remember the wind that day happened to be from the north-west which meant a short landing run across the aerodrome. Just to make matters more difficult, the approach from the direction of St George's Hill was over the River Wey while an overshoot meant finishing up in the sewage farm!

By tradition, a first solo called for a round of drinks and it was with acute embarrassment that I found myself standing a round at the British Automobile Racing Club bar in their club house near the paddock on the finishing straight, being shy and out of my depth in such company. Nevertheless, I felt honoured to be surrounded by the high and mighty of the motor-racing world, my schoolboy heroes.

Two years before I had seen the first British Grand Prix motor race when a chicane was introduced into the finishing straight, attracting the cream of the drivers from the European circuit. Divo, with a new Talbot, was an exhibitionist and aided by the very open cockpits of the racing cars of the day, he drove spectacularly, his check cap back to front, arms waving, skidding through the artificial corners then accelerating away with the new supercharged engine making a noise like a stuck pig. Benoit, on the other hand, in the very latest supercharged Delage, had much more finesse but, although he was probably equally fast, his exhaust blew a gasket and orange flames could be seen through the louvres of the bonnet as he opened the throttle. Every few laps he had to pull into the pits where he jumped out and put his feet into a basin of water to cool them down.

Parry Thomas, a world speed record holder had designed his own road racing car, the Thomas Special, known locally as the 'flat iron'. Its main feature was that it was very low with the driver sitting practically on the ground but it did not seem to handle too well. Segrave, true to form, stuck to his Sunbeam which, if I remember correctly, was not supercharged and could not compete on performance.

On completing the required three hours solo I was ready to take the tests to obtain an aviator's certificate which was issued under the authority of the Royal Aero Club who were solely responsible for the conduct of private flying. A member of the club, in my case one of the instructors, had to certify that the required tests had been satisfactorily completed but this amounted to little more than a demonstration that the pilot could handle an aeroplane. The test entailed three take-offs and landings, one of the latter without using the engine, a figure of eight at 1500 feet and the ability to recover from a spin.

Armed with the aviator's certificate and a letter from my doctor I applied for my private pilot's licence which arrived a few weeks later in a manilla envelope. Inside was Private Pilot's Licence No. 1560 issued by the Air Ministry, signed by the Director of Civil Aviation himself, General Sir Sefton Brancker who was later killed in the disastrous 101 Airship crash.

I had achieved one of my ambitions by the age of twenty but I had been unsuccessful in my search for employment. My parents had returned from France and built a bungalow in Constantine Bay in Cornwall where I went to join them as I had no funds with which to support myself. I was desperately unhappy until my father saw an article in a newspaper announcing that a new airline in Canada had been started by a friend of his, General McBrien. My father immediately wrote to the General asking if he could find me a position in the company.

CHAPTER 3

Hungry Beginnings

The epic flight of Charles Lindberg in May 1927 fired my imagination still further. The flight from Long Island, New York to Paris, France, not only inspired me and many like me but it encouraged investors both from the US government and the private sector to pour money into civil aviation. This was the boom time before the Wall Street crash of 1929 and produced a number of small companies which manufactured and operated aircraft.

This increase in commercial interest provided me with the opportunity to travel and so began my life-long relationship with and love of Canada. The letter which my father had sent to General MacBrien brought a response within weeks offering me a position as air engineer at the Head Office of International Airways of Canada. I was to be based in Hamilton, Ontario and would be paid $100 a month. My father had come to know General McBrien during the time he had spent in Kingston, Ontario soon after I was born and they had kept in close contact during the war. The General had been head of the Canadian Expeditionary Forces in Europe and was well respected throughout Canada.

Although my family had left Canada when I was four years old I still have memories of Quebec City where we lived on the Plains of Abraham for a year prior to our return to England. Most of the houses were made of wooden cladding (clapboard) and one night the house opposite to ours caught fire and was reduced to ashes in half an hour. I was at such an impressionable age that from that time I developed a fear of fire. One day I was told to look up at the sky; my mother told me there was an aeroplane up there with a man in it! To a small boy it seemed unreal, unbelievable and it remained as such until I saw the aeroplane close up on the beach at Hunstanton in 1917.

England was at that time in the depth of an economic depression with an unemployment figure of two million but this economic instability had not yet reached North America – the New World, full of confidence, optimism and money. With a sense of relief I said goodbye to England with no intention of returning.

I travelled by Cunard ship, the *Ausonia*, disembarking at Montreal full of hope and excitement, riding on the crest of the economic wave unaware that, not long after my arrival, the wave was to break.

I arrived at Hamilton at the western end of Lake Ontario, where International Airways owned the local aerodrome, in early September 1928. It was little better than a marshy field, used until a new one was built on higher land to the west. There was a strange mixture of aeroplanes in use at the field; the Curtiss JN4, or Jenny as it was called, had an OX5 V8 engine and had been the standard trainer for the American Army, the equivalent of our Avro 504. There was also a Fokker D12, presumably acquired as part of the German reparations after the First World War; this had been the main German fighter. It was a cantilever winged bi-plane with a water cooled engine and what must have been unique, a fuel tank mounted externally between the wheels as a protection against the pilot being burnt in flight, a not uncommon experience in air fighting. There was one relatively new aeroplane, a Waco two-seater bi-plane, designed for the developing civil market.

Shortly after my arrival at Hamilton a visiting aircraft landed on the new aerodrome which was still under construction. On taking off again with two or three passengers on board, it was seen to climb away very steeply, lose flying speed causing it to stall and fall out of control. It caught fire and all aboard were killed. It came as a great shock to me even though I did not see the crash happen. The next day I visited the crash site where I noticed the crankhandle of the longitudinal trimmer which was mounted in the roof over the pilot's head, had been wound fully clockwise to the nose up position instead of being in a neutral or halfway position. Obviously the pilot had not noticed the control was wrongly set for take-off but it made me realise that a careless mistake by a pilot is unforgivable and irreversible.

Within three months of my arrival in Hamilton, Ontario, I was sent to Ottawa to be in charge of the office of the photographic division. Our company was engaged on a government contract for aerial mapping and making a survey or assessment of the quantities of timber in Northern Ontario by taking oblique photographs of the forests. The timber, used as pulp in papermaking, was one of the main sources of wealth in the vast northern area.

Life in Ottawa was very different to that in Hamilton, it being the seat of government, and the photographic surveys we carried out involved making close contact with government officials. The only other employee in the office was a woman of about 30, a stenographer who dealt with all the film processing and liaised with the officials. Although I was officially in charge, she ran the office leaving me with very little responsibility. Every month the head of the field operations would return from the north with films and then proceed to spend his time in the beer halls in Hull, the town on the opposite bank of the river Ottawa in the Province of Quebec which had different laws to Ontario. Every afternoon he would insist that I accompany him across the snowbound bridge to spend hours in dark and dingy cold beer halls drinking one beer after another. It was not my scene at all and I was always glad when he returned north.

I bought myself a new Model A Ford for $500 which took me to the many parties held at the Country Club on the far side of the river. I made friends with a group of young people and we took to skiing, practising after work at a small park in Rockcliff, a residential area. At the weekends we would take a local train to the Laurentian mountains, stay the night in a large hostel and ski the twenty miles back to Ottawa next day. I had one or two special girl friends but I felt like a fish out of water not having had any real social contact with the opposite sex, always having lived in lodgings, with aunts or my grandmother. I was very ignorant on the subject of females so I found myself keeping them at arm's length.

My main interest at that age was flying, not the 'city life' and I felt quite frustrated in that respect, being in Ottawa, but it was a good life for young people, being much freer than in England and it gave me the opportunity to find my own way in this new society.

I had no imagination as a young man and, although I ignored the dangers of flying, in other respects I was inexperienced and rather like a frightened little boy, terrified of putting a foot wrong. I remember an incident when I was called upon to intervene in an emergency but I felt quite inadequate to do the job. The company aeroplane, a three-seater, open cockpit bi-plane called a Swallow and used for joyriding, was involved in an accident about 25 miles down the river Ottawa and Head Office asked me to go there and report back to them. The aircraft was on skis with a tail skid of extra large area. Where the tail skid arm entered the fuselage there was a gap through which snow had entered and become packed tight into a solid lump. The additional weight in the tail, together with the two passengers in the side-by-side rear seat, had moved the centre of gravity aft and the pilot had evidently got into a flat spin during a turn. The aircraft hit the snow-covered ice on the river in a horizontal attitude very hard indeed with the result that the pilot's seat had collapsed across the legs of his two passengers who both had broken legs. They were in hospital feeling angry and very sorry for themselves, demanding to know how much compensation they would be getting from the company. They were French Canadians and with my limited French and inexperience I fear that my explanations and apologies were not satisfactory.

The Wall Street crash of 1929 left the financial market in chaos with the operation of civil aircraft being the first industry to be hit as it depended heavily on government subsidy. It had a devastating effect on the whole country as it seemed to come in two waves. During the first fall, people did not believe it, the apparent cheapness of shares tempting those with money back into the market only to see it finally crash.

By the spring of 1929 General McBrien must have realised that the promoters had merely used his name, and resigned, so with the financial squeeze which was taking place, the Ottawa office was closed. It was very unexpected but I was fortunate to be sent, as an aircraft engineer and aerial photographer, to Fairchild Aerial Surveys at Grand Mere, Quebec, a subsidiary of International Airways of Canada. The sensible thing for a young man would have been to settle down in Ottawa and make money but I was happy to follow my instincts and move to Grand Mere, a small town halfway between Montreal and Quebec, where I hoped to be able to resume flying.

Grand Mere was the maintenance base for our flying activities, a well organised undertaking financed by the big pulp and paper company there. There were a number of English pilots retired from the RAF – Wardle, Bythell, Troup and Lumsden being the most experienced ones – but it is interesting that just ten years after the war there were only about 170 Canadian licensed pilots out of the 10,000 or so trained pilots demobilised in 1918.

The company was an agent for the American Fairchild Aircraft Company and had a number of Fairchild FC2s, some fitted with the 400 hp Pratt & Whitney Wasp and others with Wright Whirlwind J5s of 220 hp. The FC2 was a rugged, highwing monoplane, strut-braced with a welded tube fuselage which could carry about 1000 lbs. We had a contract to support an exploration and gold mining company prospecting in an area north of the transcontinental railway in northern Quebec; a shuttle service from Oskelaneo to the camp at Chiboucarman ferried in supplies daily. I had hoped to do some flying but found instead, that my time was taken 'gassing up' and keeping the aircraft serviceable. As there was no road from the station, getting the 45-gallon drums of fuel to the base was quite a problem. It entailed rolling the drums off the railway trucks, down a slope into the lake where we would lash them together and tow them to our operating base behind a small motor boat; as petrol (or gas) is lighter than water, the drums floated satisfactorily.

At the base there was a pet bear which had been captured when its mother was shot. From playing around the camp like a puppy it quickly grew into a fierce animal. We tethered it to a cable stretched between two trees so it could move around but if one passed within its reach, a friendly pat of its claws became a vicious swipe, so we decided to release it. Lifting it by its collar, a leather bootlace, we lowered it into a sack and took it to the other side of the lake where it shook itself free, cocked its leg and scuttled off into the bush.

Back at Grand Mere there was a Liberty-engined Curtiss HS2L flying boat, a salvaged relic from the war. Its flying speed was around 70mph and it was the only aircraft, to my knowledge, in which it was possible for the off-duty crew member to climb out of the open cockpit and sit on the wing with his back to the flying wires, enjoying the sun. The engine, a 400 hp V12, was a nightmare to keep serviceable as each cylinder had a separate water-jacket with flexible connections; I think the Jubilee hose-clip must have been invented around this time. This engine was built in quantity by the Americans and had been the most powerful engine available to the Allies in the first world War. Two unusual features of this engine were the coil ignition system and the narrow angle of the Vee between the cylinder banks which reduced the frontal area. The only British aeroplane in which the Liberty engine was used was the de Havilland 9A, a day bomber of the late 1920s.

One of our main activities was aerial survey when we flew back and forth in the HS2L over the centre of Montreal, taking photographs for city planning purposes. Later, we flew over the proposed routes for the extension of the electrical powerlines. This had the advantage that a close study could be made of the various properties and farms which would be affected without the owners' knowledge of the survey. Not perhaps quite ethical but arguments could be advanced both for and against the practice and I have little doubt that it still goes on today.

It was a carefree, casual life; one evening while taxiing in our Vickers Vedette flying boat to the small landing stage on the lake near Grand Mere, Lumsden cut the engine a bit late and I could see we were clearly going to hit a wooden post at the end of the jetty. Seeing a figure running down to ward off the blow, Lumsden, with his service background and in his inimitable style, called out just before the crunch, 'It's alright, there are lots more where this came from.' Unfortunately the figure was not amused as he happened to be the president of the company.

The bombshell came in October 1929 when it was announced that the company was closing down and we were all sacked. The Wall Street crash was already beginning to bite in Canada, bringing an impending depression. Unlike England, which even after years of depression had its social structure intact, Canada had no such stability. The reality of having no job just as the winter months were setting in came home to us quickly. Some old family friends in Toronto, who had a large house in the best residential area with two cars and a steady business in tobacco broking, suddenly went bankrupt. Thousands of other families were made penniless overnight as it became impossible to raise cash from anything; even cars became unsaleable.

In our optimistic naivety, the English employees moved from Grand Mere to Montreal, the business centre of Canada and well known for its excellent entertainment and restaurants. Thinking we would soon find employment, Lumsden, Bill Wardle and I shared rented rooms in Peel Street and proceeded to spend our savings freely; Peter Troup even moved into the Windsor Hotel for a time. Alcohol flowed while I acquired a taste for whisky to the extent that I could distinguish one brand from another.

During a party in Troup's hotel room one night the manager of the hotel rang up to complain, 'It is very late to be entertaining a lady in your room sir,' he said, to which Troup replied, 'Oh no you are quite wrong, she is entertaining me!'

On another occasion I took a friend to dinner in the Grill Room and having waited a considerable time for the bill, I put the money on the plate and seeing no sign of the waiter, we left. We were stopped at the door, however, and accused of not paying the bill; apparently an old trick but leaving me with no choice but to pay again. This frivolity and irresponsible behaviour faded as our savings ebbed away and the reality of not finding a job and hunger set in.

Montreal was the Paris of North America, very attractive to the Americans who were suffering from prohibition laws in New York. In the Canadian Provinces alcohol was sold at liquor stores during shopping hours but it was forbidden to drink in public which meant one took it up to the hotel room. A hip flask was carried or a bottle was hidden under the table in a restaurant while a bottle of Canada Dry Ginger Ale prominently displayed above; ginger ale looked remarkably similar to a whisky and soda. Taxis would drive people to selected houses in the suburbs where a sum of money was deposited in the mail box then, having circled the block, the money would be miraculously exchanged for a bottle. The effect of prohibition in the United States and the control of spirits in Canada had the effect of putting large sums of money into the hands of the most undesirable people, bootlegging money being the foundation of the Mafia empire. The weekend Friday night train from New York would run in up to fifteen sections, flooding the city with visitors.

It was exciting but very expensive and soon we were living a life of austerity. Getting up at midday to save energy we would seek out cheap eating places where we would have our one meal a day. I found a place in the French quarter where I could get a large plateful of hot soup with plenty of vegetables for about a dollar, maximum volume for the minimum price.

I kept enough cash on one side in case I had to buy a steerage passage to England, meanwhile learning what it was like to be really hungry. The word hungry is used in a very loose sense in everyday conversation; the reality is quite different. Canada was no welfare state and to be unemployed in the harsh winter weather was no joke.

By early December 1929, when my funds had been exhausted apart from the reserve for my passage home, I received a telegram from an American in Edmonton, Alberta. He was a strange character whom I had met in Montreal when he had tried to persuade us to pilot flying boats between Nassau and somewhere vaguely off the coast of Florida but out of sight of the US coastguard! He was now a consultant to a new aviation company in Alberta which was offering me a job as an engineer. In triumph I stepped onto the next train, using my reserve money to buy the ticket for my four day journey.

A long train journey was a new experience for me and I felt a sense of adventure as we set off from Montreal on the first leg of the journey to Winnipeg in Manitoba. The passenger coaches were big and heavy with sleeping berths which swung down from the roof over the day-time seats. The conductors were all cheerful, black men who made up the berths and brought round food and drinks on trolleys; there was a restaurant car but I could not use it on account of the cost.

On reaching Winnipeg we were transferred to a similar train for the second stage of the journey west, the original train being taken out for servicing in preparation for the return journey to Montreal. Each coach had its own electric dynamo driven from one of the axles by a belt, and evidently a source of trouble when operating in ice and slush. The train rumbled on across the snow bound prairies at about 35 to 40 miles an hour, stopping at Saskatoon before reaching Edmonton in Alberta, 24 hours later.

CHAPTER 4

Airmail to the Arctic

O n my arrival at Edmonton I was met by my American friend who kindly invited me to stay with him a short while before flying north. My host lived on the border of the old town on the road which had recently been built leading to the new Edmonton Air Harbour, two miles from the centre of the city. This aerodrome has now become the Municipal Airport for local flights only as it soon became surrounded by buildings and unable to cope with the larger air traffic. The local people were very proud of the Air Harbour, anticipating that it would make Edmonton the hub of international travel in that part of the world. Edmonton is now reported to be the fastest growing city in North America with the International Airport fifteen miles outside.

Edmonton was a typical railway town with the railway tracks running through the main streets. Before the railway, the Canadian National, had arrived, there had been much local land speculation as it had been assumed that the line would run south of the Saskatchewan River, thereby avoiding having to build a bridge. In the event a high level bridge was built, followed at a later date by a secondary low level bridge which gave a direct route to Calgary, thus confounding those who had hoped to make a killing on the south side. The MacDonald Hotel, owned by the railway company, became the natural focal point and the city grew around it.

It has now been largely forgotten but the bait offered to the railway promoters to build railways from coast to coast across Canada was a strip of land ten miles either side of the tracks. Both the Canadian Pacific and the Grand Trunk companies raised their finances in London, but after Herculean efforts to complete the first transcontinental route it was quickly found that the traffic did not justify the two railways and the Grand Trunk went bankrupt. The Canadian Government took it over (without compensation) and called it the Canadian National.

Edmonton became the capital of Alberta and the natural departure point for all forms of exploration and prospecting for minerals in the north. It is difficult to build railways in those marshy treeless areas – the ground is frozen to a depth of several feet and any steel structure such as a railway track or radio mast attracts the sun's heat, causing the foundation to melt and become unstable. Rivers all flow north or north-easterly into the Arctic Ocean which, for all practical purposes, is not navigable by sea-going ships.

The company I was to join was Commercial Airways Ltd of Edmonton, formed on the strength of one government contract to take the mail to all trading posts on the Mackenzie River. Mail carried was not subject to a surcharge but any letter, for example one posted in the United Kingdom, went automatically by air. Up to the start of the scheduled weekly air service, all mail had been carried by dog team in the winter and an old steam stern-wheeler owned by the Hudson Bay Company, called the Northland Echo, in the summer; just two deliveries a year.

Our aircraft were painted red and carried the Royal Mail cypher on each side, while the operational staff were officially sworn in as authorised to carry mail. We also carried printed cards to enable us to swear in temporary postmen to take over the mail in the event of failure to reach our destination. The carriage of mail is not to be treated lightly and its safety is paramount. Although other claims have been made to being the first airmail service, to the best of my knowledge these were subject to a surcharge and not at ordinary rates.

The managing-director of Commercial Airways Limited was Cy Becker, one of Canada's great aces of World War I with 28 enemy aircraft to his credit, and he was still an active pilot. He ran the company from the Edmonton office which was convenient as a centre of communications, allowing him to keep in contact with the Alberta Government and also with the administrative headquarters of the Northwest Territories at Fort Smith, one of the weekly ports of call on our route north.

On 11 December 1929, pilots, engineers and passengers set off from the Air Harbour at Edmonton in three aeroplanes for the company's operation base at Fort McMurray, situated on the Athabasca River at the end of the railway, 200 miles north of Edmonton. McMurray had one dirt road and a population of about 200 or 300 which, since the discovery of oil, has now risen to approximately 40,000.

My arrival at Fort McMurray was not auspicious. I flew up as a passenger in the Vega with Cy Becker and without any heat in the cabin I became thoroughly chilled. On landing, Cy Becker got stuck in the snow and, unable to get the aircraft moving again, I got out and by pushing the tail sideways, managed to free the skis so that he was able to taxi on to park. On joining the others after a struggle to make my way through 200 yards of deep snow, I was greeted with the news that my nose was frozen. Tim Sims, who had come up to McMurray as a representative of the Wright Engine Company, acted very promptly, rubbing my nose with snow and a fur glove. This action saved my nose but it was covered with water blisters and to lose a layer of skin at the beginning of winter was unfortunate. It does not take long to freeze anything in the propeller slip-stream when the temperature is 30° F below zero but that was something I had to learn. Twenty-five years later at a party in London given by Jack Davis, who was working for Canadair, a comparative stranger came up to me and said, 'I once saved your nose.' He had recognised me after all that time and I was indeed grateful to him.

Cold in the north is relative; zero weather, that is to say 32°F of frost, is cold and 50°F below zero is very cold. Fortunately very cold weather tends to be still and calm but any wind at any temperature makes life difficult and one is forced to seek shelter for protection. Even a deep breath catches in one's throat as the frost tries to freeze one's lungs. One learned not to grasp any metal door handle with the bare hand; even inside a front door handle would freeze to the skin and required the protection of gripping the metal by insulating one's hand with the fabric of one's coat pocket.

Suitable clothing was a problem although the local general store had rough shirts, mackinaws and breeches. Most of us wore leather flying helmets, the airman's equivalent to the city gent's bowler. Mine was a white chamois leather one from Herbert Johnson of Bond Street, London, and quite unsuitable in the cold. We gradually acquired all the desirable extras: Royal Canadian Mounted Police uniform breeches, fur mittens, Eskimo parkas and sealskin mukluks. The latter items were only to be obtained on a barter basis, there not being much use for bits of paper on the Arctic coast. Parkas were made of untanned caribou skin with trimming of different markings to denote the particular tribe. A very special one would have the hood part trimmed with wolverine, the only fur which has the unusual property of not freezing to your face from condensation of your breath.

Extremities such as hands and feet were particularly vulnerable to the cold, so we wore woollen gloves and normally kept our gloved hands tucked into huge fur mittens slung from a cord round the neck. No shoes, particularly if leather or rubber soled, could be worn, only a kind of boot made of sealskin called a mukluk which becomes soft and pliable after being well chewed by Eskimo women! Spare socks are important and it became routine practice to hang up one's socks by a fire every night so as to ensure absolute dryness. One of the main secrets of keeping warm is never to get hot from over-exertion; sweating is not only a loss of energy but will cause condensation and one's outer clothing then acts as a form of refrigerator.

The weekly train brought the mail from Edmonton to Fort McMurray and from there we flew it north to the various fur trading posts. We also carried passengers when space was available; Hudson Bay officials, prospectors, trappers and Roman Catholic priests. There were isolated Roman Catholic, as well as Anglican, missions at three or four of the trading posts, teaching the Indian and Eskimo natives.

Once a year we would fly Bishop Breynant of the Northwest Territories on his rounds, our arrival being greeted by a turnout of the entire settlement. He gave me a Bible suitably inscribed as a momento of one of these tours and I had it in my possession until it was burnt during the London Blitz.

The route north was down the Mackenzie River to Chipewyan on Lake Athabasca and Fort Smith, an Alberta Government post on their northern border with the Northwest Territories from where it was but a short distance to Fort Fitzgerald at the lower end of some unnavigable rapids. Fort Resolution, an important settlement on the Great Slave

Lake, was our weekly destination and we often had enough mail to require a second load. Hay River, on the south coast of the Great Slave Lake, was a very small settlement at the time but in later years was destined to be the terminal for the railway from Alberta. Fort Simpson which was our terminal every third week, was another trading post and could be reached by the Liard River from Fort Nelson in the foothills of the Rocky Mountains. Once a month our schedule called for a flight to Aklavik on the river delta before it flowed into the Arctic Ocean. En route we called at Wrigley, Fort Norman, Good Hope and McPherson, a total distance of some 1600 miles.

The fleet consisted of five aircraft, two Bellanca Pacemakers, two Bellanca CH300s and a Lockheed Vega. The Vega was a beautifully streamlined highwing monoplane of wooden monocoque construction, quite unsuitable for the north and it was quickly withdrawn.

The Bellancas, which differed only in the undercarriage design, were strut-braced highwing monoplanes, the main feature being that the wing struts and the whole fuselage were of a lifting section. With a 300hp Wright Whirlwind J6, it would cruise at about 100 mph with a useful payload of 1000 lbs.

'Wop' May, another World War I Canadian fighter pilot, was Chief Pilot. He had had considerable experience flying in cold weather and our aircraft had been modified locally to incorporate his ideas; skis were of ash and hickory with laminated pedestals. The oil pipes had been lagged with asbestos string and the oil tanks enclosed in a felt and canvas jacket to retain the heat. With a similar object, every aperture in the engine cowling was blanked off. Very large hand-operated draincocks were fitted to the oil tanks to drain the hot oil and thereby prevent the engine stopping. Special containers were made up to collect the oil and then used for re-heating it over a camp-fire or blowtorch before start up in the following morning. The danger of the oil freezing in the aircraft's oil tank was a constant worry and the engine could never be idled for more than a minute or two as slow circulation would lead to the oil congealing in the pipelines and a build-up of pressure in the system. Overnight, an engine would freeze rigid and before it could be turned it was necessary to apply heat. We carried heavy canvas and felt covers with an asbestos trunk into which was placed a plumber's blowtorch. On an average winter's day the engine would come free after about one-and-a-half hours and the propeller could then be turned. An alternative type of cover consisted of a heavy tent over the engine which had the added advantage of warming up the engineer as well. Engine starting was by a hand-cranked inertia starter which gave us independence from any outside source of power. Having taken so much time and trouble to warm up the engine and the lubricating oil before take-off we found that sometimes the oil would overheat as we reached cruising altitude. An air-cooled engine relies heavily on its circulation of oil for internal cooling and this overheating was a serious matter.

It was only when we fitted external air thermometers that we discovered that in the cold of the north there is often a big temperature inversion. Normally the air gets colder with height by about 3°F per 1000 feet but not infrequently we found a 30° F temperature rise in the first 1000 feet; a suitable modification to the engine installation overcame the difficulty.

As we had no radio and 'blind flying' instruments had not been invented, all flying was visual so that we kept under the clouds and followed the rivers. If the visibility, for example in snow or low cloud, forced us to a dangerously low level, we turned back to whence we had come. Alternatively, if we had seen from the air a cabin obviously inhabited with perhaps snow tracks visible, we would land there and stay until the weather cleared. If the owner was away but it was an emergency, we would take shelter in the uninhabited cabin. To land away from any shelter in the winter entailed setting up camp, a major undertaking. In summer, while on floats, one just pulled in to the river bank or perhaps remained on board floating for an hour or two.

A forced landing in the north can be dangerous. Our survival kit weighed about 160lbs and tended to get bigger with experience. An axe, tent, snow-shoes, rifle, fishing gear, collapsible stove and food were all stowed in the rear fuselage, while our personal sleeping bags and clothing went into the main cabin. A camp-fire is extremely inefficient and burns a lot of wood so we decided to carry collapsible stoves which could be used inside a tent thus providing warmth as well as cooking facilities with much less effort, an important consideration when the conservation of body energy was vital. We carried matches separately in a corked bottle in a convenient pocket; it would hardly be possible to survive even one night during the winter in the far north without a source of heat.

Fort McMurray was on the junction of the Athabasca river and the Clearwater River but fortunately, at some time a channel had been gouged out between the two rivers by the ice breaking up and causing a flood. This snye, as it is called, provided a perfect base for maintenance purposes with smooth ice in winter and little current in summer. A shed on skids called a nose hangar, with a canvas curtain on one side capable of being drawn tight round the back of the engine bay, provided with a stove, gave good facilities for engine maintenance while parked on the ice.

There was a hotel of sorts owned by a Mr O'Coffee but understandably living conditions were somewhat elementary with the sole provision for washing being a barrel of water in the kitchen and an outside privy. The single living-cum-dining room had a large and effective wood stove which warmed the whole building, including the bedrooms which opened on to an inside gallery. Outside the front door was a thermometer which I have seen indicate 50° F below zero in winter and 90° F above in summer.

Of all the pilots and engineers based at McMurray, there was only one who really knew the north and that was Jack Bowen who had lived there most of his life. For eight years he had driven his dog team taking the mail from Fort Smith to McMurray and had also been a driver for the Royal Canadian Mounted Police. Breaking a trail on the first trip of the winter or after a snowstorm was very tough going and other travellers would wait for Jack to leave before following quickly behind. The distance covered in any one day varied greatly according to the weather and surface conditions. A frozen lake is easy going whereas fresh snow means that the lead dog has to make progress in a series of leaps, hardly conducive to fast travel.

A good time for the journey from McMurray to Chipewyan would be about five days for the 160 odd miles. Jack Bowen once made the journey from Fort Norman to Cambridge Bay, about 700 miles, without a map but just on hearsay: 'turn right at Bear River, follow along the north shore of the lake, follow a river draining from the north east corner, cross two lakes, etc. etc.' Dark growth on the tree trunks gave the direction of north, the sun at mid-day, if out, gave south. For food he carried bacon, flour, sugar and tea, supplemented by rotten fish from Eskimo caches near the Arctic coast; an incredible journey through totally uninhabited wastes. His only comment was to wonder how the dogs survived on half a frozen fish a day!

Compared with Jack, the rest of us were a lot of greenhorns so far as survival in the real north was concerned but I think he must have learned a thing or two from us when it came to aeroplanes. During World War II, he became engineer in charge of maintenance at the Edmonton Flying School which produced thousands of pilots and navigators for service in Europe.

I was detailed off to fly with 'Loopey' Lumsden whom I had known at Grandmere. He was an ex-service officer whose uncle was Lord Trenchard, the 'father' of the Royal Air Force. He was a first class, very polished pilot who liked his comforts, and we got on well together. In many ways flying in the north is like sailing with a companion on a passage in a small yacht; mutual respect and the ability to work together under adverse conditions without a clash of personality are very important.

Although I was employed as an engineer, my pilot's licence was current and I usually did a lot of the routine flying. There was no training like flying with experienced men in the days before radio, weather reports and air traffic control; the pilot was in supreme charge and made all the decisions. Knowledge of the route and the weather conditions likely to be encountered were important but, above all, airmanship and knowing when to turn back can only be acquired by experience and by building up hours in the air. In flying with experienced men I was indeed lucky.

After two months of flying with Lumsden, I was transferred to 'Wop' May. In the previous year, he had made an emergency flight to the Peace River district where there had been an outbreak of diphtheria. He and his friend Vic Horner set out from Edmonton with the antitoxin in an open cockpit of a de Havilland Moth in sub-zero temperatures.

This episode, together with his wartime experience of being under attack by the famous Baron von Richthofen at the very moment when the greatest German ace was shot down by another Canadian, Roy Brown VC, had made him famous. He had kept part of one of the splintered propeller blades of the red Fokker Triplane as a relic and reminder of his luck.

'Wop' had, by the time I got to know him, become a tough, hardworking serious person with a bent for engineering. From the moment of leaving McMurray with the mail until our return in a fortnight or so, we were together constantly and came to know each other well. He was always very conscious of the degree of cold and, of course, being a Canadian, had the right clothes for the job but I could never understand his habit of opening his side quarter window, taking off his glove and putting his fingers outside in the airstream to feel the temperature. One good tip of his was to put a fur rug over our knees and the controls to retain the heat from a rather inadequate so-called heater, rather like a couple of old women out for a drive in their carriage in the park.

It was company policy to allocate specific aircraft to the various pilots and so we naturally took over the latest Bellanca to be delivered, the Pacemaker. The new type of undercarriage, replacing the old shock cord, became very hard in the extreme cold and I replaced the hydraulic fluid with paraffin. Some of the landing areas were of soft snow where it was like landing on a feather bed; others, in particular Fort Resolution on the Great Slave Lake, were fully exposed and rough. The wind would blow the snow over the smooth ice into waves which would freeze into hard ridges eighteen inches to two feet high. Take-off and landing in these conditions imposed very heavy strains with a further hazard being the snow horizon which would sometimes merge into an overcast sky, making the judgement of height in the approach and hold-off very difficult.

Arrangements were made with the local trading posts to lay out a line of spruce boughs to indicate the smoothest runway and these eased the landing problem as they gave a good definition of height. Another problem was the lack of any indication of wind direction or speed, although sometimes it was possible to pick out, against the snow background, a wisp of smoke from a log cabin.

On our first flight to the Arctic we were diverted to take a prospector from Fort Norman to Fort Franklin on the Great Bear Lake which had once been the most westerly of Franklin's winter quarters when searching for the North-west Passage. Prospectors were understandably secretive in their searches for minerals and did not encourage questions but about this time, 1930, a French Canadian prospector called Labine discovered pitchblende or uranium ore at what was later to be called Eldorado. Flying along the east side of Great Bear Lake in a Fokker piloted by Punch Dickins of Western Canada Airways, a rival company, he noticed that, on an outcrop of rock, a certain area was bare of snow and deduced this was due to some radiation activity.

Up to that time the only known source of pitchblende ore was the Belgian Congo and with such a monopoly of the supply, the price of radium was in the region of £30,000 an ounce. It was mainly used in the treatment of cancer but the Canadian source was, I believe, used for the first atom bomb.

The Northwest Territories, an enormous area uninhabited except for a few Eskimos, Indians and isolated trappers, was administered by the Federal Government in Ottawa. There was a small establishment at Fort Smith on the Slave River just over the border from Alberta, through which all travellers from or to the north had had to pass – before the day of aeroplanes, there was no alternative route.

It had a small hospital, the only one in the whole area, and we were often called upon to pick up injured and sick people, not to mention a number of expectant mothers. The latter were a menace to us as the journey was often left until the last moment and in the event of bad weather there was a tendency to press on to our destination incurring risks we would not otherwise have taken. On one such flight, en route from McMurray to Edmonton, we were forced to turn back after completing most of the journey to pick up an expectant mother. Landing after a bumpy, three hour flight we were just in the nick of time. We had no medical facilities on board and in winter, no heat, so with only sufficient room for the passenger to sit, the only comfort we could offer was a sleeping bag to wrap round them. It would have been my job to deal with the problem but I was completely ignorant of anything to do with health and even more ignorant about women.

There were three radio and weather reporting stations on our route, one at Fort Resolution on the Great Slave Lake, one at Fort Simpson and the most northerly one at Aklavik on the Mackenzie Delta. Advance weather conditions were not available and with no blind-flying instruments, our time of departure was radioed ahead and in the event of non-arrival, the authorities would be notified. The Mackenzie River itself had been surveyed and mapped but the tributaries and outlying lakes were only shown dotted; presumably the information had been supplied by odd trappers and prospectors.

The settlements along the river were at intervals of about 200 miles. These fur trading posts had been established by the Hudson Bay Company but were then being challenged by Northern Traders who were cutting in on the old HBC territory and were regarded by HBC as upstarts. The sign 'H.B.C' over the store was usually referred to by their rivals as 'Here Before Christ'. As postmen, we were made very welcome by them all but we were also aware of the competition, even at these lonely outposts.

The relatively frequent deliveries of mail which we made were not regarded by all with favour. Instead of one annual return of trading to the Head Office, they were pestered with form filling, fur market prices, statistics and all the paper work of bureaucracy. In compensation, our aircraft were never 'dry' and there were many Scotsmen, manning these HBC posts, who appreciated a nip or two. It was absolutely forbidden to give or sell alcohol to the Indians whose stomachs were not accustomed to it but every white man was allowed one case of spirits a year. The cases arrived in mid-summer, on the annual visit of the Northland Echo, and were disposed of usually within a week.

I was learning to fly in totally different conditions to those in England where I had first gained my pilot's licence. Flight has a mysterious quality in that, on leaving the earth and all its worries, one is in another world. It is entirely different with another set of rules to guide one and perhaps the first impression is of instability and loss of locality. The third dimension is not a natural world for man, nor is the question of height and the combination of all these factors during one's first solo flight is to increase the feeling of tension, if not of fear, of the unknown. Familiar places such as neighbouring towns, fields, woods and even one's own home are difficult to recognise but instead one sees rivers, lakes and railways, all of which become implanted on one's mind.

The most important sight of all is the horizon on which one's sense of balance depends, whereas the sun becomes a vital point of reference for direction. More subtle is the distance travelled from one's base which is estimated in terms of speed and time rather than distance. The third dimension is height for which the pilot refers to the altimeter but the altimeter really measures the air pressure which decreases with height and which is subject to many possible errors and of course measures at best the height above departure point and not above the ground.

The human brain is not accustomed to all these factors but the pilot has the priceless asset of sight. In mist or poor visibility it is much more difficult to fly and instruments become necessary, but in the late twenties blind flying instruments had not been developed, nor of course had radio communication in flight, so all commercial flying was by sight of the ground. On our runs to Aklavik all these facets of the human brain and the body's resilience were tested.

CHAPTER 5

Aklavik Run

My last flight with Wop May in the winter of 1929 to the most northern outpost was a memorable one and very nearly my last – although at the time, in my innocence, I did not think of danger, being perfectly willing to gamble with my future so long as it involved flying. The fact that I was crewing as an engineer to such a well known hero was a great honour and I put my heart into it. The very thought of seeing the real north was exciting and to be accepted by such a company of real men in a man's world gave me confidence.

I was 21 years old and up to that time my own life had been influenced by the war, causing the interruption of my education and my family life, resulting in my leaving the country of my birth and emigrating to Canada. Life there was a substitute for a formal education and was almost entirely involved in aeroplanes and engines. I had had no experience of the humanities – nothing except a material outlook. The wide open spaces and the simple life of the north was a great teacher. A man stood on his own two feet and was judged, not by his background, but for himself and for what he had to offer. Money had little value and in parts none at all. Food was important for life itself but not for pleasure; heat and warmth were essential to ward off death. None of these things were really concerned with flying but it added a touch of drama and provided the satisfaction of bringing people closer together by taking the mail and providing transport in emergency. In other words, life became very basic, eliminating all the minor worries of a civilised existence.

The success of our flying was very dependent on the weather although, because of its consistency, we could anticipate it. These long periods of stable conditions were largely due to the fact that the prevailing winds were from the west and therefore downwind from the Rockies which had already squeezed out most of the water from the moist air coming from the Pacific Ocean but in the summer, when it did rain, it usually persisted for a week at a time.

In the area north of the Arctic circle, sudden winds of great strength would occasionally develop. In the high latitudes near the North Pole the wind has no obstructions and it tends to blow directly from an area of high pressure to one of low. Further south, on the latitude of Great Britain for example, the rotation of the earth has a centrifugal effect on the atmosphere which causes the wind to circle anti-clockwise round an area of low pressure and clockwise round a high which reduces the speed.

On occasions, however, we were unable to anticipate the conditions and this precipitated some dangerous situations. Up until that flight to Aklavik in March 1930, my flying experience had been in fair weather but that trip was to be a tussle with nature herself.

From the first it was a tough trip with bad visibility, snow and heavy winds and in addition to a great deal of mail we also had two Norwegian passengers, neither of whom could speak any English. They were going north to establish a base for a large herd of reindeer which were being driven across the Beaufort Sea over the ice north of the Bering Strait, from Siberia to the Arctic Coast, then on to the Mackenzie Delta. The Canadian Government had bought the herd from the Russians with the intention of providing Eskimos with an alternative source of food and transport; an ambitious scheme and one which is well documented in the Canadian Geographic Magazine published in October/November 1978.

We left Fort Simpson on the morning of 18 March and were scheduled to land at Wrigley, but the river there flows fast and the ice had broken into huge and jagged chunks leaving only a narrow smooth strip near the bank. Wop decided that landing was too risky and so, having thrown out a bag of mail, we pressed on towards Fort Norman.

The weather started to close in with heavy snow and a 50mph head-wind, meaning that we were flying at about the limit of our Bellanca's control. Looking down from about 200 feet I could see that the snow was being picked up from the ground, forming a sort of mist through which the vertical visibility was not too bad but horizontally it was probably less than two hundred yards. From my position in the cockpit I could see a thin layer of clear ice, about 1/16th inch thick, building up on the leading edge of the wing. In the very dry atmosphere of the north the snow normally does not build up on the struts or windscreen but just gets blown clear. Wop did have a rag and a bottle of alcohol which was used occasionally to clear the windscreen by reaching round to the front through an open window of the cockpit.

The gusts were so fierce that the airspeed indicator was jumping between about 70 and 100 mph and Wop was using more or less the full movement of the stick and heavy bursts of power to maintain control of the heavily-laden aircraft. There was no question of being able to make a turn at that height and we could only keep on following the west bank of the river ahead with me following every turn and landmark with my finger on the map, rather like a rally driver's navigator. Fort Norman, on the east bank, was very exposed and our only possible landing place was a cutting, parallel to the river, which had been gouged out by the floods in the annual break-up of the ice; it was vital to land straight ahead and not to overshoot. I have never flown in such bumpy air before or since that day.

After three hours and twenty minutes in the air I told Wop that I thought we were nearly there. We landed blind in deep-driving snow with no sign of our cache of fuel drums as we taxied slowly ahead.

Our fuel caches near the settlements, had been put down on the river bank without much thought for convenience; those who have ever tried to roll a 45-gallon drum of petrol through snow will appreciate the problem. We soon learned to park as near as possible to a cache and not to roll the drums but to tip them end over end. One also became very expert at opening the screw on caps with an axe; a few well-directed blows were more effective than any spanner. We carried our own wobble-pumps and hose and each aircraft had a very special elaborate filling funnel with a chamois-leather filter and water trap. Although in England the standard of maintenance insisted on by the Air Ministry was higher, the Canadians and Americans gave much greater priority to the fuel system. For instance, all the engine fuel filters could be flushed in flight in the event of an accumulation of water whereas in England they were not only bolted but wired up and were not part of the daily inspection routine; the one thing which will stop an engine dead is a fuel stoppage.

If the aircraft was brought to rest in deep snow it would often stick and the only way to get moving again was to rock the wings by heaving up and down on the struts or sometimes by pushing sideways on the tail. Similarly, if the aircraft was left overnight the skis would freeze on the snow surface. A routine was evolved by which before stopping, we would taxi in a figure of eight patting down the snow with our skis and then stop with them straddling two tree trunks with the underside of the skis clear of the snow. I was particularly keen on this technique after having once been left to walk a quarter of a mile through deep snow after unsticking; a more exhausting form of exercise is difficult to imagine.

Our landing at Fort Norman incorporated all these problems and more. As we taxied along searching for the fuel cache an extra gust of wind would suddenly lift the aircraft six feet into the air and using the engine we had to land again and again. After about half a mile I spotted a drum and while the aircraft was held stationary on the throttle I managed to get a rope round the drum and attach it to a wing strut. The Norwegians then helped and we rolled the other drums on top of the skis with drifts forming immediately behind these, effectively holding the skis down. I attempted to dump the oil but it froze in the draincock.

Our passengers were fortunately accustomed to winter conditions but because of the mail bags stowed just behind us we had been unable to see or speak to them, and were oblivious to the fact that they had been airsick and were very frightened.

Although safely down we were still in considerable danger of exposure but in circumstances such as these one seems to be given the extra strength needed to push and heave drums of petrol, using them as anchors to hold the aircraft down. The settlement was two miles away across the river and with visibility in the blizzard down to twenty yards there was no possibility of reaching shelter. An aircraft's cabin can get very cold and normally one would always set up a tent and build a fire but this was impossible as we dared not go out of sight of the aircraft. Fine snow was drifting into every nook and cranny through ill-fitting windows and doors but by shifting the mailbags on to the front seats and hanging one sleeping bag across the front of the cabin we made it as sheltered as possible. Meanwhile the aircraft was lurching about on its undercarriage and every now and then the tail would lift off the snow and drop back down with a bump. I dared not attempt to light the blowtorch to get some heat and in any case my hands were too cold. It was a miserable night. We huddled together two to a bag, head to foot, to preserve what warmth we could, eating slabs of frozen chocolate and taking nips of rum. No-one slept much that night.

At about six the next morning, there was a lull in the storm and we immediately set off on foot, single file across the river. Progress was slow, climbing over jagged pieces of ice six feet high, but we finally reached the opposite bank. The locals were astonished to see us and could hardly believe that we had flown in the previous day. The lull in the storm at dawn that day was unbelievably fortunate as we could not have survived with only the shelter of the aircraft's cabin and no heat – there was no timber on that particular stretch of river, all having been swept away by floods. We were especially fortunate at being able to get to shelter because the blizzard closed in again and it was three days before we were able to make an expedition across the river to see if the aircraft was still safe.

It took me a day's work to thaw out the oil trapped in the tank and to brush out the drifted snow. The space between every cylinder fin was packed solid as was the back of the engine, including the magnetos. The rear of the fuselage was also full; fine snow seems to get through the tiniest hole. Nothing had been damaged and after four days we were able to continue the journey in glorious sunshine but as there was no radio station at Fort Norman we could not report ahead that we were safe. Our departure from Fort Simpson would have been relayed to Aklavik where our arrival was well overdue so it was important to get on before any search was started.

The last port of call before Aklavik was McPherson on the west side of the Mackenzie Delta. The snow looked perfect from the air but on landing we sank deeper and deeper until the aircraft was resting on its belly with the propeller cutting itself a groove. On climbing out of the cockpit I sank through the snow into water! I learned that this phenomenon was called 'overflow' and was caused by the lowering of the water level in the river during the winter causing the unsupported ice to crack in the middle; water flows up through the cracked ice and floats off the snow giving no indication of the danger.

Freeing the aircraft was hard work, the first step being to cut down some trees to provide a rough base for jacking. Having jacked up the skis high enough to clear the water the next step was to shovel the snow away to make a clear path exposing the water. This path had to lead to the bank of the river where the ice was not flooded. While we were working we were inevitably floundering in and out of the water shovelling and jacking. We ought to have built a fire and removed our wet clothes to dry while the water that had been cleared of snow froze over but, being inexperienced, I failed to do so, only returning to the river water to prevent my trousers and mukluks from freezing solid. However, in the end we managed to get the aircraft free and taxied close to the bank on solid ice then, knowing that it was only 50 miles to Aklavik, we decided to fly on immediately.

This decision almost proved fatal when, having climbed to 5,000 feet to get a good view of the delta, Wop put the aircraft into a shallow dive for Aklavik which was in sight ahead. Suddenly there was a thud followed by the nose going down into a gradually steepening dive. I looked out and could see that the ski on my side had twisted round its axle and was lying with the tip down at about 45 degrees to the airflow. Wop had the stick right back and was twisting on nose-up trim as hard as he could go to give the tailplane downward thrust. Scrambling out of my seat and over the top of the mail, I joined the two passengers on the back seat, trying to move the centre of gravity as far aft as possible. Slowly the nose came up and by the time Wop had reduced speed to 80 mph the ski had returned almost to the horizontal, normal in-flight position. I could see clearly what had happened; the elastic shock-cord used for holding the ski in the correct position against the check cable had become frozen while under water in the overflow and had lost its resilience.

We landed safely at Aklavik but as soon as I got out I realised that my leggings were frozen rigid and the locals, seeing this, lifted me onto a dog sleigh and rushed me off to the nearest warm cabin. There, my feet were placed into buckets of hot water and the ice thawed. My legs and toes were still all right but another twenty minutes and the story might have been different. Inexperience in the Arctic is dangerous and I was left in no doubt about this by my friends in Aklavik.

Aklavik, near the open sea, was a convenient trading post for the Eskimos and although they had no money, they brought their furs and skins for barter. It boasted a radio station for weather reports, a small cottage hospital, a Roman Catholic Mission, the Hudson Bay Store, Northern Traders and of course the Royal Canadian Mounted Police. The river had a deep channel to the Arctic Ocean a few miles away and the Eskimos, who normally live on the coast, frequently visited the settlement.

I had little contact with the Eskimos but those I did meet were always cheerful and held in high respect. They were a stocky, tough, independent people, still living by hunting and were constantly on the move. By contrast, the Indians, whose population had been decimated by a flu epidemic in the early 1920s were very poor specimens. On coming into contact with the white man and abandoning the tribal life, they seemed to have lost their will to live; health habits which might have been acceptable in nomadic conditions led inevitably to disease when they took to living in shacks and when feeling ill they just gave up, waiting for death.

Even small communities such as the one at Aklavik have their social order, keeping their distance and only meeting on special occasions. The local Northern Traders with whom we dossed down for a couple of nights were, however, very excited as they had recently rigged up an aerial which they shared with the RCMP and they found that for some reason they could listen in on all their private conversations!

The two stations which provided the best reception on the wireless were Schenectady,

New York State and London 2LO. It was strange to hear Carroll Gibbons and his Savoy Orpheans, as London seemed so far away but of course the distance over the Pole was much shorter than the way I had travelled.

I noticed small mounds of snow distributed around the settlement which turned out to be huskies chained up and living permanently outside without shelter. During the night one dog would start a mournful howl, sitting back on its haunches with its head thrown back; no sooner would one start then several others would join in, making sleep impossible, but if someone gave a loud shout they would all stop howling and for a while a deathly silence would follow. Huskies are not domestic dogs but are often a cross between a German police dog and a wolf and on no account to be patted! A lead dog in a team can find, and will always use, an old trail even though it is covered and hidden with fresh snow. It is able to feel the old path with its paws and in this way avoids some of the effort of breaking a fresh trail. It is interesting that, within the first mile or two of starting a day's journey, when a dog feels the call of nature somehow the lead dog gets the message and stops, the dog concerned instinctively moving off the trail to have its easement rather than fouling the trail for the future. If two teams, travelling in opposite directions, happen to meet on the same trail, a fight to the death over right of way is likely to ensue and in order to avoid this happening, quite a large detour must be made. This right of way also has its parallel among some human beings; who has not seen two motorists, meeting face to face on a narrow passage, refusing to give way..? Huskies also seem to have a great sense of pride in their strength as, however tired they may be on reaching a settlement at the end of their journey, their tails will go up, they will step out and enter with all flags flying!

Aklavik had one very strange inhabitant. This was a horse which had been brought in by barge all the way down the 1600 odd miles of the Athabasca and Mackenzie rivers to this isolated trading post 300 miles north of the Arctic Circle. Its owner was a man called Peffer who fed it on seal meat and fish, hiring it out for dragging timber and other heavy loads to the settlement. It seemed to thrive on this diet for a number of years and in the words of a Canadian pilot, Stan McMillan, with whom I flew later that year, 'It was well respected by man and dog.'

I too began to have a greater interest and respect for the animals in the north. They really own the vast spaces of this desolate land, with man being the intruder. The Arctic coast line provides a bit of living space for the very sparse Eskimo tribes who derive sustenance from the sea and live during the winter almost entirely on fish and seals. They have no houses or settlements but they hunt caribou for meat and clothing, fashioning tools from bone. Animals in the wild migrate with the seasons generally following regular trails across the tundra, the birds migrating to the southern states of America. There is a pattern or rhythm to their lives in which each species seems to have found a niche.

Our flight back to McMurray took two days with seven hours in the air on the last day; altogether we had made eighteen stops on the total sortie, covering 3200 miles. Apart from the flying, we also had to do all the parking, re-fuelling, morning warm-up and handle all the mail without any outside help.

By the first week in April, the ice at McMurray was getting rotten and most of the snow had melted from the surface of the river ice. We removed the skis and replaced the wheels for the take-off for the flight to Edmonton Air Harbour where our arrival was always quite an event. After a few months in the north our eyes had become so accustomed to whiteness everywhere that the first sign of colour or green fields was unbelievably brilliant and good.

Having marched into the foyer of the Shasta Hotel clad in furs and looking like an Eskimo it was a joy to have a hot bath, clean clothes and a well-cooked meal. Our arrival in town was reported in the press and it was not long before a party developed, in fact there were so many parties that in the end some of us were glad to get moving again, away from the artificial life and the bright lights of the city. This reaction may have been due to the sudden and complete contrast to the life of austerity and adventure to which we had become accustomed while flying in the north. Our city acquaintances were curious to hear about our experiences in the north but they had their own lives to lead with their own problems. It felt like being an utter stranger, not really able to communicate. As winter faded away we began to prepare for the next very essential phase of our year, the overhauling of the aircraft.

CHAPTER 6

Flying with Monkey

S pring at Fort McMurray lasted for about two weeks from the time the river ice became rotten to the first signs of summer. The snow had disappeared, the mosquitoes and blackflies were out in force and grass and trees showed signs of growth. The blackflies were a pest, penetrating the soft skin such as the neck and when walking by a lake in the evening, the flies would create a sort of ground mist up to two or three feet above the water.

Most of the snow on top of the ice had melted and we installed the main wheels, taking off through pools of shallow water for the flight to Cooking Lake, twenty miles east of Edmonton, landing in a small grass field by the lakeside. Using a tripod to lift the aircraft we removed the wheels and land-undercarriage and fitted the Edo floats. Cy Becker, our managing director, did the test flight and on 13 May we returned to Fort McMurray.

The more northerly parts of our route were still not completely free of ice, some large chunks being stranded on the banks or in shallow water. We operated the same mail route throughout the summer as we did in the winter but the scheduled flight times were more frequent as we carried a few passengers and were called upon to make various side trips for prospectors. I liked flying in floatplanes and, although they required more maintenance, at least we avoided the morning engine and oil warm-up. It was good experience to have to land on glassy water or quite large waves in strange places. On a map, Canada looks like a large land mass but, in fact, about one third of the area is covered with lakes and it is possible to fly right across Canada using an aircraft with a short range, provided it is equipped with floats.

I met some very interesting characters during my time at Fort McMurray and they were as keen to share their experiences with me as I was to listen to them. One of the engineers I came to know well was a Dutchman called Van der Linden who had worked for KLM before going to the United States where he enlisted in the US Naval Airship Service. He described life on board these big ships which would make flights lasting four or five days at a time, cruising at quite a low altitude of about 1000 feet. The crew would have to carry out maintenance during the flight, constantly repairing leaks in the internal gas bags. These leaks were caused by the fabric chafing on the alloy rib structure and repairing them was quite a difficult job, rather like reefing sails on a square-rigger. The Americans had one big advantage over both the British and the Germans as they used helium not hydrogen for lift, which eliminated the enormous risk of fire. Van der Linden described the sleeping accommodation as a hammock slung between two girders with nothing between you and Mother Earth except a piece of outer fabric covering; in bad weather the whole structure creaked and flexed like a jelly. In spite of his description I have always wanted to make a trip in one but the opportunity has not arisen. During the First World War the Royal Naval Air Service used a type of non-rigid airship, called 'Blimps', for spotting submarines; about 250 were built, equipped with 80 hp Renault V8 engines.

On returning to Fort McMurray from Edmonton I became acquainted with Archie McMullen, a Canadian pilot trained in Alberta. He used to help out at our operational base on routine maintenance but I never had the opportunity to fly with Archie. Before learning to fly at a civil flying school, he told me that he had worked on the Canadian Pacific Railway as a locomotive fireman, a job which I thought entailed simply throwing coal into the firebox, but apparently it is skilled work. The fire must be built up into a horseshoe of flame, backed by fresh coal and if the wheels slip and race, this tears the fire apart, causing loss of steam pressure and provoking a few well chosen words between the fireman and the driver.

By far the most colourful character was 'Monkey' Sherlock, a brilliant pilot, with whom I had the good fortune to fly with for most of the summer. He had originally been in the Royal Flying Corps and after the First World War, had fought in the expeditionary force which Britain had sent in order to help the White Russians fight the Bolsheviks. They had been stationed at Grozny near the mouth of the Volga River under Commander Bowhill, where Sherlock flew DH9A aircraft. I gathered that there was more drinking than flying involved, this being the country of the Cossacks and honour demanded the upholding of the British spirit.

Retiring from the Royal Air Force in 1929, he had come to Canada to continue his easy going lifestyle as a bush pilot. Like all fighter pilots Monkey was a 'press-on' type, always ready to have a go, but fighter aircraft up to that time had been very compact, lively biplanes with thin wing sections which were liable to sudden vicious stall making, so understandably his flying technique was not ideal for commercial flying with nervous passengers. In the approach to land he would 'stir the pudding' as he described it, moving the stick around feeling for the weight of the control and the aircraft's response to the movement, thereby assessing how near a stall he was. On the other hand, in taking a heavy load off calm water, he had a delicate touch, just sensing when the lift was at a peak in relation to the combined drag of water and air. Similarly in flight, when turning back due to bad weather at very low altitude, he would use a lot of power and make a very gentle turn with a small angle of bank allowing the aircraft to turn gently without increasing the wing load due to G. One way and another he was a natural born pilot and I am very grateful to have been fortunate enough to fly as his No. 2. He used to hand over to me to do the routine flying when conditions were straightforward and I did all the navigation, which was not his strong point, whenever it was called for.

Our Bellanca, CF-A1A, became, for all practical purposes, our own personal transport and for most of the time we were out of touch with the office and were our own masters. To spend the night in a bed was an unaccustomed luxury. The normal routine was to sleep on the floor in one's own sleeping bag using a sweater for a pillow. Washing facilities were non-existent except for a washing up basin and, in winter, water was a problem because the heat required to melt snow or ice came from burning wood which had to be cut down, chopped up and dragged to the cabin.

If we ever had to make a forced landing we would always pick an inhabited cabin if we could find one, but failing that it was an understood thing that one could go into any cabin and help oneself to shelter, warmth and food. Before leaving, one wrote a message for the owner but, far more important, one left kindling ready to make an immediate fire and any food which was used had to be replaced as soon as possible. Life in the far north has some elementary lessons for the so-called civilised man as money ceases to have value in the fight for survival and to leave money in payment for food used could well lead to death for the owner of the cabin.

The cabins were usually owned by trappers who were lonely men and usually bachelors, although sometimes there was an Indian woman in the background. They came from all walks of life, of different education and who, for one reason or another, preferred a solitary life looking after their traps and selling some of the finest skins to be found anywhere in the world. No-one inquired into their backgrounds which is probably what attracted them to that life. There are people who criticise the killing of animals for furs but little do the critics realise the skill and hardship entailed in obtaining the skins; the real money is made by the middleman and furrier, not the trapper.

Some of the rules of air safety were not adhered to, especially when it came to loading the aircraft. Scant attention was paid to the weight allowance authorised in the Certificate of Safety of the aircraft; one simply took as much on board as one could lift off the water. There was an additional limitation for us as the Bellanca cabin was designed as a six-seater and mail is very bulky in relation to its weight. The question of stowage required skill as every available square foot would be utilised and it saved work if it was stowed in sequence for off-loading. A heavily loaded floatplane has to overcome a critical stage during take-off in getting 'over the hump' at about 15 to 20 mph. Resistance reaches a maximum as the floats try to start planing before the wings give the benefit of much lift.

The engine of a floatplane inevitably receives a severe beating at full power with little airflow to cool the cylinders; on a hot summer's day the attempt to take off was sometimes prolonged or even abandoned due to overheating. On CF-A1A, I reset the adjustable pitch propeller to give us more revolutions per minute which enabled us to take off with more load, although once airborne our cruising speed was lower.

Whenever pilots met there was often an argument about the best technique for getting a heavily loaded floatplane off smooth water, some arguing for the 'rocking' of the craft to get it onto the 'step' followed by the single leap method while others argued for the gentle touch. Similarly, there was disagreement as to whether to try taking-off downstream with the current giving more airflow over the wings, or upstream against the current with more speed through the water and more dynamic lift on the floats. These questions were never completely answered as conditions were never identical but the handling of the controls at take-off required the greatest skill if a heavily loaded aircraft was to become airborne.

One danger was in landing on very calm, glassy water as the judgement of height is difficult under these conditions. On a river, one landed close to the side using the bank as a reference line, but on a lake it was better to throw something overboard, such as a newspaper or cushion, and land on that as a reference. Another hazard for a floatplane is a floating log when, in the spring, the rivers rise and all the stranded logs float off. Usually these float horizontally on the surface and can be seen, but if only one of the aircraft floats rides over a log it sometimes tips up and is struck by the revolving propeller. Later in the year waterlogged tree trunks or dead-heads will float vertically with only the tip on the surface and striking one of these will rip the bottom out of a float. Putting a patch on a partly submerged float is an unenviable job but it is surprising what you can do if there is no alternative transport and you are 1000 miles from home.

Normally the weather in the north becomes very stable and settled for long periods but from time to time patches of low cloud and rain persist for over a week. We had one such spell in June 1930 on a flight to McMurray from Edmonton with three passengers, when we were forced to land on an unknown lake surrounded with reeds and marshes which made it impossible to get ashore. It rained all night and none of us got much sleep sitting in the cabin, cold, miserable and damp with the aircraft pitching just enough to add a slight feeling of sickness. By morning we were hungry but the emergency rations were stowed in a locker in the rear fuselage which I found very difficult to reach from a float. I had not previously realised the difficulties of actually living on a marooned floatplane; even the most elementary demands of nature called for an acrobatic balancing feat our passengers did not appreciate. I did manage to make some flapjacks and tea for them on our primus in the cabin, an action which the Civil Aviation Authority would hardly have approved of, especially with 100 gallons of petrol in the wing-tanks above us, but needs must when the devil drives.

As morning wore on there was a slight lift in the low cloud so we took off. It was still hopeless but while airborne we saw an isolated cabin on the edge of the lake and landed near it. We made fast to a rickety wooden jetty which several children were running down to see the aircraft followed by their mother and father. He was the only one who could speak any English and looked either Scandinavian or Polish; as an immigrant he had been given a piece of land and had literally carved a living for himself and his family from the virgin bush. I do not think the children had ever seen strangers before, behaving in a very shy manner and not wanting to come near us.

Their mother made some hot soup as we were wet and cold and in return a bottle of our rum was contributed to the party. The mother would not touch it but the father took a liking to it, becoming very excited, and by mid-afternoon he was singing and dancing, our own party fully entering into the spirit. It was a strange scene with six rather drunk men behaving like lunatics surrounded by half a dozen surprised and scared children and a resentful mother. It was not an episode to be proud of and by evening when the clouds again showed signs of lifting, it is doubtful that we were in a sober condition when, anxious to get away, we decided to take off.

Our navigation by dead reckoning was now adrift and, in any case, the map only showed the Athabasca River with no other details, so we took a north-westerly course hoping to hit it. The weather was still bad with a cloud base at about 200 feet and on seeing a stretch of water ahead, we landed. Unfortunately, the river, as such it turned out to be, was very fast flowing; almost a rapid with steep banks. A floatplane has a strong tendency to weathercock into the wind and turning downwind can present great difficulties as, by using a lot of power to give the necessary turning effect from the rudder, the craft itself gathers too much speed and this increases the turning circle. In the circumstances we had no option but to get airborne again.

We spotted a small lake and for 'want of a better hole', settled there. A second cold, wet night on board certainly had a sobering effect especially as we were getting low in fuel. Every full-power take-off uses a great deal of fuel and as we still did not know how far we had to fly before reaching McMurray, the situation was getting critical. The Bellanca fuel gauges were glass tubes on the cabin end of the wing tanks, rather like a water gauge on a boiler; very accurate.

We had already flown nearly six hours since refuelling and there was little fuel showing on the gauges but we had been flying too low to drain either tank completely. By leaning out the mixture, and cruising at reduced speed, I estimated that at best we had another hour's endurance. As luck would have it, next morning the weather improved and we were able to make it to McMurray in forty minutes flying time – a bit too close for comfort.

On 26 June 1930, Monkey Sherlock and I flew from McMurray to Aklavik, making ten stops *en route* to drop mail and to re-fuel, arriving at about two o'clock in the morning to find everyone up and about. In midsummer, of course, there were 24 hours of daylight, which I found most disconcerting; to arrive at Aklavik at that hour in the morning to find people having their main meal of the day seemed wrong when we wanted our breakfast! It is interesting to note that Aklavik is nearly 70° north and as far west as halfway to Honolulu from San Francisco. One is moving up round the top of the world.

It had taken us $11^3/_4$ hours flying time and was the first flight from the 'end of steel', the railway terminus at Waterways near McMurray, to the Arctic Ocean in a day. Those who fly seaplanes will know that one's anxieties are not over until the aircraft is safely secured on dry land. It was a very long day but we found the most restful part was while we were actually flying.

Our flight, although carrying only a few hundred pounds of useful load, was well covered by the Canadian press because it showed how effectively the aeroplane could, in a few hours, bring civilisation to the remotest parts. Today there are two flights a day to the Mackenzie Delta, only a short distance from Prudoe Bay, the largest source of oil on the North American continent whereas, on the Canadian side of the border, an oil and gas field is still waiting to be exploited. Little did Monkey and I know what lay below those barren wastes because no-one had even scratched the surface then.

The two Norwegian herdsmen who had flown with us to Aklavik in the previous winter were now ready to set up camp in anticipation of the reindeer's arrival. We flew off with them along the coast in an easterly direction from Aklavik on a beautiful sunny day with unlimited visibility – the barrier ice could be clearly seen a few miles to the north. Our passengers picked a suitable looking place with a sandy beach and low hills behind. While unloading their gear, two of us decided to have a bathe. With a hot sun on the shallow water for 24 hours a day the water was reasonably warm! The place chosen was completely barren but on a high bank, well above sea level. At the time we named it Reindeer Point but later it turned out that it was called Kittigasuit, an Eskimo name. Both Monkey and I felt badly about leaving these men so sparsely equipped in such a desolate spot.

The 3000 reindeer which were to be driven by Andy Baker, a 60 year-old Laplander, for the last lap from western Alaska to Kittigasuit, did not arrive until February 1935, which meant it had taken over five years to complete the great drive. They endured unbelievable hardships of extreme cold, exposure and lack of food *en route*. The herd had a compulsive urge to return to their former home range which made the journey almost impossible and the final crossing of the Mackenzie River Delta took two years! By the time the herd finally reached the eastern side, the reindeer were weak and dying and some even had to be carried on dog sleds to their food supply.

The Canadian Government paid only $65 per head for animals delivered safely to the corrals at Kittigasuit and the final count was 2382 head. Only 20% bore the markings of the original herd, the others were born on the trail and in fact 800 fawns were born in the next couple of months, a magnificent achievement. By 1978 the herd had 9000 animals providing employment, food and hides for the Eskimo and Indian natives of the area.

On the route south we were diverted from Fort Norman during a special charter flight for the Imperial Oil Company. In 1924 oil had been discovered on the east bank of the Mackenzie River, 50 miles down river from the settlement but, as there was no demand for oil in the north at that time, the well and other equipment had been abandoned. We were to visit the site and make a report but, on our arrival at Fort Norman, the manager of the Hudson Bay Company Store arranged a drinking party for us with two or three others.

Before going to Canada I hardly drank anything, even beer, because it was too expensive. All the flying people drank spirits, however, and one had to join in to keep them company.

By the age of 21, on joining Commercial Airways, I had learned to tell the different brands of whisky by their taste and after three months flying with Monkey, I had taken a liking to his usual drink, brandy which is the real drunkard's drink. It is a very different drink to whisky which up to then had been my choice, but it does have a stimulating effect. It is known as 'eau de vie' and of course is used for medicinal purposes.

About midnight, although there was still daylight, I went off to sleep leaving the others to it, but about five in the morning I was woken with the news that we were just going off to the oil well. I did not immediately realise the state that Monkey Sherlock was in, not that I could have done much anyway, but we set off with two passengers in the back of the cabin. We found the site easily and went ashore to inspect it.

Everything moveable had been taken as every boat going down river must have landed there to help themselves. Not knowing anything about the oil business I was surprised to find a pipe sticking out of the ground with a tap on it still intact but with the stopcock padlocked. With the judicious use of an axe I freed it and oil squirted out and finding an old empty food tin we filled it with the brown, dirty-looking liquid. To our surprise it proved possible to light it with a match without difficulty so presumably it was unusually volatile and I would guess that it could, after filtration, be used directly in a diesel engine. During World War II a pipeline was constructed from this area, running for a few hundred miles over the Rocky Mountains to the new Alaskan Highway. This project must have cost a lot of money and it would be interesting to know how successful it proved to be.

Our flight back to Fort Norman from the oil well was a frightening one. Monkey, still suffering from the night before, kept turning round to talk to his two passengers on the back seat but in the middle of the conversation he gently pushed the stick forward until his passengers were suspended in mid air due to negative G! There were no such thing as passenger seat belts in those days nor was there anything for them to hold on to and their faces of surprise and alarm merely goaded Monkey on to do it again! He finished off by looping the loop which I knew was taking the wings and structure of the aircraft very near the limit of strength but although we had the extra weight of the floats, we fortunately had no load in the cabin and little fuel. Commercial aircraft are only designed for a wing strength of about four times that of a normal full load and this is easily reached in a pull out from a dive. The whole episode was a shattering experience. However, I thought I could stop him flying in the future while in that condition and nothing like this ever happened again.

After that trip I swore never to drink brandy again and as, at about that time, I noticed my hands were getting shaky, so shaky in fact that I had to use both hands to steady my glass to prevent it spilling, I decided not to drink anything at all before flying. Even now, 60 years later, I cannot drink brandy without a pounding heart. It certainly makes you live faster but you have to pay for it!

All our maintenance was carried out at McMurray, each engineer looking after his own aircraft. Wright Whirlwind engines were very reliable, the ignition being by dual Scintilla magnetos which had rotating field magnets with fixed make-and-break, a great advance over any British magneto at that time. Engines were returned to the factory for major overhauls which became due at, I believe, 600 hours, but we did our own period checks and top overhauls.

One day I was greasing and adjusting the valve clearances when, on turning over the engine, I suddenly realised that it had started and was idling over slowly! At that time I was standing on a plank straddling the two floats with the propeller hub at about chin level. Not daring to move I shouted to someone to come and switch off, in the meantime holding myself clear of the hub with the blades whirling past my toes. It was a nasty moment and I can only assume that I must have knocked 'on' the American type of swinging arm contact switch with my knee while climbing out of the cockpit.

In the early summer Lumsden heard he had been given the sack. He was too much of a man of leisure to stand the pace and was considering leaving anyway when the message arrived. It placed him in a dilemma, however, as there was not much money in the kitty with which to buy his train ticket back east and the problem was whether he should travel the four day journey to Montreal first class or whether to go 'tourist' and take some bottles of whisky. Being a very human person who liked meeting people, you can guess which alternative he took.

The availability of our aircraft gave prospectors a wonderful opportunity to search vast new areas for minerals. Their interest was primarily in gold and other rare metals which could easily be transported as, although there is an abundance of other minerals such as zinc and copper in the Northwest Territories, these are more easily obtained elsewhere. We often flew these men and their supplies into some remote place in the early spring arranging to collect them in the autumn before the freeze up. These camps were not identifiable on any map for the simple reason that no maps existed but they relied on our sense of direction and memory. It always worried me, therefore, that should anything happen to us or our aircraft, they would be in trouble and would, at the very least, have to wait until the freeze up before being able to walk or canoe to the nearest trading post.

On one such trip we were persuaded to carry a canoe to the site. It had been done before and using a good deal of rope lashings we fastened it under the bottom of the fuselage where it fitted surprisingly well. However, when taking-off, a large quantity of spray found its way inside the canoe which put the centre of gravity of the aircraft right outside the aft limit. In flight the water sloshed backwards and forwards making it impossible to hold a steady flight path. Fortunately, the distance was only 25 miles but we were glad to land safely and never took the risk again. In fact, it was our own fault because, although we knew canoes had been flown before, neither of us had actually seen it done. The proper method was to tip the canoe on its gunwale and lash it upside down onto the outside of the struts of one float so that water could not collect in it.

In mid-July we were recalled to Edmonton to embark a party of politicians who wished to make an election tour of the Peace River District. The Peace River flows from the foothills of the Rockies in a north-easterly direction, feeds into the Slave River and ultimately flows north to the Arctic Ocean. This area must have been one of the last to be populated in North America as, although it was potentially good farming land, it was relatively inaccessible, being north of the main trans-Canada railways.

After a flight of two and three-quarter hours we landed on the McLennan Lake. From there the election tour really started with daily flights in different directions but it was a very sparsely inhabited region which meant the meetings only attracted a few people. Although the charter was successful from our Company's point of view, I cannot believe the outcome of the subsequent election had any significant effect, except that it was the first electioneering tour by air of what is now a very wealthy oil-bearing area.

During the summer an old stern-wheeler called the *Northland Echo*, made its yearly trip to Fitzgerald taking passengers and supplies. Fitzgerald was at the top of the rapids on the Slave River, the rapids marking the dividing line between the Province of Alberta and the Northwest Territories. During the summer of 1929 our fuel dumps had been established in time for the start of the winter flying service but in 1930 the steamer was unable, or unwilling, to do this and so the Company was forced to do it itself. A wooden barge and petrol-engined tug were built and the whole outfit set off on the long journey. The Mackenzie flows very fast in places, with sandbars and minor rapids, making it uneconomic to attempt to return against the current, so that everything that was used for the journey north had to be abandoned there. By the time the fuel was delivered to the most northerly trading posts it was very valuable and precious. From time to time one found a drum empty, lost either from evaporation or theft; for us this was almost as serious a matter as being short of food.

Most of the operational crews moved out of O'Coffee's Hotel in the spring of 1930 and joined together to rent a house, employing a Chinese cook who more or less ran the place. As we were never there together it can be imagined what chaos this led to. I had never realised before how thin the veneer of civilisation really is; manners disappear, bad habits develop without check and untidiness and dirt accumulate everywhere. There was a hip bath which one emptied out of the window onto the snow below but the water was quite expensive as chunks of ice had to be chopped from the frozen river and melted. Our only relaxation was to listen to the wireless on earphones.

The next year, from September 1930, I was sent on special assignments which expanded my range of experiences.

CHAPTER 7

Nahanni River Hunting Trip

At the end of August 1930, CF-AlA, which by now I regarded as my own aircraft, was allotted to Glyn Roberts, an ex-Royal Air Force Welshman. We were given a most interesting job to fly a party of American big-game hunters into the Rocky Mountains to try to obtain specimens of the special mountain sheep which were known to live in those remote parts.

It had been decided to establish a camp at Dead Man's Creek on the Nahanni River, about 250 miles west of the Great Slave Lake. It was inaccessible both on foot or by canoe as the river flowed through a deep gorge which cut through a ridge of hills on its way to join the Liard River, a tributary of the Mackenzie. Everything had to be flown in, including three hefty men and supplies for a month.

We waited three days at Fort Simpson for good weather, finally leaving on 10 September. From the air the whole area beyond the gorge looked formidable with high, snow-covered peaks falling away to a heavily timbered valley. The river was fast flowing but it was straight for about a mile before the rapids leading through the gorge. On landing safely we taxied into the west bank and set about making a clearing, felling some timber for the camp. I joined one of the party who was fishing for the evening meal; it was unbelievable as every cast seemed to produce a beautiful large fish – it had evidently never been fished before.

That night we had a further surprise. While sitting round our camp fire, what I believe was a pack of wolves came to have a look. Their eyes reflected the light from the fire but after taking a shot at one of them they turned tail and slunk away. The valley was teeming with game of all sorts but it was not a place to go off casually shooting for the pot; crossing one of the dried-out river beds we found the trail of a large grizzly bear whose prints were a good twelve inches long! After this we never left camp without rifles; a grizzly is one of the few animals which will stalk and attack a man without provocation.

I had learnt to handle a gun in Scotland shooting grouse, walking over the moors with pointers and also stalking deer using a rifle. Searching for game around our camp in the Nahanni Valley was the first time I had carried a gun for defence and it certainly made me more alert.

The hunters set off to climb the surrounding mountains while we went to collect the next load of supplies. However, our landing back at the camp three days later very nearly turned into a disaster. As previously mentioned, the river was flowing at about 6 knots and at the same time there was a wind upstream of 15 mph. Understandably, Glyn Roberts chose to land into the wind but downstream. The width of the river was about 100 yards with banks lined with small boulders. Owing to the combination of wind and current making the aircraft weathercock and not being equipped with water rudders, we found it difficult, in fact impossible, to turn upstream. Every time we tried to turn we finished up heading straight for a bank, so finally, with the rapids looming up ahead, Glyn Roberts ran ashore into one bank at considerable speed. There was a great grinding and bumping of the floats over stony shallows as we were carried downstream. By climbing out and wading in the icy river I was able to swing the aircraft's nose up river and so to taxi back to safety. We had not improved the floats but they still seemed to be watertight and at least we would be able to fly out again successfully. I took the precaution of mooring the aircraft tail to the bank as I knew that with leaking floats or even a lowering of the river water level overnight, a floatplane parked nose towards the shore can finish up with the tailplane under the water.

The party were successful in their hunt and obtained some good 'heads' of the rare species for which they had been hunting. Mr Shultz, who was the leader of the party, was very pleased with their trophies, the horns of which were rather similar to a bull's but corrugated and curled round more at the tips.

About a month after his return to civilisation a large packing case arrived at McMurray filled with an assortment of socks. It turned out that he was the president of the largest sock manufacturer in the USA! My share lasted for years but Mr Shultz told me that the better the quality, especially of wool socks, the shorter the life, so there must have been little wool in them.

The charter must have been one of the first hunting expeditions in the north using aircraft. It was an ambitious sortie and the visitors were fairly tough types – building the camp, cutting wood and cooking far from civilisation. There are now hunting and fishing lodges in the north, built on a permanent basis to attract tourists, rather like the dude ranches in Texas for the city cowboys.

Before returning to the Nahanni River at the conclusion of the hunting trip, we were recalled to Edmonton where, to my surprise, my brother David, who was four years older than me, had turned up unexpectedly.

I had not seen him for a couple of years but I had heard that he had left the Stock Exchange where he had been since he left Rugby. He hated life in the city and finally had a nervous breakdown. He was a keen yachtsman and had done some sailing on the east coast where he kept a small yacht and he also crewed for Bobby Somerset, one of the leaders in the early ocean racing days, and in fact had sailed with him in the first Fastnet Race. He had a natural feeling for the sea in the same way I loved the air while my brother

Jack, the eldest, hated both but liked to hunt and shoot.

David had apparently left the city and gone to Finland where he signed on as a seaman in the *Olivebank*, a four-masted square-rigged ship of 3500 tons with a crew of 25, departing in ballast for Australia. He was returning to England by steamship across the Pacific and Vancouver, hence his arrival in Edmonton.

He told me of the 168 days he had spent at sea and the hardships of manning such a large sailing ship. The English Channel, with the prevailing wind from the west, was a difficult route owing to the lack of manoeuvrability of square-rigged ships and so they had gone round the north of Scotland where the wind, sea and cold had been grim. In addition, as the ship had no power, there was neither electric lighting nor heat except for the galley located on the main deck and in a really rough sea even that would get flooded. To change tack was a major operation calling for all hands on deck and then wearing round, that is to say putting the helm up and the stern through the wind. As with most ships the most dangerous manoeuvre was running down a strong wind when they are liable to broach out of control.

David had always been rather a strange character but in later years he married an artist, lived on a Thames barge at West Mersea and St Tropez before it became fashionable, then with their son they went to Papeete, the French tropical island in the Pacific. He also sailed alone across the Atlantic twice, on the second occasion being caught on the edge of hurricane Diane. His log describes the seas as monstrous and his little Vertue class boat pitch poled but survived, probably because David had prepared her well for this very eventuality occurring; he was a real sailor. It was strange to meet him in Edmonton, our lives had diverged so completely but in a way I knew we both liked a life of freedom and independence. He only stayed a couple of days in Edmonton when after taking him for a short local flight, we both went our own ways.

Returning to Fort Resolution on the Great Slave Lake, we received a message to go to Fort Rae on the north shore of the lake to take some mining engineers on a reconnaissance flight. Most of the places we used to land while on floats were well sheltered but Resolution was fully exposed and on this particular day there were some big waves.

The lake is like the open sea being 250 miles long by 100 miles wide, and as we were carrying two 45-gallon drums of fuel in the cabin as well as two passengers, we were on the upper limit of load. After a few violent bumps and premature leaps into the air, Glyn Roberts managed to get the aircraft airborne without damage.

Although the Bellanca never gave any structural problems, there were a number of features which would never be accepted by civil aviation authorities today. The main throttle control was only a piano wire sliding through a tube; even the main elevator control cable ran over a sheave which relied on a weld to attach it to the middle of a cross tube of the fuselage.

Any aircraft which became damaged in the north was a write-off unless it could be patched up and flown out. There have been a number of amazing recoveries including one

STAN McMILLAN FINDS PADDY BURKE'S JUNKERS ON THE LIARD RIVER, DECEMBER, 1930

Stan McMillan finds Paddy Burke's Junkers on the upper Liard River under the winter's snow in December 1930. (Note that it is still on floats.)

STAN McMillan

The salvaged Junkers at Atlin B.C on 11 February 1931. From left, the author, Stan McMillan, Van der Bill and Joress, the two pilots who flew it out. (Note the snowshoes in the cabin, even the paddle did not help!)

Mail for the North being loaded into a Bellanca Pacemaker (300 hp Wright Whirlwind J6 engine) on 11 December 1929, flown by celebrated Canadian bush pilot, Wop May (right) and the author (centre).

The local dog team owner collects mail from an aircraft at Fort Resolution.

Curtiss H.S2L flying boat with 400hp Liberty engine. One of the last stick and string aeroplanes built in the first war. Used in Canada for forest survey and photography.

Wearing my fancy mukluks, with the Lockheed Vega at Fort Mcflurray in January 1930. The Vega was the first aerodynamically 'clean' aeroplane, except for the undercarriage. It had a monocoque structure and a cantilever wing. (Note skis on laminated wooden pedestals with wire and rubber check cables.)

Crew and passengers at Edmonton, Alberta, at the new Municipal Air Harbour before departure for Fort Mcflurray on 8 December 1929 in Bellanca Ch 300's nos CF-AJQ, CF-AJR and CF-AAL. *Rear row* (left to right): I Glyn Roberts, pilot (ex-RAF); Cy Becker, pilot and company managing director; John Melvin, Hudson Bay Company Inspector; AW Hale, Post Office Inspector; Maurice Burbridge, CFI, Edmonton Flying School; Ted Watt, reporter. *Front row* (left to right): Don Robertson, an air engineer and a licenced pilot; Reg Jackson, office manager; 'Boom' Lumaden, pilot (ex-RAF); ARC McMullen, pilot; Stan Green, air engineer.

The Argosy's passenger cabin – in 1927, aeroplane designers had the final say, not an interior decorator! Argosy 20 passenger cabin with wicker chairs and a discreet curtain at the rear, no special ventilation or heat.

Evocatively photographed in flight over the city of London, the Armstrong Whitworth Argosy giant airliner for Imperial Airways with a 20 passenger cabin, made its maiden flight in 1927. (Note the pilots' open cockpit.)

The staff of the Henderson Flying School, Brooklands 1928. AVRO 504 with 80hp Renault V8 Engine. (Note the engineers clothes and the racing track in the distance.)

1923 GN Air cooled twin cylinder with a multiple chain drive. The Author's brother David teaches him to drive.

Granny's 1912 Minerva

Ella on our honeymoon June 1936. 1922 Hispano Suiza type Monza with body by Kellner of Paris. No luggage space in boot, but spare wheel.

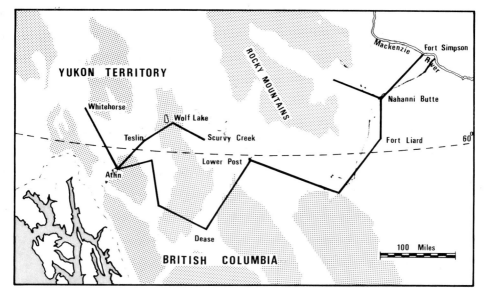

Map of Rocky Mountains showing our course to Atlin and Whitehouse from Fort
Simpson on the McKenzie River. The mountain area was not fully surveyed in 1931.

Fort Norman N.W.T on 22 March 1930. Wop May's visit after the storm on a tour
of inspection. The snowdrift over the skis saved the Bellanca, a typical carryall and
dog team bringing help.

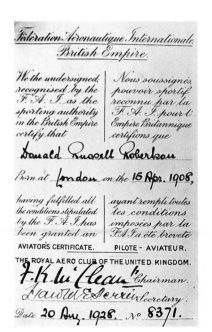

The author's Pilot's Certificate of competency.

Don Robertson at maintenance base Fort McMurray, Winter 1929/30. (Note nose hangar with curtain in background.)

case where the crew made their own replacement wooden propeller, another when a badly twisted and broken rear fuselage was lashed up with wooden splints and galvanised fencing wire! The prospect of being marooned hundreds of miles from home without transport certainly proves the old saying 'necessity is the mother of invention'; improvisation is the order of the day, safety rules taking second place.

We made the final mail delivery to Aklavik on 5 October 1930 before the winter freeze-up. It was getting late and the weather was cold when trouble developed in the engine oil system. As we were still on floats, no winterisation of the engine had been thought necessary but suddenly the oil temperature started to rise above the upper limit. Four times in one day we had to force land on the river to allow the oil to cool.

The type of oil supplies, incorporated the very latest advances in this field – in fact we were being used as a kind of guinea pig. Unfortunately, it foamed badly and from the quantity of oil covering the exterior of the engine it was evident that a lot of pressure was building up in the crankcase. Although we reached home safely, the trouble was almost certainly due to either the breather pipe becoming frozen or possibly coring in the oil scavenge line to the tank.

After a year of intensive flying I had acquired the airman's habit of thinking in terms of time to one's destination, not the distance. This is entirely rational as up to the establishment of air routes, one thought of the distance by sea from say Bangkok to England via the Indian Ocean and the Suez Canal, whereas by air one goes the much shorter route via the Himalayas and Moscow. One's whole conception of the world changed, it became much smaller. When I decided to take a holiday in England in 1930 I travelled for four days by train to Montreal and eight days by sea. At that time it did not occur to me that it was unusual to undertake such a long distance journey as that from Edmonton to England simply for a two weeks holiday.

It was good to be home and to see my family in Cornwall but England was a depressing place. My parents had moved to their Constantine Bay bungalow in North Cornwall and although I was keen to tell them all about my adventures in Canada, my mother was not well and in fact, although I failed to realise, it was the first indication of a serious illness. My father, a keen golfer, had fallen out with the local Club Secretary and had no partner with whom to play golf. Altogether it was a cheerless situation not helped by the three million unemployed at that time. I suppose the life I had been living was unusual but one could not help contrasting the stodgy established order of things with the freedom of Canada so I could hardly wait to get back and the urge to fly was still very strong.

The return journey on the *Europa*, a crack ship of the Hamburg America Line, to New York and via Chicago by train was interesting. Transatlantic voyages in the big liners provided a great opportunity of meeting all sorts of people and for those who wanted a social life it was almost a continuous party with invitations to the Captain's drink parties, various dinner parties, cocktails and every kind of entertainment and sporting event.

Aeroplanes and the established air routes of the world cannot provide these social contacts for passengers – many lifelong friends and business acquaintances began on board ship.

On this particular journey I met a Wall Street banker who was involved with the building of the Woolworth skyscraper, then being built. He kindly invited me to visit the site and we went up in the workmen's elevator to the fourteenth floor. It was just a bare skeleton, steel structure but he proudly told me that they had built this far in the astounding time of fourteen days; a storey a day! When finished it was the tallest building in New York but was soon exceeded by the Chrysler Building which added a light tapering spire.

From New York I boarded the Twentieth Century Limited, a well known train to Chicago, which made the trip overnight with a guaranteed arrival time of 9.00am. There was even a refund on the fare of a dollar for every minute it was delayed!

I stayed with friends of my family in Chicago but not having room for me in their apartment, I was made an honorary member of Mr James's club, a very sedate English type of establishment. The year 1930 was the height of gang warfare in the city and I was given strict instructions that, if stopped on the street, I was to hand over my wallet immediately without argument, any foreigner being fair game. My clothes and hat were quite ordinary but were probably different enough to look unusual in a mid-west city before universal television and rapid communications.

Mr James, an Englishman who ran a big power station, The State Line Generating Company, had a daughter, Margaret, a vivacious redhead with expensive tastes. She was studying sculpture and in the interest of my artistic education, she took me to the opera; it was fun for a few days to enjoy a life of luxury.

I took a second class seat on the train which rumbled over the bleak snowbound prairies for four days only to find that there was no aircraft flying north to McMurray, leaving me with no alternative but to take the weekly mail train. This was a new experience. The mixed freight-cum-passenger train consisted of four freight cars and one passenger coach and was due to take 24 hours for the 200 mile journey. The coach had a cooking stove at one end and a lavatory at the other. My fellow travellers consisted of about twenty rough and tough looking characters but we very soon came to know one another over crates of whisky and rum! A game of poker started on leaving Edmonton and was continued all day as we crawled slowly north. We stopped at every wayside halt and even log cabins where the engine driver and fireman would descend and have a chat with the locals. By evening the party was in full swing with singing and dancing (alas no girls!) until it gradually subsided into a drunken stupor. The next morning we crept into Waterways, the terminus near McMurray in a very subdued state.

The most derelict taxi imaginable – which was open and had no hood – ran the final five miles. The radiator had to be filled for each sortie and leaked like a sieve but it was better than hiking through the snow with luggage. The owner driver who was probably of Scandinavian extraction, knew only a few words of English, nearly all swear words, but he made himself clear enough!

CHAPTER 8

Yukon Salvage

For the winter of 1930-31 I was to crew Stan McMillan, the celebrated Canadian bush pilot. In the previous year, 1929, Stan had been one of the pilots of the two seaplanes, one a Super Fokker, the other a Fairchild FC2-W2, lost for 54 days in the Barren Lands in the Arctic when Colonel MacAlpine, President of Dominion Explorers and his party, had been visiting some of the company's prospecting parties in the area who were making the first organised search for minerals in the far north. The aircraft had left Chesterfield Inlet on Hudson Bay in the late autumn, intending to fly to Bathurst on the Arctic Ocean but they failed to arrive. No expense was spared in the search which was immediately organised as the freeze-up was expected shortly, making floatplanes useless until equipped with skis. Most of the fuel caches were used up throughout the north before a wireless message came from Cambridge Bay of their safe arrival on foot. They had waited for the sea ice to form and been guided there by Eskimos. They had force-landed out of fuel at Dease Point.

The world press had been following the dramatic search in the Arctic Barren Lands and their subsequent rescue. The experience gained of operating aircraft under such adverse conditions owed a great deal to the fortitude of the pilots concerned. In all, five aircraft were lost through failures or accidents but no lives; sadly, several of the pioneering bush pilots who took part were killed in the following years.

Many bush pilots have disappeared without trace in the north because an aircraft is difficult to spot, especially in winter when the top surfaces would probably be covered in snow. Our Bellancas were painted post office red which stood out well but nowadays fluorescent orange is used as the colour is easier to see.

It is a strange fact that when a pilot is lost it has been found that he tends to turn in a westerly direction so when first searching for him, the search is always initiated on that side of his planned route. Perhaps a psychiatrist could give an explanation of this phenomenon but, of course, on the North American continent, immigrants always tended to go towards the under-developed west. The usual comment to the ambitious was 'Go West Young Man' where there was free land and even gold to be found. Years later when staying with a friend in Vancouver who was in charge of the coastguard operation and rescue service at Vancouver International Airport, he told me that they were often called out to search for suicides who had been seen to jump off the Lion's Gate Bridge which spans the deep water channel at the entrance to the main harbour. Those seeking a better life cannot go further west than this and it is sad to relate that the average number of suicides per year in the late 1980s was fifteen.

Stan was a very different character to Monkey Sherlock, being quieter and far more painstaking in planning a flight; furthermore we never carried any alcohol! His experience the previous year when the MacAlpine party came so near to starvation may have made him more cautious but he was a good steady pilot who never took any unnecessary chances. He realised, as I began to realise, that the hazards of bush flying are as great on the ground as they are in the air. The north is such a vast, almost totally uninhabited and inhospitable area that any unexpected minor mishap can easily lead to disaster. Stan knew how to survive and I could hardly have had a more experienced true bush pilot to teach me.

After a few northern flights with mail we were sent on an entirely different and unusual charter trip which came about as the result of someone else's misfortune and tragedy. A Junkers F 13 flown by an Irishman, Paddy Burke, and carrying a prospector and an engineer, had been forced to land on a river in bad weather during a flight in Northern British Columbia. It was a sad story with Paddy Burke, an ex-RAF pilot, being persuaded to make the prospecting flight late in the autumn.

Following a river through the Rockies he had been forced by bad weather to fly lower and lower until he had no alternative but to land. The floats, being damaged, filled with water and the aircraft was left with the floats submerged but the fuselage and wings high and dry. The three men on board waded to the bank and set up camp but with the oncoming winter, no rescue was possible until the freeze up. After a few days they decided to try to walk to Wolf Lake which they knew was at the head of the valley about 75 miles away.

As none of them had any real experience of living rough and off the country, Burke, a German engineer called Emil Kading and a city-type mining engineer, made all the mistakes one might expect. Seventy-five miles may not sound too far but there was a great deal of undergrowth along the banks of the river, all the icy tributary streams had to be crossed and they had to carry all the camping gear. On top of this they had little food. After a week on the trail they had covered 20 miles then had the luck to see a deer but unfortunately they had failed to remove the grease and oil off the breech of the gun and it had frozen. During the autumn most animals are to be found high up near the tree line but fortunately another deer was seen and they shot it. None of them had ever gutted an animal before and in their efforts with a knife, wasted much of the meat. After feeding themselves up they set forth again but three days later they were so hungry they went back for the head and other bits. By this time Burke was becoming very weak and a few days later he died while the others managed to reach a trapper's cabin on Wolf Lake.

The river where the aircraft had come down was shallow but a rock had punctured the floats. Although otherwise undamaged, the aircraft was resting on the river bottom and the insurance company thought it might be possible to salvage it, commissioning us to do the job.

We left McMurray on 27 January following the scheduled route as far as Fort Simpson where we loaded all the fuel we could carry into drums and branched off to the west, landing at Fort Liard on the Liard River. After staying the night we set off next morning to fly over the Rockies for Atlin, British Columbia where the land undercarriage for the skis and other spares were awaiting collection. The only map we had was one of Western Canada torn out of an atlas with a scale of about 80 miles to an inch which showed the distance as the crow flies as being about 340 miles. It appeared as if the best route would be to fly up the valley of the Dease River, over the height of land and by steering west we should then hit a river which flowed north-westerly, taking us in the direction of Lake Teslin and so to Atlin.

We followed the Liard River with the mountains rising steadily on either side. Carrying about 80 gallons of extra fuel in the cabin we had hopefully expected to pump this into the main wing tanks during flight. I could not make the lash up system work and in any case it was bumpy and some of the precious fuel was spilling. I had had no experience of mountain flying nor I think, had Stan but it became evident that with an adverse wind and the heavy load, trouble lay ahead.

Although the Whirlwind engine was mildly supercharged, the impeller was more to improve the distribution of the mixture than to provide power at altitude. The height of land we had to cross was about 10,000 feet but the westerly wind was pouring over the top like a waterfall and as we approached, our rate of climb turned into a rate of descent. After three hours in the air, Lower Post, where the Dease River joins the Liard River, came into sight, only 160 miles from our point of departure.

Here was the first sign of human habitation, a log cabin with smoke and trails leading to it so we landed in very deep snow to be greeted by a very surprised Scotsman. I do not think he had seen another human being for a year or two and certainly not an aeroplane. For us it was a relief to have landed safely and to have found shelter as well as receiving a warm welcome in such inhospitable country. The snow was so deep it was like a feather bed and Stan and I were forced to use snow-shoes but all was well when we took off the next morning reaching McDame, a small trading post, an hour later. There I pumped the remainder of the fuel into the tanks and was glad to get it out of the cabin. We stayed the night before setting out on the final leg.

The height of land was a flat, featureless, snow-covered plateau, 50 miles across, but there was no sign of any river or valley to guide us to Lake Teslin. I was beginning to think that the position of the river had been inserted on hearsay! The lie of the land and mountains was in a north-westerly direction so after turning that way, a long, narrow lake eventually appeared which proved to be Teslin. The route onwards to Atlin was through a narrow gap in the mountains which acted like a funnel for the strong westerly wind, bumping us violently all over the sky; I was glad that most of our fuel had been used as I looked anxiously at the flexing of the wings.

Atlin, a gold mining town on Lake Atlin, duly turned up but to our embarrassment we saw that the lake was open water and we, of course, were on skis! Not much hope of landing there. Luckily we had spotted a small lake about five miles away which was frozen and hardly had we landed than a snowmobile or tracked Model T Ford appeared with many helpful people. I think we must have been the first to fly over the Rockies in such northerly latitudes. It was strange to find relatively mild weather with over twenty feet of snow and of course, we were definitely wrongly dressed for the occasion with our parkas, mukluks and Arctic gear.

I was glad, however, to reach there as a large boil had developed on one of my fingers and it was beginning to affect my left arm. All was well after it had been lanced but it took quite a long time to heal up in the cold weather.

Gold was still being mined near Atlin and somewhat to my surprise the manager offered me a job at twice my salary to look after the mining machinery. A nice cushy job with no risks but I was not in the mood to be tempted. We immediately started making plans to fly the skis and other equipment to the wrecked aircraft but before doing so we had to report to the provincial authorities at Whitehorse across the border of British Columbia in the Yukon because the wreck was in their territory. The flight there was via the White Pass on the old Klondike route from Skagway; it looked very desolate as no doubt it had to those who took part in the gold rush of 1898. The landing strip was a clearing in the forest a couple of miles from what remained of the ghost town of Whitehorse which, at one time, had a population of some 30,000. The reception party took us straight to the police station before joining us for a meal. It was the only occasion in my life when I was asked to produce my licences both as pilot and engineer and I felt we had come a long way into the wilds to be so insulted!

Back at Atlin Emil Kading and a freelance pilot called Van der Byl were waiting. It was then that we heard details of the difficult journey to Wolf Lake and, understandably, the engineer was not too keen about going back. Nevertheless, next morning one ski for the Junkers was lashed under our fuselage and we all left for Wolf Lake *en route* to the accident. The trapper at Wolf Lake had more or less nursed Kading and his companion back to life using up many of his precious provisions on the starving men so he was very glad to see us and the food. He made his living by shooting wolves and claiming from the government the bounty of eight dollars per tail. It takes all types to make a world but this must surely have been one of the loneliest of men, completely cut off from civilisation, content to live a life of isolation.

We found the Junkers somewhere on the Upper Liard River and gave the place the name Scurvy Creek. The aircraft looked like a sort of white scarecrow, all the upper surfaces were covered with the full winter's snow, about three feet on the wings, yet the struts of the floats held the aircraft well above the surrounding snow bound river. On examination, I was doubtful whether it could be salvaged as the wing tips were sagging downwards at least a couple of feet under the snow's weight. The first job was to establish camp on the bank near the aircraft. We had no intention of going short of either food or drink. First, fresh spruce boughs were laid on the snow followed by a ground sheet, tent, collapsible cooking stove and even a stove pipe. The first night we were all in a fairly relaxed mood having celebrated well and truly before crawling into sleeping-bags, but during the night I crept out quietly in order to relieve the call of nature and, looking round, saw a rifle pointing at me through the flap of the tent. One of the party had woken up, seen a shadow outside and, assuming it was a bear scavenging around, was just about to take a shot when he heard my shout! We had, as usual, left a loaded gun handy just in case of intruders but for me it was a lucky escape. After that we took more water with the rum!

In the small clearing near the aircraft which had been used by Paddy Burke and his crew, there was a tree with a flat surface which had been hacked out with an axe. On it was carved an arrow and a message: 'Leaving for Wolf Lake, October 1930 – Burke.' We cut the tree down and took back the part with the message for his widow; a somewhat macabre present but we felt she might like it, although I never heard if she received it.

The usual method of clearing snow or frost off the wings was to throw a rope over the wing and for two people, one either side, to 'saw' the rope backwards and forwards, gradually moving inwards from the wing tip. It was most successful on the Junkers until suddenly there was a 'thump' and the aileron flipped up as it was relieved of the weight of snow. The other aileron went down hard to its maximum travel – so hard, in fact, that it bent the lever arm slightly. The control circuit was not designed for that particular load but we were pleased to see the wings spring back without any apparent set or damage from the weight of snow. We were more accustomed to a powdery dry snow, known as sugar snow, which does not pack, rather than this heavy damp snow.

Stan and I made three more flights to Atlin to pick up the second ski and various parts of the undercarriage while the engineer began checking everything. The Junkers was an all-metal low wing monoplane which was a very advanced design at the time. The aluminium sheet covering both wings and fuselage was corrugated to provide stiffness and this type of construction was still in use by a German manufacturer during World War II when a three-engined design, the Ju 52/3m, was used as troop transport. Another unusual feature of the F 13 was that the aircraft had an open cockpit for the pilot and an enclosed passenger cabin.

My first flying instructor, Colonel Henderson, was killed flying a similar aircraft while returning to Croydon from Le Touquet with a party of well-known celebrities. The aircraft was seen to dive into the ground at Meopham and it was later reported that the cause of the disaster had been due to the top engine cover becoming loose, swinging back and covering the cockpit.

Fitting the undercarriage was not easy but with the use of jacks and several tree trunks it was finally accomplished. Then the even bigger problem arose of removing the float struts of which there were a large number – anyone who has tried cutting through steel tube with a hacksaw will appreciate how easy it is to snap the blade. It was a question of whether the supply of blades gave out before the F 13 was free although in an emergency it is amazing what can be done with an axe!

The big moment arrived with the starting up of the engine, a six-cylinder Junkers L5. Water-cooled engines are not the preferred type for use in the north but all was well with it firing up immediately and running smoothly. Both aircraft took off and flew in company, the F 13 being flown by Van der Byl, and we landed safely at Atlin after brief stops at Wolf Lake and Teslin.

Stan McMillan and I took a good view of Atlin and northern British Columbia. Although only 100 miles from the Pacific Ocean, it is separated from the sea by the long narrow strip of Alaska which runs 350 miles to the south nearly as far as Prince Rupert. Whoever drew the boundary between Canada and the USA seems to have made a mistake here but perhaps the separation and consequent isolation was the key to the independent, free life the people seemed to live. I do know that the frontier between the mainland of Canada and the United States, the 49th parallel which sub-divides the Island into two, led to many disagreements over Vancouver island. In the end the British won the argument without having to go to war again!

After two days celebrating in Atlin, which to us was civilisation, we set off home. *En route* for the Mackenzie we landed at Lower Post with a present of liquid refreshment for our trapper friend who had been so kind on the way out. He was very pleased to see us but unfortunately for him the weather closed in and during the ensuing two days the supply dwindled a bit.

The flight time to Fort Simpson was six hours including stops at Nelson Forks and Liard to top up with fuel from the drums which we carried in the cabin. One more day picking up mail at the usual trading posts found us back at McMurray.

As the engine of the Bellanca had, by now, reached its normal time for an overhaul it was decided to remove it and return it to the manufacturer – but it did not go according to plan. The replacement engine was in the manufacturer's standard large packing case and as this had two convenient wooden beams underneath, we used them as skids and asked Paddy, the local 'jack of all trades', to drag it down to the river with his horse. In the meantime I had disconnected the various pipes and controls from the old engine in preparation for pushing the aircraft out of the nose hangar to lift the engine out. It was a cold, crystal clear night with a bright moon and we had a good fire going in the stove so as to be able to work in comfort. When the time came to slide the aircraft backwards I found the skis had frozen to the snow and, using the usual method of rocking the wings by pushing up and down on the main struts, proceeded to heave away. What I had completely forgotten about was Paddy's horse which had been waiting patiently under the other side of the wing. The sudden battering of the wing on top of his head took him by surprise and he bolted with our precious engine disappearing at speed round the bend and out of sight up the Clearwater. A search party was quickly organised but it was three hours before the whole outfit was retrieved.

Glyn Roberts also excelled himself about the same time when the weather was clear but exceptionally cold, around 50 degrees below zero. As was his usual morning custom, he used to take a blow lamp with him to the privy to warm up the place and with an extra touch of delicacy, he would complete the job by running the flame round the seat. On this particular morning Glyn came rushing out clutching his trousers and shouting for help. The badly singed seat was never the same again!

CHAPTER 9

Farewell to The Barrens

To fly in the Barren Lands of the far north is a lonely and yet a very satisfying experience. In winter the landscape, as seen from 2000 or 3000 feet, is featureless as far as the eye can see in all directions and everything is still. There are no trees to move, no water to ripple, no smoke to be seen, often there are no clouds or wind to blow the surface snow, no sign of man; in fact there is utter peace. I had never really felt the romantic call of the wild and the wide open spaces before as my mind had been entirely concerned with the material side of life. Flying does, of course, give one a great sense of freedom but it also gives self-reliance and discipline as the safety of all on board is so dependent on having done all one's work precisely so that nothing is forgotten.

I remember one flight during which I could not recall putting back a split pin locking the throttle control rod after I had been working on it, and as it was under the dashboard it was not accessible in flight. On landing I found that I had omitted to replace the safety locking pin so that control could, with vibration, have become disconnected from the engine, leaving the pilot without control over the throttle. Flying permits no mistakes and this incident gave me nightmares. Your ears become attuned to the steady beat of an engine and even the slightest change in the sound brings your heart into your mouth! It was a strange life with nervous tension in flight, contrasted by isolation, total silence and extreme cold on the ground.

Our mail route did not cross the Barren Lands but followed the course of the mighty Mackenzie River making its way to the Arctic Ocean. The banks had a fringe of trees and scrub but in flat areas, what would normally be called marshes, was muskeg. Here, even in summer, the ground was frozen two or three feet below the surface so that no crops or food could be grown and even the burial of the dead presented a problem!

The Mackenzie River drains an enormous area of Canada but it is unusual in that the flow is northwards into a frozen sea. For all practical purposes the Beaufort Sea near the delta is not navigable by ships and this is the reason why the area with all its minerals and possible oil fields had not been opened up; it was the arrival of aircraft which changed the picture.

The normal magnetic compass becomes very unreliable and finally useless in the area of the magnetic north pole which is not located at the true North Pole but 500 or 600 miles to the east of Aklavik. The magnetic compass in an aircraft is always a bit misleading when flying on a north-south course as on banking into a turn, the needle gives momentarily the wrong direction because the lines of force are not horizontal to the earth's surface near the poles but dip downwards towards the earth. At the magnetic north pole itself, the lines of force are vertical and therefore the north seeking end of the compass needle, which is mounted horizontally, cannot respond. Many aircraft have been lost in the far north for this reason. For any long journey over the Barren Lands towards Hudson Bay, the only alternative at that time was a sun compass and that was simply a sundial, the base of which was revolved by clockwork at the speed of the rotation of the earth. In order to hold a course, the shadow was kept lying along the central line but it had its limitations!

Following the opening up of a new prospecting area at the eastern end of Lake Athabasca, there was a great stirring of activity in the mining world towards the end of February 1931. Stan and I made a number of flights from McMurray carrying personnel and their gear, landing them at Crackingstone Point, Fond du Lac and Stoney Rapids. Sometimes one was at a loss for a name to enter into our log book and the map was of little help. Early explorers put their own name to places and rivers or picked up local names from Indians or Eskimos. These names live on but visits by aviators were often too transient to leave any record of their ever having been there.

Whenever the aeroplane delivering the mail was due, the children would run out to greet its arrival, this being the big event of the week but this practice, together with adverse weather conditions, caused a tragic accident on one occasion.

It was an overcast day when one of our aircraft was attempting to land at Chipewyan on Lake Athabasca. The conditions made the finding of the direction and strength of the wind very difficult. Smoke from a chimney merges into the snow background and any movement of trees or cloud shadow was, of course, not visible. To make matters worse a recent early spring thaw had been followed by frost leaving an icy surface on top of the snow. After flying round, the pilot decided to land along the row of spruce boughs which had been laid out to indicate the best landing strip. Unfortunately he landed with a 5 mph tail wind and on touch down the aircraft just skidded along the ice with no resistance, running helplessly a considerable distance while gradually losing directional control. The children, waiting for the pilot to land, did not realise that the aircraft was out of control as it ploughed towards them, hitting one child who later died.

From the air, the trading posts looked tiny consisting of a warehouse and only three or four cabins with a population both white and native, of perhaps a dozen souls. Quite insignificant in comparison to 'God's own country' as it has been called. Some of the men living in these outposts had no wish to return to civilisation or the outside world and were unkindly described as being 'bushed'.

During a late trip to Aklavik, the last of the 1931 scheduled winter services, the Royal

Canadian Mounted Police asked us to fly two officers to Blake's Cabin on the Porcupine River about 50 miles away, where a man had been found dead for no apparent reason but murder by poisoning was suspected. We waited while the grisly job of removing the intestines was performed by two totally unskilled surgeons and departed with a strange looking object in a jam jar pickled nicely in alcohol.

It seemed a waste of good alcohol but we could think of no alternative and in due course it was delivered safely to the hospital in Edmonton for analysis. They say the Mounties always 'get their man' but as so often happened, we never heard the end of this story.

During the flight south we picked up a trapper who was taking with him his entire catch of white fox and a pair of live wild mink in a box. He was hoping to catch the market early in the season and so obtain a better price for his fur whereas the live mink were fetching a very high price for breeding purposes. Mink farming was a development which came later and of course, led to an enormous expansion in the market for expensive coats. I thought the white fox was a beautiful fur and the trapper picked out a good one for me which I bought to give to my mother when I returned to England. Later, however, when I gave it to her she did not seem very enthusiastic and years afterwards she had it dyed. I had not known but apparently white fox at that time was the standard fashion worn by 'ladies of the town'! So much for innocence on my part.

The settlement of Good Hope was one of the scheduled stopping places on the route but it only received a mail delivery occasionally. It happens to be almost exactly on the Arctic Circle but its only claim to fame concerned the manager of the Hudson Bay Post there. The story goes that year after year, in his returns of stocks and request for stores, he would put in a demand for two gallons of red ink. After this had finally been noticed by head office in Winnipeg they had written to ask why he was using such an exceptionally large amount for the limited office work involved. What they apparently did not realise at head office was that red ink is almost pure alcohol!

By the early part of the century the buffalo in Canada was almost extinct. As the tide of immigrants flowed westwards with the coming of the railways, so the buffalo herds were slaughtered for food and driven out. Some of the early conservationists in Ottawa had designated an area to the north west of Lake Athabasca as a reserve and our company had received a small contract to make a survey and report.

The government was particularly interested in a census of the animals which had been preserved. The reserve was not clearly shown on our map but covered an area to the west of the Slave River and north of the Peace River where the land was relatively flat and partially wooded. Stan and I flew to the Government Hay Camp, a log cabin where the warden lived and we flew all round looking hopefully for buffalo. Although I had expected to find a few silhouetted against the snow there were, in fact, two big herds with animals packed together but as soon as we flew low to make a count they stampeded, hurling themselves through the deep snow in panic. This meant we could only make a rough estimate of their number but at least they seemed to be thriving. Looking back it is interesting to see how the Canadian Government even 60 years ago, was concerned with its wildlife. During 1930 we had received two small contracts in connection with animal welfare, the reindeer on the Arctic coast and the buffalo in northern Alberta.

About 25 miles north of McMurray, the Athabasca River showed signs of a black tar-like substance oozing through the sandy banks. We sometimes landed there, an unscheduled stop, to deliver mail to the single log cabin. We thought the man living there was a trapper but he must have been a mining engineer as the area is now the world's largest oil bearing sand discovery and is of immense value. Until recent times it was not known how to separate the oil economically from the sand, especially as the ground is permanently frozen a few feet below the surface. However, with the current price of oil and with the expenditure of very large capital sums on extraction plants, the Alberta tar sands are now producing oil in quantity.

The economic exploitation of oil from the tar sands, as well as from other sources, suddenly changed Alberta from being one of the poorest provinces in Canada to nearly the richest. They formed a Heritage Fund for the surplus wealth and Edmonton and Calgary flourished. There were some complaints as there was no oil in eastern Canada and the Alberta oil was taxed, the taxes being used to subsidise the eastern Provinces using the more expensive oil from the Middle East, Venezuela and Mexico.

We made our last flight north as far as Resolution on 10 April 1931 before the break-up. By then the sun was getting high and the ice at McMurray began to look rotten with pools of water lying on top of it. When the ice breaks, the river carries it away very suddenly but large chunks of ice jam together or get stranded in shallow water. Where this occurs a barrier can form and within minutes the river will rise twenty or thirty feet and overflow its banks. After 24 hours it will flow clear of ice. A week later the snow will have disappeared and the mosquitoes will be out in force. The break-up is of course, the onset of spring and is a very positive moment in time, a time for rejoicing and celebration. Every year a sweepstake was organised estimating the exact time of break-up, taken from a timing clock, which was linked to the first movement of the ice. The winner of the sweepstake was the person whose guess was closest to the actual time.

Another sign of the arrival of spring was the return of the snow geese. One day we were following the course of the river, flying just below the low cloud at about 200 feet, with the tops of the trees on either bank hidden in the cloud but with visibility beneath being about a mile. Suddenly about 200 yards ahead at exactly our height we saw a skein of geese flying in Vee formation in the same direction and there really was not room. We were cruising at about 90 miles an hour and our closing speed seemed quite slow and prolonged. Finally, when we had almost joined their formation, the leader must have spotted us and they scattered, missing us by inches.

One would have expected the wing birds to break first but they neither saw nor heard us, or at least took no action until the leader gave the signal. I suppose they had as much right to the route as we did but it was surprising to be in a traffic jam in flight.

Communications between our operating base at Fort McMurray and the Edmonton Head Office were few and far between and the brief announcement in April 1931 of the company's take-over by Western Canada Airways, was a shock. Up to that time the life in the far north had been isolated from depression which followed the collapse of the Stock Markets. Commercial Airways had been financed during the public euphoria for aviation generated by Lindbergh's flight across the Atlantic and the easy money of the Wall Street boom. The whole staff were given the sack but some were offered jobs with Western Canada Airways at greatly reduced salaries. Most of us spurned the offer thinking we could get better jobs elsewhere but unfortunately there were no such jobs and aviation, being largely dependent on government support, entered the very depths of hard times.

My salary had been $100 a month and 2 cents a mile. Out of this I had saved some money, so on reaching Edmonton I went to the Canadian Pacific office and booked a passage home to England going westwards across the Pacific, picking up a P & O liner at Hong Kong. To me it was just another way back to England and I knew nothing of our ports of call.

Before leaving Edmonton I said goodbye to Stan whom I had come to know well during our flights together. Sharing the hardships, the frustrations, indifferent food and all the hazards of the unknown cements a friendship and it was a strange experience to meet him and his wife Dot, when I returned to Edmonton years later, in 1977, with my wife, Ella. They were just the same welcoming friends and Stan and I, in spite of the lapse of time, picked up exactly where we left off, the real test of friendship.

He still has a flying licence after 22,000 hours and has retired but he takes an active interest in Canada's Aviation Hall of Fame, a museum in Edmonton dedicated to bush pilots and other famous Canadian pioneers. He showed us some cine camera films which really brought back memories.

One particular sequence was of our trip through the Rockies to Atlin, another was of McMurray which had looked exactly like a typical western town film set; a single dirt road with a raised wooden sidewalk and flat fronted clapboard houses with ridge roofs. It now has high rise office blocks and a population of 45,000. He also took us to see Vi May, Wop's widow, and out to Cooking Lake where we used to change over from skis to floats. Stan had just set up a small company to market an invention of his which was a very simple marker light for runways in the north. These consisted of a plastic cone with reflectors, like those on motorways. The aircraft's landing lights picked up the markers for about half a mile enabling a bush pilot to make night landings where no electric power was available. Before we left Edmonton Stan took me out to a local airfield and gave me a demonstration.

On another trip in 1987, Stan and Dot met me at the International Airport, ten miles south of Edmonton. I had travelled there by Wardair and Stan told me that he had sold Mr Ward his first aircraft, a Fox Moth, sometime in the 1930's. One of Wardair's Jumbos was named after him and he went over to France to name one of the new Airbus aircraft which

Wardair had bought. Stan and Dot drove me on to Vancouver where I took him out in our new twin-engined hovercraft which our English manufacturing company, Griffon Limited, had built for our American agent and which was used as part of the transportation system at Expo '87. As a momento of our flying together, Stan sent me a signed print of the painting showing him standing in front of the big Bellanca in which he flew for three years transporting the pitchblende ore from Eldorado on Great Bear Lake to the nearest railway for refining in Southern Canada.

It was time to leave Canada so I boarded the *Empress of Japan*, a new ship, at Vancouver for my journey back to England. There were few passengers but with a largely Chinese crew of 600 we received a lot of wonderful attention. The first evening at sea, on going down to the dining-room, I told the Chief Steward I was travelling alone. He gave me a table for two and I thought nothing of it although the ship was not full. About a quarter of an hour later he appeared with a beautiful Canadian girl who was also travelling alone, and asked if she could sit at my table! Needless-to-say that, although at 23 I was very shy and lacking in knowledge of the opposite sex, we managed to get along well together. What I did not know or realise during the journey to Honolulu was that the other passengers thought we were on our honeymoon and they kept well away! Five days later we sailed into Pearl Harbor to be greeted on the quay by an Hawaiian band and Hawaiian girls placing a lei of flowers around our necks. The taxi ride to the Royal Hawaiian Hotel on the beach at Waikiki was almost unbelievable. I had never been to the tropics before: the Jacaranda trees, vivid colours and warmth were such a contrast to the frozen north to which I was accustomed – it was like entering another world.

Unfortunately my new found girl friend was staying with friends in Honolulu but before the ship left I invited her and several of her friends and relations on board to see the ship. Although it was about 2 o'clock in the morning, within a few minutes of pressing the bell in my cabin, a friendly Chinese steward brought us drinks and fresh sandwiches – real service.

After calling at Tokyo, Osaka, Shanghai and Hong Kong the ship went on to Manila in the Philippines of which my chief memory was of a visit to a cockfight. We then returned to Hong Kong where I spent a week seeing the sights and waiting for the P & O ship which duly arrived for the six-week journey back to England. It gradually filled up with civil servants, planters and serving officers with wives. It was a long, dragged out voyage with my savings dwindling to practically nothing before arriving in Plymouth where I was met by my father.

CHAPTER 10

Down to Earth

In 1931 with a world-wide recession, aviation was still so dependent on government finance it was hardly surprising that it was one of the first industries to feel the squeeze. England was technically very much in the vanguard of progress and had won the Schneider Trophy twice running but when it became our turn to stage this international seaplane race, the government flatly refused to pay for the building of an aircraft to defend the title. It was only through the generosity of a private individual, Lady Houston, that the £100,000 required was found. The Supermarine S6B not only won the race outright at an average speed round the course of 340 miles an hour piloted by Flight Lieutenant J N Boothman, later to be my Commanding Officer, but soon gained the world speed record of 407 mph. The design team headed by Mr R J Mitchell, CBE went on to design the Spitfire, based largely on experience learnt from the S6B.

Through the influence of my aunt who lived at Itchenor House, near Chichester, I was introduced to Sir Henry Royce who had retired and lived nearby. He thought there might be an opening for me at the factory at Derby but after a long delay they wrote to say that having just won the Schneider Trophy Race and World Air Speed Record, they were reducing the numbers of development engineers and therefore could not offer me a job.

On arrival back in the UK I lived with my parents at Constantine Bay, North Cornwall, a very beautiful coast with sandy bays between the rugged rock cliffs but a boring place for a young man. My father, who was still partly incapacitated from war wounds, was able to play a gentle game of golf and I accompanied him, although not very enthusiastically as I was too impatient to be any good. I went for long walks by myself to get exercise but my mind was still thinking of aeroplanes. David was living on his Thames barge with his artist wife and Jack, retired from the army in 1931, had joined Wedd Jefferson, the family firm in the city.

It was difficult to find a job in aviation in 1931 as the country was in the throes of widespread unemployment and a business slump. There were still a number of aircraft manufacturing companies building aircraft but they only survived on small government orders for military aircraft, the main object being to keep the design teams together. On the civil side, where we lagged sadly behind the Americans, the only serious operator was

Imperial Airways which was responsible for carrying airmail to the Commonwealth countries.

I applied to them for a post and was offered a job as second pilot but I found, on presenting my Canadian licences to the Air Ministry, that they would not accept them. After passing the required medical examination for a 'B' licence, I borrowed £150, joined the London Aeroplane Club at Stag Lane and hired a Moth. The necessary hundred hours solo flying took only two months but, on returning to the authorities for the licence, I was told that I was no longer fit and had tachycardia (abnormal rapid heart beat). In spite of all my efforts and pulling every string, they were adamant. It was a bitter experience as I lost the offer of the job, I was left in debt and could see no way of carrying on with my career.

Twelve months later, by which time my self-confidence was at a low ebb, I was glad to be taken on as a clerk in the city at £5 per week. I lived with my grandmother at Ingatestone in Essex for a year before moving to London to share a mews house with Peter Cazenove. Although he too worked in the city he had no relationship with the large broking firm of that name. We were both short of money for most of the time but Peter managed to find sufficient to live very much as a man-about-town; I think his name helped.

We only had the upper floor and in order to make the most of the space available, someone had installed a bath in the narrow kitchen, the hinged wooden cover of which acted as the kitchen table. It was convenient to be able to lie in our bath on a Sunday morning and regulate the gas stove cooking the joint! A year or two later we moved to a better mews house just behind the Brompton Oratory. It had two bedrooms, a good sitting-room and the old hayloft which we converted into a kitchen/bathroom. It also had a long double garage all for a rent of £80 a year!

I was grateful to have a job and I met many interesting people in the city but I was no clerk and I hated it. After a year in the office where I was mercilessly teased about my past life in Canada, they moved me down to the floor of the Stock Exchange. In 1934, following the retirement of one of the partners in Wedd Jefferson, I was offered a job as an authorised dealer which meant that one dealt, as a jobber, directly with brokers. It was a very responsible position buying and selling with the firm's money. By 1938 I had become a junior partner just in time for Hitler's entry into the various countries in Eastern Europe causing dramatic upheavals in the markets for gilt edged securities. The Stock Exchange, at that time, was a mixture of many types of men from the nobility to the penniless East End and yet it had a strong cohesive whole, the one essential being honesty as all deals were carried out by word of mouth!

My original private 'A' licence was still current and somehow I scraped enough money together to do the necessary three hours a year for its annual renewal. In 1935, however, an uncle died and with a legacy of £1,000 I bought a Klemm, a light, low-wing monoplane, which was kept and looked after by my old training school friends at Brooklands. The Klemm was unusual as it had been built in Germany which was forbidden to build aeroplanes under the terms of the Versailles Treaty. I think it must have somehow been built as a glider (the German gliders were very advanced and successful) and then taken over the border to Switzerland where a French engine was installed.

It came to me from an aeroplane broker who had an office in Piccadilly so I never knew who the previous owner had been. The Salmson was a 7-cylinder air-cooled radial of about 45 hp. It had single ignition and a bad habit of oiling up the lower plugs so that, after taxiing out to take-off, it would often only be firing on about five cylinders.

Although I flew it for only a few hours before selling it I did have one memorable flight. This was after a weekend sailing at Itchenor when a friend, Pat Wigan, joined me for the return flight to Brooklands. We had intended to leave immediately after dinner on Sunday evening but, having wined and dined exceptionally well, we were late taking off, leaving just enough time to get there before dark. As luck would have it there was a thunderstorm inland and it became darker and darker until we were flying in pouring rain and visibility of about a mile. Neon lights and streams of car headlights appeared but with no cockpit lights, I continued hopefully on course thinking that I was bound to hit the main Southampton to Waterloo railway. Finally the four-track railway appeared but no aerodrome, which was hardly surprising as it had no lighting. Turning west I saw a large field and decided to land.

The Klemm fortunately had a low landing speed and we settled gently into a crop of fully grown barley. Rather shaken, we picked up our weekend kit which included a half bottle of brandy and made our way to the railway. By now we were soaked to the skin and glad of a nip. After trudging along the edge of the tracks for two or three miles we came to a station which turned out to be Winchfield where the ticket clerk was somewhat startled to see, on a Sunday night, two city gents complete with bowler hats, soaking wet and rather the worse for wear, asking for tickets to London. When we said that we had just landed from an aeroplane he obviously thought we were quite mad.

The only damage in the whole adventure was to the farmer's crop for which he charged me £5. Passing the spot many years later in a train I saw how lucky we had been as a high tension line ran right across the field – but of course I don't know if it was there on the night of our landing!

During the winter of 1935-6 I went to Switzerland to ski. Although lacking experience in this sport, apart from some skiing in the Laurentian Hills in Ontario, I went off confidently down the Swiss mountains only to fall heavily, twisting my ankle. I returned to England limping badly where one of Peter's friends, Ella, an Anglo-Argentine girl whom he had known in Argentina, looked after me. I was unaccustomed to female company, certainly no ladies' man and I had insufficient funds to entertain in the London night clubs like Peter. Ella was kind and I was vulnerable so my thoughts were beginning to warm to her. She worked as personal secretary to an Argentine shipping magnate and was completely bi-lingual in Spanish and English. Her mother and father had both died and Ella had been brought up by her English aunts but she had inherited a sum of money from her parents and had spent it travelling to the United States and on to Paris where she had a rich uncle before returning to England.

I decided to sell the Klemm and buy a car which I could keep in the garage below and it just happened that Jock Leith, a distant cousin, wanted to sell his 1923 Hispano Suiza type Monza, a two-seater sports car which had recently been completely overhauled by the manufacturer. A more unsuitable car it would be difficult to choose but as a bachelor I was selfish and could not resist this magnificent vehicle so I gave Jock £160 for it.

The car was one of only four that had been constructed about the time of the building in Italy of the Monza racing track near Milan. It was fitted with a French two-seater open body by Kellner of Paris to the order of Count Zabrowski who used to race the famous Chitty Bang-Bang at Brooklands and was reputed to have won its class at the Monte Carlo Concours d'Elegance. Later it belonged to Clive Gallop and was used by the 'Bentley Boys' as a hack car for learning race circuits before the event. It was then owned by various keen motoring types before Jock bought it. He had bet a friend that he could beat the Flying Scotsman from London to Edinburgh so starting very early one summer morning he did the journey in 7 hours and 40 minutes and won his bet! The car's engine, however, was in a mess and he had to take it to the parent company for a major overhaul and with all his spare money gone he was forced to sell it.

For its date it was amazingly in advance of its time. The engine, about 7 litres, had an aluminium block with steel liners, overhead camshaft, dual coil ignition and a dual carburettor, all spin-offs from their famous aeroplane engine used in fighters of the first war. The chassis had four wheel brakes servo-assisted by a mechanical device on the gearbox and later copied by Rolls Royce. The electrical system, all made by the manufacturer, employed two batteries. One could be used for cranking the engine while the other provided ignition or the second battery could be used to boost the cranking. The three-speed gearbox with outside gear lever was a weak point but the engine had big torque and it was high geared. With 1000 rpm in top, giving 35 mph, 2000 rpm – 70 mph and 3000 rpm – 105 mph was about the limit. A well engineered exhaust cut-out, operated by a lever by the passenger's foot, produced a shattering noise but when closed it was as silent as a Rolls Royce.

A few months after my purchase of the Hispano, Jock had invited me to join a party of friends at his large estate which he had inherited in Glenkindie, Aberdeenshire. As a source of income he used to let the grouse moor every year to rich American and French sportsmen. In the party was Robert Ropner who had a 38/250 Mercedes and so had Jock – so on the first wet day we all drove over to Aberdeen and, having antied up into the kitty, we bought £25 worth of fireworks and explosive as well as several cases of champagne!

The rest of the holiday was a mad – you might think childish – party. I was not the first to get back to the house and by the time I arrived the courtyard was full of rockets being let off without sticks on the gravel. This was highly dangerous as they whizzed in all directions from under the cars. That evening Jock searched the attic for old junk and produced a commode, an umbrella stand and other odds and ends. These were all ceremoniously blown up outside the garden door but the set piece was the bomb which we made using his grandfather's tin wig case (he had been a judge) to hold the gunpowder and a few rocks. Having dug a two foot deep hole in the garden and attached a suitable length of fuse, we all retired to one of the turrets with our drinks. All the cows in the adjoining field were interested and came to peer over the iron fence. Unfortunately the fuse seemed to have failed and after fifteen minutes it was getting cold in the turret,but just as we were about to leave…Bang!; large clods of earth shot into the air pattering down as mud all over the well-kept garden. The cows bolted and everyone was happy except the gardener who gave Jock his thoughts on the matter that night. The next day we set up the ceremonial cannon but not having any shot we found a suitably sized turnip and stuffed it into the barrel. I expected it to break into bits but instead it sailed off into the distance in one piece, breaking the garage door over a hundred yards away.

One night after a good dinner, we had a bet on who could make a circuit of the front and back drives fastest. There was a little strip of road outside which we had to use but at that hour, about midnight, there was no traffic. I went around about a half a dozen times and so did the two Mercedes. I am not sure who won but next morning there were deep grooves in the gravel which on the corners had been effectively swept off the road and which would have to be relaid; it became known as the Glenkindie Grand Prix. Before leaving Jock stacked all the empty champagne bottles on the front drive forming a pyramid about three feet high. With our host spreadeagled over the top, it made a memorable photograph!

It was not long before I proposed to Ella and she accepted. No-one in my family had met her or even heard mention of her so it was a great shock, particularly to my mother. She was devastated and even more so when I told her that Ella was a foreigner. I had always made snap decisions in my life acting on the spur of the moment but on this occasion I had not appreciated the cruelty of my actions. My mother had not been very well and she must have been suffering the first effects of cancer of which she died two years later. She was so upset she refused to come to our wedding although thankfully, she did change her mind at the last moment. We were married on 4 June 1936 when I was 28 and Ella was 27.

On our honeymoon we drove down to Spain having stopped for three nights at Biarritz where we had been lent a house by Ella's boss. The Black Panther, as the house was called, was luxurious with a butler and servants to look after us and there was another honeymoon couple staying there. Ella, alas, had a very sun and windburned face after the journey in the open car and was laid up in bed, while the husband of the other couple was also unwell, so I sat down to meals with his wife, a beautiful French lady!

We crossed over to Spain through a little-used pass at the other end of the Pyrenees near Andorra and on crossing the border the road led through straggling villages. In one of them the street was deserted except for a Guarda sitting on a doorstep asleep with a gun across his knees. The road led straight to a ravine with a bridge only 100 yards away and, after crossing it, the road ran along the opposite side. As we drove past the road we had just left, I caught sight of the Guarda standing up and, seeing a puff of smoke, assumed he was taking a shot at us! I thought at the time that it was an unfriendly gesture but we drove on and ultimately lost our way near Barcelona. Although Ella kept asking, in her fluent Spanish, the way to Tossa, everyone just turned their backs and walked away. Finally a doctor spoke to Ella and said that we had overshot the turning to Tossa by twenty miles. We turned around and found the signpost directing us to Tossa where we spent a couple of weeks by the sea in what was, at the time, only a small fishing village, before returning to France.

I had noticed that there seemed to be a number of soldiers about, particularly by the bridges, but took no great notice – after all we were on our honeymoon. A week later, however, the Civil War started and several years later I learned that the Spanish monarchy always used Hispano Suizas. As that part of Spain was very communist we were fortunate to have been blissfully ignorant!

During this trip Ella had wanted to visit Milan to see the cathedral. I had no objection to driving into Italy but, because of my deep interest in motor cars, I wanted to see, not the cathedral, but the new motor track at Monza. I am ashamed to say that my wishes prevailed.

I was keen to see the Alps and I liked driving so we came home via the Stelvio Pass, one of the highest, not entirely without incident. We paused for a drink at the top where one can look down on the endless hairpin bends and we saw a car stuck or broken down about 500 feet below. We went down and towed him up the last bit so that he could freewheel all the way into Italy to get the car fixed. Going on through Austria we crossed into Germany where I took Ella to Friedrickshaven. There we visited the Zeppelin works and I was able to see one of the civilian craft in its hangar. Under the Versailles Treaty they were forbidden to build military airships or even aeroplanes but by then it was obvious that these restrictions had been ignored.

Having sold the Klemm and being determined to keep my flying licence, I took to hiring aircraft. The Cierva Autogiro Company at Hanworth was at the time trying to popularise their new C19 autogyro and was offering an hour's flying to any 'A' licence holder for £5. This was, to the best of my knowledge, the first rotating wing aircraft to obtain a certificate of airworthiness. The rotor was spun up on the ground to about 180 rpm by the main engine through a hand clutch and lightweight transmission. The pilot then disconnected the drive by de-clutching, released the wheel brakes and with full power, took off in about twenty yards. All the flying controls were similar to a fixed wing aircraft with rudder, elevator and ailerons mounted on stubby wings. It flew extraordinarily well and could be landed in its own length but one had to be careful not to raise the nose on the approach as an autogyro will fly backwards as well as forwards and this can be embarrassing. In spite of all the early development of rotating wing aircraft which took place in Britain this was abandoned on the outbreak of war, leaving the whole field open to the Americans, – another of our lost opportunities.

As a hobby I built many model aeroplanes to incorporate the tiny petrol engines which became available about that time. Ella was very patient as the kitchen table was the only flat surface for glueing all the bits together. I used to enter the aeroplanes in various trials with some success and I learned a great deal about stability and automatic control. When one has spent hours building a model, the first true flight is quite an event and it may go anywhere and often did – straight into the ground!

In one event in 1939, Richard Fairey, the head of the aeroplane company of that name, allowed our club to use the far western quarter of Heathrow, a grass aerodrome which his company owned. On this occasion, just before the war, I had taken two models to the event but was only allowed to enter one, so the older one, I entered in Ella's name. My new craft crashed spectacularly in a full power dive but Ella, who had never flown one before, won the competition!

Shortly after returning from our honeymoon we had taken a lease of a flat in a new block in the Brompton Road, opposite Harrods. We were on the third floor where we could see the famous store's show windows while doing the washing up. I had been convinced that war was coming and was not, therefore, surprised when Chamberlain made the announcement, but I was surprised when, a few hours later, the air raid sirens went and we all trooped down to the basement expecting to be bombed at any moment.

In 1938 when the war had seemed inevitable, I applied to join the Royal Air Force Volunteer Reserve but was again rejected as a pilot for a new reason; I did not reach the required standard of eyesight. Meanwhile the government came forward with a scheme for support of the flying clubs, called the Civil Air Guard. One of the conditions of obtaining cheap flying was an undertaking to assist in some way in the event of an emergency. I immediately joined this as I was a member of the London Aeroplane Club at Hatfield.

Later I learned that no pilot, other than those trained in the service, was acceptable to the RAF and consequently many civilian pilots joined the Air Transport Auxiliary who collected the new aircraft from the manufacturers and delivered them to the squadrons and maintenance depots.

Everlasting arguments between the Royal Air Force and the Navy over control of air defence at sea had only finally been settled in May 1938 when it was decided that in future all shipborne aircraft were to revert to the Navy. This was fortunate for me as it left the Navy, on the outbreak of war and the withdrawal of RAF personnel, extremely short of experienced pilots and engineers. The result was that medical standards and other requirements, such as age, were relaxed and a considerable number of civil pilots were engaged purely for second line or training purposes.

Being very short of money in 1939, I laid up the Hispano Suiza at my sister-in-law's house near Haslemere but eventually the old car had a sad ending. A friend of mine in Cornwall, Humphrey Pellew, whose father ran a hotel, had asked for first refusal when I came to sell it, so I let him have it for £35. He put it up on chocks and went off to join the Tank Corps but was killed quite early on. In 1942, while serving in HMS *Victorious* in Iceland, I received a letter from M. Chevrollier, the French agent for Hispano Suiza who knew the car well and wanted to know where it was. This I was able to tell him and he bought it from Pellew's executors. Chevrollier sold it to General Giroux in Algeria but the ship transporting the car out there was torpedoed in the Bay of Biscay and sank! A sad end for a great car.

PART 2

Naval Wings

CHAPTER 11

Fleet Air Arm

W ar was declared on Sunday 3 September 1939 when I was 31 years of age and Ella and I had been married for 3 years.

On the Monday morning, armed with my log-books and Canadian licences, I went to the Admiralty. Goodyear, the Chief Instructor of the London Aeroplane Club of which I had been a member for years, had given me the name of the recruitment officer. Entering by the side door near Admiralty Arch in the Mall, I asked to see the officer. To my surprise I was immediately ushered into his office and within a quarter of an hour emerged with the promise of a flying commission provided I was passed by the medical examiner. There were a number of recruits milling round the converted offices in Lower Regent Street where medical officers were doing the tests and I passed without any trouble. In the rush and confusion it did not take much sleight of hand for one recruit, who thought he had diabetes, to find an obliging friend to give the necessary sample! On 15 September an impressive document arrived, signed by Admiral Little on behalf of their Lordships appointing me Temporary Acting Sub-Lieutenant (A) RNVR. Some months later I was 'called up' by the RAF to join the Balloon Corps and it was with some satisfaction that I was able to report that I had a flying commission in the Royal Navy.

The assessment of the new officers' flying ability was carried out at Eastleigh, which was at that time a naval aerodrome but shared with Vickers Supermarine who were building Spitfires in the old hangars on the west side. By a stroke of luck the Chief Instructor was Lieutenant Commander John Wintour whom I knew well. He had been axed from the navy in 1931 under the ten per cent economy cuts and, like me, became a clerk in the Stock Exchange. We often had lunch together at Lyons Long Room in Throgmorton Street where we reminisced about aeroplanes. Even more fortunate was that he and his wife Daphne had taken a house in Southampton and they invited my wife and I to share it with them.

Tests of flying ability were carried out in a Miles Magister and on passing these, we were initiated into flying a variety of service types. We all had considerable civil flying experience so after being shown the taps, off we went. After a short period we were selected and sent to report to the various observer, air gunner and wireless operator training squadrons, the object being to release the fully trained regular naval pilots for the first-line duties in operational squadrons.

All the aircraft were deck-landing types, mostly by Faireys although there was a sprinkling of more modern bi-planes made by Hawkers, including the Osprey and Nimrod. These two aircraft were naval versions of the RAF Hart and Fury, the last of the bi-planes, beautiful aircraft in their day, very eager and responsive to fly, having been developed to the 'nth' degree. The new monoplanes just coming into service, namely the Hurricane and Spitfire, with their much higher performance, made the bi-planes obsolete almost overnight but I am glad I had the opportunity to fly them and to handle a Rolls Royce water-cooled engine for the first time. A rare antique collector's piece was a Fairey Seal in good condition and complete with wire and interplane struts in two bays all arranged to fold back along the fuselage. The air-cooled engine, a 600 hp Panther, was mounted alfresco in a prominent position on the nose; this was kept very busy in flight.

As the headquarters of the Fleet Air Arm were at Lee-on-Solent, an ex-RAF station renamed HMS *Daedalus*, Ella and I decided to rent a small house on the seafront and I settled down to flying air gunners and radio operators on their various exercises.

The Blackburn Shark was a strutbraced bi-plane with folding wings and an Armstrong Siddeley Tiger engine of 760 hp. It was a well-engineered aircraft, rugged but heavy. Standard practice in all military bi-planes was to arrange for the pilot to be positioned with his eyes in line with the upper wing in order to give the least obstruction to his view both upwards and downwards, but in the case of the Shark this drew attention to two unusual features. One was the very steep angle of glide, and secondly the fact that in heavy rain, rivulets which formed on the upper surface of the centre section, ran uphill and forward, indicating a less than perfect airflow.

The navy had recently taken over control of shipborne aircraft with the naval air stations being handed over from the RAF. The question of the defence of aerodromes was a point of contention between the RAF and the army until the Aerodrome Defence Regiment was formed from RAF personnel. In the meantime, however, the navy decided it knew how to defend itself so drew up its own defence plan at Lee-on-Solent. This consisted of a large number of officers and men being posted all round the perimeter of the aerodrome every night to watch for German parachutists. We adopted a shift system of naval watchkeeping hours, marching up and down between all the tents. If we had had enough men we could all have held hands and our defence arrangements would then have been perfect. We all carried revolvers and there was even a Maxim machine-gun, a relic of the Boer War, on the watch hut overlooking the slipway.

The injection of a relatively large number of wartime RNVR personnel, many of whom had run their own businesses, inevitably altered the well-established routine of service life at Lee-on-Solent. The navy makes a point of trying to fit square pegs into square holes and gradually people found their feet. In my own case this was a transfer from an observer training squadron into the Service Trials Unit commanded by Lieutenant Commander

Kilroy, a tough regular naval officer and an exceptional leader. The unit had been formed as the navy had no facilities for undertaking any special trials that the Admiralty required.

In the spring of 1940 we were joined by Lieutenant Lewin DSC, just back from the *Graf Spee* battle in the River Plate where he spotted for the guns of HMS *Exeter*. Lieutenant Commander Grenfell, a retired naval officer who had been axed in 1931, was our Senior Observer and an expert on communications. To be appointed to the Service Trials Unit was indeed lucky for me.

One of our two Fairey Swordfish had an extra petrol tank taking up a large part of the observer's rear cockpit and I was sent off to do some trials to make sure it functioned properly and that it drained completely, as well as to do a check on the engine fuel consumption. Having completed the tests, Robin Kilroy took the aeroplane away for the weekend but weeks later I heard that he had in fact flown it from an RAF station in Norfolk to somewhere in Norway, which was occupied by the Germans, presumably to pick up a passenger. He never gave the slightest indication that he had been on a secret mission and he had even made the flight in his everyday working uniform without any extra warm clothing; not much fun in an open cockpit. Kilroy was like that, however; he had complete control of mind over matter and incidentally was a gifted painter.

As a number of reports of anti-submarine bombs failing to explode had been received, we were instructed to carry out some trials. These consisted of loading a stick of six AS bombs onto a Swordfish, flying round the east end of the Isle of Wight, which was a prohibited area, to St Catherine's Point where, having checked there was no shipping, we dropped the bombs and counted the duds. There were plenty.

The Blackburn Skua was the most modern aircraft in use by the Fleet Air Arm, a two-seater monoplane fighter with the 820 hp sleeve valve Bristol Perseus, a two-position fine and coarse pitch propeller and a retractable undercarriage. Unfortunately the centre of gravity of the prototype was found to be too far aft and about eighteen inches had to be added to the engine mounting to make the aircraft stable aerodynamically. However, the undercarriage was still in the same position, with the result that a touch on the brakes or a soft bit of ground led to a tip up on the nose. The second time I flew in one I was sent to Farnborough to pick up Ralph Richardson, the actor, who had just delivered a Proctor there. With the wind in the north-west, the grass field was very short, especially coming in over the hill and trees from the south-east. It was good training for deck landing but 75 knots with the nose well up and lots of power does not come naturally to a land-based pilot.

Two of our aircraft, a Swordfish and a Walrus, were fitted with such highly secret equipment that I was not allowed to see it or even go aft of the cockpit. However, we used to fly south into mid-Channel and from the directions which I received from the observer, usually Harold Grenfell, it soon became obvious that the equipment was used to intercept ships when they were out of sight.

Air Ship Visual (ASV) as it came to be called, was a very early version of radar. The range was ten to fifteen miles but this depended on the size and silhouette of the ship. After an interception we would fly down to bridge height to read the name and obtain her tonnage from Lloyds register but of course most ships' names had been painted out so often a name board would be held up for us to read. Sometimes reflections picked up by the antenna would give a false reading and I would be directed off on a wild goose chase and find nothing.

A key man in these trials was Able Seaman Banner who had also been axed from the navy in 1931, becoming a managing-director of one of our largest radio manufacturing companies in the meantime. His company had made the ASV sets which were fitted to our aircraft. After each sortie Banner, Harold Grenfell and a captain from the Admiralty would sit down together to discuss and decide on the next step, an unprecedented break with naval discipline.

As part of the trials I flew down to Tenby in South Wales with the Walrus, Ella following by car. Being posted to Tenby made a welcome change with Ella being able to be there with me and for years after we still talked about the super Dover sole we had at one meal at the Imperial Hotel where we were given one of the best rooms overlooking the sea.

There are a number of small islands off the coast and we used these to calibrate the radar tube. On crossing the coast I would shout 'Now!', at which point Banner would pencil a mark on the tube. By repeating this at various heights and crossing the coast at different angles, a fair polar diagram was established.

One day, when we were grounded by bad weather, Grenfell and I went for a walk and he started talking about ASV. Apparently their Lordships were not convinced of the use of ASV for the navy so decisions to proceed were painfully slow and money was sluggish in being forthcoming. Grenfell was impatient, to put it mildly, and he told me that he had given Mr Banner an order for twenty sets which he himself promised to pay for if the navy would not. I never heard the final outcome as our paths went different ways but after the war I read that he had become chairman of one of the biggest mining companies in Africa. It now seems incredible that the usefulness of airborne radar could have been questioned.

At Lee-on-Solent there were still a few floatplanes which had been pensioned off as the catapults were removed from the larger warships. They were like magnets to me after my years in Canada where half my flying time had been on floats. Lieutenant Commander Esmond, an ex-Imperial Airways flying boat pilot and later to win the VC for leading the torpedo attack on the *Scharnhorst* and *Gneisenau* in the Channel, cleared me for flying the Walrus and I went off by myself on the floatplanes. The Blackburn Aircraft Company had modified a Roc – a gun-turreted fighter – to a floatplane using floats designed for the Shark bi-plane and as there was, at the time, a very urgent demand for a fighter in Norway, someone must have thought that this aircraft could be used from the fjords and decided to have it tested for that purpose. It had a two-pitch position propeller and after a tremendously long run from Lee Tower to Calshot Spit, I left the water; in another five minutes 1000 feet was achieved but, on going into coarse pitch, height could barely be maintained! It was not a great aircraft and the final straw occurred when, on reaching the slipway, a pebble went through the bottom of a float on beaching. The floats had been designed, probably from lack of practical experience, without any external keel but with a beautiful smooth bottom. It was an interesting experience for me but not much help to the war effort and, of course, the project was dropped.

Lieutenant Commander 'Butch' Judd, in command of the Walrus training flight, was a fierce-looking character to any young pilot coming for a conversion course on boats with his red beard and abrupt manner. The Walrus was not fitted with dual control and it had a strong tendency to swing on take off so Judd's method of training was to grip the trainee pilot's right ear and twist it until the message got through to check the swing to the right.

In his midshipman days he had been a shipmate of my friend, John Wintour, and one evening during a party in his cabin, they found themselves short of a glass. Judd went to John's cabin to borrow his tooth mug but, finding some water in it, he threw it out of the scuttle. Next morning John could not find his false tooth which he had acquired following a fight that had taken place with Judd many years earlier!

The Fairey Albacore, a larger version of the Swordfish, was the first aircraft to do its acceptance trials at the Service Trials Unit. The navy was less interested in its speed or rate of climb than in its range and weight carrying capacity and its Bristol Taurus sleeve valve engine was also, I believe, an unknown quantity, as it had not previously been used in any production aircraft. I was detailed to carry out some of these trials, providing me with the opportunity of putting in many flying hours. Most sorties were away from the heavily defended south coast area and I came to know the geography of the west of England and the Cornish coast well while doing long flights measuring consumption.

Being a naval aircraft, the radio and other electronic equipment represented a heavy electrical load and, in fact, the generator could not cope with even the windscreen wiper – which had to be discarded, I invented a small device to move the wiper aerodynamically and to my surprise it was not only put into production but, years after the war, I received a cheque for £50 with 'their Lordships' grateful thanks.

The Admiralty was for some unknown reason interested in the installation of automatic pilots and one of the early designs called the PB which operated the rudder only, was fitted to one of our Swordfish. It was obviously a hand-made prototype and occupied most of the rear cockpit. One day, flying along peacefully on the automatic pilot at 2000 feet somewhere between Winchester and Salisbury, the rudder bar suddenly whipped over to full lock. I could not get at the override release quickly enough and the aircraft did the first half of a flick roll before I was able to regain control. The gyro must have toppled when the power supply failed and there was no automatic disconnection as is the case in the very sophisticated systems fitted to today's airliners.

In the spring of 1940 the new naval aerodrome was being built at Yeovilton and I was sent down at regular intervals to take aerial photographs to record its progress. A big debate took place in the ward room at Lee as to whether the ammunition dump should be placed next to the officers' quarters or the WRNS quarters on the opposite side of the main road. In the end it was decided that it would be safer to put the dump next to the officers' quarters.

On one occasion some urgent ferrying was required and three of us were ordered to fly the Skuas up to Evanton in Scotland. The supply depot was at a secret underground hangar at an aerodrome in the Midlands where the aircraft were stored tipped up on their noses and nestled together like chairs in a public hall to save space; it was a surprise to find such quantities. We heard that the three Skuas were to be embarked in an aircraft carrier at Invergordan and flown to the Finnish north coast. I understood that Churchill himself had decided on this operation as a gesture of help for the Finns who, at that time, were fighting the Russians single-handed. This bitter Winter War must have been one of the biggest bluffs in history as it made the Russians appear incompetent with their obsolete equipment and untrained soldiers but at least it persuaded the Germans that they would be a pushover.

I had never been to Finland but my father had been Military Attaché to the Embassy in Sweden from 1921-24 with Finland under his supervision. He had made an official visit to Helsinki, travelling via northern Sweden and Lapland on the Arctic coast, and had told me all about it. There had been a revolution in Finland shortly after the one in Russia in which the Bolsheviks had been driven back and he had been able to see some of the difficulties of fighting in extreme cold and snow.

The journey up to Scotland was a bit of a nightmare as the weather was bad and we were aware of the aircraft carrier waiting at Invergordon to take the three aircraft. We flew together in a group but at Blackpool the cloud came down to sea level and the leader turned back to land at Squires Gate. When the clouds lifted we again took off and flew round the coast to the Firth of Clyde but first we had to refuel at Donnibristle, a naval aerodrome.

Rosyth, the big naval base just above the Forth Bridge, was bristling with balloons and we had strict instructions to fly ten miles north of the river. On reaching Donnibristle I was horrified to see how small the grass aerodrome was with a low hill on the approach and an iron fence at the far end of the landing run. It was a real test, especially as I had hardly flown a Skua and it was very nose heavy on the ground, making use of the brakes hazardous. We squeezed in, however, but were once again grounded by weather.

Signals flashed back and forth from RNAS Evanton but it was two days before we finally crept all the way round the coast right down on the water and delivered the aircraft safely. The political position had become critical by that time with the Germans having succeeded in pushing us out of Norway. The Russians, who were our enemies and allies of the Germans, were to become our allies when Germany invaded Poland. Fortunately, in my opinion, at the last moment someone in Whitehall persuaded Churchill not to send these aircraft to Finland at all.

After this experience I always preferred to fly alone, not in a group. I could trust my own navigation and follow the maps closely so that if bad weather made me turn back I knew my exact position and was not dependent on others.

Delivery of aircraft was, in the early days of the war, a very haphazard business with no pre-flight planning, no weather report and no radio; only a signal from the watch officer to the intended destination to notify the departure time. The number of accidents was staggering until the Air Transport Auxiliary pilots took over. I had great admiration for these men and women who, for one reason or another, were unable to pass the stringent tests for active service but who came forward to help their country.

In June 1940, during a search operation in the Channel by one of our aircraft carriers, an Albacore had been forced to land at Jersey with high oil temperature. I was sent there in a Walrus to accompany the aircraft on her flight back to the UK. The weather was poor with low cloud and rain but after passing Cap de la Hague, Jersey appeared right on the nose. A Wellington landed just behind me and the pilot was very annoyed because he had been fired at by French guns at Cap de la Hague. I think they must have been alerted by my noisy Walrus but they were obviously very nervous with the German panzers sweeping down the French coast roads behind them.

During lunch at St Helier the radio broadcasted the surrender of the French. It came as a bombshell to those at tables around me as they realised the possible implications for themselves. Before departure an official from the governor's office gave me a letter to be delivered to the C-in-C Portsmouth and I also bought some wine and brandy thinking it would be a pity to leave it for the Germans. The letter was, I believe, a request for ships to be sent immediately but what I did not know was that the British Government had already decided that it would not be in the country's best interests to evacuate the civilian population and it would appear that the Governor had not been advised of the original policy decision. The population of Jersey were abandoned to their fate.

They were obviously very nervous with the German panzers sweeping down the French mainland.

CHAPTER 12

Fighter Course

T he Fleet Air Arm was very heavily engaged in the Norwegian campaign of 1940 when the Germans invaded from the south. As the distance from the United Kingdom was too far for the RAF to give fighter cover to our troops, an endeavour was made to provide this from aircraft carriers.

During the three months before our final evacuation, losses in pilots had amounted to 30% of the first line strength. These men were part of the peace-time regular navy, the natural leaders for the growing number of RNVR pilots who were being trained to fly in Canada and elsewhere but were not yet ready as replacements. These losses were serious and consequently left the service desperately short of pilots.

The fall of France and the call for the 'little ships' to help take off our troops from Dunkirk suddenly brought the war closer and was followed immediately by an Admiralty request for volunteers for first-line pilots. So far most of the RNVR pilots, like myself, had been confined to training air gunners, wireless operators, positioning aircraft and such activities; this was our opportunity to see active service and on 20 June I was sent to Eastleigh, Hampshire, on an air fighter course.

An odd collection of fighter aircraft had been assembled: some Blackburn Rocs, Gladiators, Skuas and, to everyone's surprise, a Spitfire which had been built at Woolston and assembled at Eastleigh. Our particular aircraft was a very early version with a manually operated retractable undercarriage and a two position propeller. After a half-hour in a Gladiator to familiarise myself with its handling, I was surprised to find myself flying in Vee formation with my CO, Lieutenant Commander Brian Kendall, leading. He took us up through broken cloud, insisting that we get closer and closer, finally breaking into clear, brilliant sunshine. The other aircraft stood out sharply, silhouetted against the white clouds or hanging stationary in the blue sky with highlights from the wings and fuselage reflecting the brilliant sunlight; I had never been so close to other aircraft in flight before.

To fly in tight formation is, in many ways, easier than in a loose formation when any loss of position takes longer to recognise, but close formation requires very heavy concentration and a determination to keep one's wingtip in the right position with your leader's wings parallel with your own. On entering a turn greater power is required by the outside wing aircraft, both in order to climb a little, and to increase the speed for the greater distance caused by the bigger radius of the turn; conversely, the inner wing man has to cut back the power sharply.

One loses sense of direction, height and even horizon in concentrating on maintaining one's position in relation to the leader and I was surprised, therefore, when ordered to lower the flaps for landing. Flaps on the Gladiator had to be pumped down with a lever on the starboard side of the cockpit which was awkward in formation as it meant releasing the throttle and changing hands on the stick. The sight of grass a foot or two under the leader's wheels then appeared and soon we rumbled to a stop.

For me the Skua was the first aircraft I had flown which incorporated all the latest devices to improve performance, such as a retractable undercarriage, flaps and a variable-pitch propeller. In order to ensure that these were correctly set for take-off, we were taught to run through the word REPUF – Rudder, Elevator, Pitch, Undercarriage, Flaps. In my early flying days one had just to make sure that the petrol was turned on while in a modern airliner the second pilot has to read out and check off a long list of at least 30 items.

Apart from the training in how to make an attack, how to make use of the sun and how to break away, the naval side also had to be covered. This consisted of simulated deck landing on the aerodrome, dive bombing, open sea navigation and night flying.

During the two and a half months of my training there were seventeen serious accidents in our squadron but the worst one of all occurred one evening to a visiting aircraft. A Lockheed Hudson belonging to the Air Transport Auxiliary landed to pick up a few pilots who had just delivered some Spitfires to the Supermarine assembly hangar for some modification to be fitted.

The whole Southampton area, which included not only the Supermarine works building Spitfires but many naval and armament factories, was defended by a large number of balloons. They were controlled by winches on the ground, their cables creating a very deadly obstruction to an aircraft in flight – but they were down when the Hudson landed. Unfortunately, an enemy air raid was reported as being imminent and the balloons went up as the Hudson taxied out, evidently intending to take off. Johnnie Wakefield, a young Sub-Lieutenant, RNVR, of the famous Wakefield Castrol Oil firm, who happened to be Officer of the Watch in the Duty Pilots Office at the time, ran out on to the aerodrome and fired a red Verey light. By this time most of the balloons were at about 500 feet but one, right in the take-off path, was already at about 2000 feet. The pilot must have thought there was a gap as, with the low, shallow windscreen of the Hudson, he could not see upwards and proceeded to take off. Again Johnnie fired another red Verey light low across his bow but to no avail. On reaching about 500 feet the aircraft struck the cable, slowed up, stalled and spun in, right into the middle of the town of Eastleigh. All eighteen people on board and two on the ground were killed. I felt sickened, as did everyone, at such a tragic accident.

Deck-landing training was usually carried out on Skuas with a special area being marked out on the aerodrome and an experienced deck-landing officer or 'batsman' in charge. By holding his bats in an upward Vee, horizontally or in a downward position, he indicated that the approaching aircraft had to go higher, was correct for landing, or had to come lower, respectively. In a ship these signals are direct orders from the batsman and so long as the instruction is followed, no blame for any subsequent crash is attached to the pilot.

The landing technique is quite different from a conventional landing on an aerodrome as the aircraft is placed and held in the landing attitude, ie. nose up, at about 200 feet and the final approach made with a lot of power. The rate of descent can be controlled by delicate use of the throttle but, being near the stall, it is against one's natural instinct to throttle back in order to lose height. If out of line, the aircraft must be eased into a gentle side slip but no attempt should ever be made to turn.

Having completed the Fighter Course we were sent over to Gosport, an old RAF grass aerodrome of the first war situated near Portsmouth. The Navy had special permission to use it for the training in the use of catapults, in this case, one which had been removed from HMS *Hood* and installed permanently on a concrete base. The catapult has a barrel and breech very similar to a Naval gun, but the barrel is a cylinder with a piston instead of a shell. This is connected by various cables and sheaves to pull a small trolley on which is mounted the aircraft which gives the aircraft very great acceleration as it reaches about 60 miles an hour in about 90 feet. This approximates to the minimum flying speed but as the catapult in a ship is perhaps 40 feet above the water the aircraft, which is at full power, can gather further speed after release by sinking slightly towards the water.

There are various types of propellant but cordite is good as it pushes harder and harder as it nears the end of its throw, whereas compressed air does the opposite. The acceleration is just enough to make one black out temporarily and providing no mechanical failure occurs, the sensation is not unpleasant.

While I was sitting in the aircraft waiting to be shot off, an RAF corporal came round to the side of the cockpit and showed me a couple of white sacks on a tray, rather like a waiter bringing a specially cooked chicken for your approval in a good restaurant. Never having seen cordite before I did not know what was going on until afterwards when I made enquiries. It seemed that there had been an unpopular commanding officer at Gosport at some time in the past who, having decided to give a demonstration of catapulting to a course under instruction, mounted his aircraft. Someone had decided to get his own back, however, and increased the cordite charge so that the aircraft went off with a tremendous kick – after which station orders were amended; all pilots were to be shown the charge before being catapulted off!

The Skua had been designed as a dive bomber to give it the capability of attacking a ship or any other small target. The technique which the navy adopted was to fly past the target at about 8000 feet and when it became visible under the trailing edge of the wing, the aircraft was pulled up into a stalled turn, at the same time partially closing the throttle and applying the dive-brake flap. In this way all the forward speed was lost and the aircraft could be pointed vertically at the ground. It was then possible to do an aileron turn to bring the target into line over the nose before gaining too much speed. The more vertical the dive, the more accurate the attack, but what feels nearly vertical to the pilot merely appears steep to the onlooker.

Part of the grass aerodrome at Worthy Down, an old RAF station recently transferred to the Royal Navy, situated about four miles north of Winchester, was used for target practice with smoke bombs and one was encouraged to dive really steeply because any bombs overshooting the target tended to land in the Captain's garden and incur his displeasure!

The barrage balloons round our home base at Eastleigh were a menace. Often, while training as fighter pilots, we would return home to find the balloons up, forcing us to land and wait at Worthy Down. The aerodrome had a ridge along the centre with relatively steep slopes on either side and although it may have been suitable for World War One aircraft, landing a Skua or Spitfire necessitated touching down short and stopping by the crest of the hill. It caught out many an innocent stranger and must have cost the country millions of pounds in damaged aircraft. I even saw one aircraft virtually written off while parked facing up the hill with the tail to the south. In the south westerly wind which was blowing, the rudder was swinging from side to side thus releasing the air pressure for the differential brake/rudder control. On finally losing all the pressure, the aircraft started to roll backwards until it reached a shallow ditch alongside the approach road. When the tail wheel fell into this, the whole fuselage buckled just in front of the tailplane.

When the barrage balloons were up at Eastleigh we would wait impatiently at Worthy Down for them to be pulled down, at which time there would be an ugly rush to get home first. The air raid warnings often occurred in the evening just at the end of the working day when the bar at Eastleigh, our home base, opened; hence the rush. One evening we heard that one balloon had broken its cable after a hang-up on the winch but it was only at the daily inspection of our aircraft the next day that two deep, ugly cuts were noticed on one of the engine cowlings. The strange thing was that the cuts were horizontal and the culprit had, therefore, been in a vertical turn. We never heard any more of the incident but it did discourage the evening race to the bar.

In the early years of flying, the accident rate was appallingly high. My own parents, with their memories of the losses in the Royal Flying Corps in World War One, had been against my learning to fly but I had the urge and, like all youth, would not listen. Even in 1928 the general attitude to civil flying was still slapdash.

Perhaps training in the armed services was better organised but even here the ratio of accidents to the number of flying hours was fairly constant. By noting every mention of an accident in the press it was possible to make a reasonable estimate of the number of hours that that particular service had flown. Every now and then there would be an outcry in the press about excessive losses in the Royal Air Force and a call for an inquiry.

I witnessed many crashes and had many good friends killed but somehow one hoped that one's luck would hold. It would be untrue, however, not to admit that I was constantly aware of the danger with one small mistake due to thoughtlessness, misjudgement, or any other human failing, being enough to cause disaster. An aircraft is unforgiving of any error: no excuse, no second try; it must be right the first time. This discipline of thought and action does not come naturally but as a result of training and experience, the lesson must be well and truly understood – 'no mistakes'. Once airborne and flying there is little danger for, as Monkey Sherlock used to say, 'It's the last half-inch which helps the undertaker!' I remember Duncan Davis, my early instructor, telling me never to make a climbing turn but to fly straight on until reaching 1000 feet, then put the nose down to gain speed before making a turn. Taking off is the most critical period of any flight and by far the most dangerous but to visit the Farnborough Air Show, England's major international air event, nowadays, it appears as though the new generation of pilots can disregard the old training. My heart is in my mouth for them when I see those frightening climbing turns.

The one thing which I believe all pilots dread more than anything is fire, the most usual outcome of any aircraft accident. The best action to take in a crash landing is always to get out as quickly as possible, even with the mildest bump. Once as a passenger in the old Canadian days, I learned a trick from Lumsden which, as a passenger, was to sit as near to the tail as possible and to open the rear door a crack by putting your foot in it! Doors almost always jam in a crash due to the fuselage distorting.

By August 1940, the Germans were only 80 miles away across the Channel and the war was in full swing. Some pilots from my course were seconded to the RAF who were short of fighter pilots but I was told to go on a week's leave.

On ringing Ella to tell her to pack her bags I was surprised to hear that Lee-on-Solent had been bombed. When the sirens had rung, Ella had crouched in the cupboard under the stairs with Pooch, our bull terrier. On hearing a series of screams followed by an explosion, Ella had thought it was simply another German bomber down, but when it was over she went out into the street and could see flames and smoke from burning hangars. She became anxious about my whereabouts so my telephone call was opportune. The attack had been made in broad daylight by 90 Stukas which had bombed Gosport and the aerodrome at Lee, although they had been intended for Gosport only which was not in use as an aerodrome by the RAF. The Duty Pilot's orders at Lee were to fire off coloured Verey lights in the event of an enemy attack or the sighting of parachutists, which, of course, he did. The Germans must have thought they were attacking the wrong target, turning their attention to Lee when they saw the lights. Gosport and the dockyards were heavily defended with anti-aircraft guns while Lee was fully exposed, virtually without defence. For fifteen minutes the Stukas, after dropping their bombs, flew round the perimeter squirting at anything worthwhile with their machine guns.

Forty-five of the forty-seven aircraft dispersed on the aerodrome were either burnt out or riddled with bullets, the two main hangars had been burnt down and everything was in a shambles.

By the time I arrived home, the bags were packed and we drove straight off to Constantine Bay in Cornwall. My parents had moved to Sussex by then so we had to stay in a bed and breakfast but it was a good break for both of us.

CHAPTER 13

To Sea in Pegasus

Returning from leave I was sent to No 807 Squadron, a new squadron being formed with Lieutenant Commander Sholto Douglas in command and equipped with the first Fairey Fulmars to come off the production line. These were, in many respects, similar to the RAF's Fairey Battle day bomber but were built to naval specification 08/38 with folding wings, four Browning machine-guns firing forward and of course, a hook for deck landing. It was a good reliable flying machine but hardly a fighter, largely because it was conceived before the days of radar and an observer was considered essential for communication and navigation at sea, hence the second enclosed cockpit.

We started working up the squadron at Worthy Down before being sent to St Merryn in North Cornwall for air firing practice. I knew this aerodrome well as my parents had lived at Constantine Bay for many years and of course I had only recently spent my leave there. It was while we were in Cornwall that I received a letter from the Army and Navy Stores in London who had been storing our possessions since Ella and I had moved out of our flat on my joining the navy. The letter stated that as a result of an 'incident' on 11 October, their depository had been burnt by an incendiary bomb and was a total loss. They went on to say that any claims were to be made to the War Damage Commission and not to them. To add insult to injury, they enclosed a bill for storage due from 1 October up to the night of the fire, for the sum of 12s.6d. Considering we had lost everything we owned it seemed a bit callous, especially as their letter was a printed form with a rubber stamped signature.

On returning to Worthy Down I was sent to Lee-on-Solent in charge of a flight of three Fulmars; I held, by that time, the rank of Lieutenant (A) RNVR. We were briefed to make an attack on an unmanned radio controlled, high speed power boat undergoing special trials operating in the West Solent. It was fun to fire one's guns at a live target but, due to the lack of good radio communications, the whole episode was a mess.

Our aim and/or gun alignment was also wide of the mark as we scored the minimum of hits on the craft during several attacks. After this I always insisted on setting up my own guns and sight, taking the greatest care to see that the aircraft's attitude was correct for the expected attack speed and that the gun pattern was focused on a point at the correct distance. Considering the cost of the weapons as a whole, the aircraft, the guns, the crew and the training, the best natural shot in the world is no good unless he knows his weapon and how it fires, yet it was surprising to find that many fighter pilots accepted a new aircraft from a supply depot without making their own check of the gun alignment.

It was while we were working up No 807 Squadron at Worthy Down that our Commanding Officer, Lieutenant Commander Sholto Douglas RN, had an extraordinary experience while driving home one evening. While driving towards Winchester he was about to drive under a railway bridge when he saw a man fall or jump from the parapet on to the road in front of his car. He was killed instantly. Sholto Douglas drove to the nearest house where he telephoned the police before returning to the bridge to wait for them. When they arrived they searched the body for his identity and then asked Sholto Douglas for his name and address. When he told them the policeman said, 'No, we want your name.' It turned out that the man lying dead on the road was also called Sholto Douglas!

While waiting to embark on HMS *Ark Royal* a signal arrived from Admiralty detaching a flight of three aircraft which were to fly forthwith to Sydenham, the aerodrome by the Belfast Docks. I believe the inspiration for this move came from Mr Churchill himself because we had been losing ships at the rate of one a day during their approach of the Northern Irish coast in convoy.

A four-engined German aircraft, the Focke Wulf FW 200 Condor, operating from Stavanger would appear off the west coast of Ireland at dawn every morning, give a weather report, position, course and speed of any convoy, pick off any stragglers with a bomb and fly on to land at Bordeaux. These convoys had no anti-aircraft defence except from their escorts and these were seeking out submarines. The object of our operation was to provide fighter defence by loading Fulmars onto a catapult ship called HMS *Pegasus*.

We towed our three Fulmars through the dockyard area early one morning and loaded them aboard, one in a hold, one on the hatch cover and one on the catapult. *Pegasus* had started life as an Italian tanker in World War One but had been acquired by the Admiralty. She was really a kind of 'Q' ship, i.e she really looked more like an old oil tanker or merchant ship, she had been converted in peace time by the Royal Navy for aircraft training purposes caterpulting and recovering aircraft at sea being used in the Solent for perhaps one afternoon a week. It was hardly suitable for the North Atlantic in mid-winter but nevertheless her crew was increased to 200 and some extra life rafts were added.

We set sail in February 1941 under the command of Captain Wodehouse, brother, I believe, to PG Wodehouse, and joined an outward bound convoy from Liverpool. The aircraft on the catapult was at immediate readiness which meant that the pilot and observer were in the cockpit fully kitted up, the engine was kept warm and ready to be fired off at a moment's notice. From dawn to dusk a fresh crew relieved those on duty every four hours and after each sortie our orders were to dump the aircraft in the sea near a destroyer or to fly back to Belfast if it were feasible. By using a secret code, the ship kept in constant radio touch with a land-based direction-finding station and as soon as the Condor broke radio silence we were informed. Having reached a position of 25° west without incident, we broke away from the convoy and wandered aimlessly about the middle of the Atlantic hoping to intercept the next incoming convoy.

We were kept informed of the position of the eastbound convoy which, due to enemy action, was running behind schedule. I was shown how to decode these signals and then plot them with the navigating officer.

Our Chief Engineer, who was nearly 70, had been brought back for war service in *Pegasus;* he was very nervous, as were we all. The area was stiff with submarines and with our maximum speed of 8 knots and no watertight compartments, we did not reckon our chances high in the event of a torpedo attack. The wardroom, however, was amidships just under the main deck and it had an old-fashioned double brass rail and glass covered hatch above the dining-room table; by removing the screws from the latches we eased the Chief's worries a little as this enabled one to step straight out from the top of the table on to the upper deck.

The incoming convoy was delayed first by one day and then another. Meanwhile, our navigator, ex-merchant navy, had not been able to get a good sight to fix our position since leaving Ireland and was getting worried, so a great cheer went up when at last smoke appeared on the horizon. We tucked ourselves into the middle of the back row; the safest position in a convoy.

That night the convoy was attacked. I was asleep when a tremendous crash woke me up and I thought the main engine connecting rod had gone through the side, but all was dark on deck so I went back to my bunk. There followed an even bigger crash which felt as if the ship had been hit with an enormous hammer. An oil tanker was on fire and another ship was burning. At dawn the tanker was still afloat and after much deliberation and signalling, one of the escort ships was sent off into the blue for 50 miles before breaking radio silence and asking for a tug to be sent. The main convoy plodded on at a steady six to eight knots with no sign of a Condor.

I noticed some drops of oil on the deck below our aircraft and, sure enough, on close examination I could detect a very small leak in the corner of the oil cooler. It was impossible to switch aircraft – even in harbour it was difficult, let alone in the prevailing sea – and so we kept the oil tank well topped up hoping for the best. A day later the Irish coast came into sight and when we were about an hour's flying time from Sydenham I was catapulted off – which seemed the simplest way of changing round the aircraft. Hardly was I airborne before oil started coming up into the cockpit through the slot of the radiator flap lever covering everything including the inside of the windscreen, my eyes and goggles. Opening the hood increased the flow and made it worse but somehow I managed to get down alright, although I was soaked to the skin in hot, dirty oil.

On landing I was immediately called to the telephone to speak to the Naval Officer In Charge (NOIC). I thought I must have broken some local flying regulation but I was surprised to be told that Ella was waiting for me in the Grand Hotel having a drink with him in the bar! How she pulled strings to get there I shall never know but she had a room with a bath, clean underclothes, shirt, socks, shoes and my No 1 uniform; I have never been so pleased to see her in my life. Ella was a wonderful wife and like Ruth in the Old Testament, would always 'go where you go' whatever the difficulty. We had, for brief periods, seventeen different homes during the war years.

Belfast was relatively free from rationing and with the bars open from morning to midnight, we all had quite a time. We even had a dinner party on board HMS *Pegasus* with a menu of Consommé Mussolini, Halibut au Fulmar and Widgeon Roti Catapultie – an unusual event in wartime.

Leaving Belfast to join our next convoy we made the routine run over the degaussing range as a precaution against magnetic mines but we promptly turned back as the ship's signature was too pronounced so, after a loving farewell in the early morning, Ella was surprised and delighted to see me back at midday. The same thing happened at least twice more as the electricians could not get the ship 'clean' to clear the range. Finally, my relief pilot, Bob Everett, the 1939 Grand National winner, arrived and I was ordered to return to my squadron, now at Yeovilton. On the following trip of the *Pegasus,* Bob was catapulted off and had a chase and a shot at a Condor. I never heard whether its loss was confirmed but Bob himself was lost shortly afterwards. The message that some of these convoys had a fighter escort soon got back to Germany as the Condor, being basically a converted civil airliner, had no rear defensive armament, making it very vulnerable to attack by fighters. This particular menace diminished from March 1941 onwards.

Back at Yeovilton I was disappointed to find my squadron had already left and was in the Mediterranean on HMS *Ark Royal* but I was glad to meet up again with a good friend, Nigel 'Buster' Hallett. We had first met at Worthy Down in 1940 on the formation of the first Fulmar squadron, No 807, when Buster was a lieutenant RN and had had a somewhat unusual career since joining the navy as a cadet at Dartmouth. After qualifying for his sea watchkeeper's certificate, he volunteered for flying in the FAA which was, at that time, partly under RAF control, with naval pilots having to take temporary RAF commission, bringing them under air force discipline when not embarked on ships, even though they wore naval uniform. The whole business of dual control of this vital arm of the Royal Navy between the wars was a most unsatisfactory arrangement.

In 1937 when Buster was flying as a young lieutenant with the Torpedo Development Unit at Gosport, he was court-martialled by the RAF for low flying over the nearby coast *en route* to the torpedo range only half a mile away. The number of his aircraft had been reported to the AOC by a local poultry farmer and it was at a time when the Minister for Air was being criticised by the press and questions were being asked in Parliament about low flying nuisances by the RAF. Buster and another naval officer had their flying careers terminated and the minister concerned was able to announce that 'action had been taken against two flying officers in order to put a stop to unauthorised low flying', though he failed to mention the true facts.

Buster immediately resigned his commission but this was not accepted by the Admiralty who sent him to sea. He left the navy shortly afterwards and was put on the Emergency Reserve List, being reinstated in 1939 when the Admiralty was at last granted autonomy over the FAA. After an outstanding war record during which he was awarded the DSC, commanded two fighter wings and a Carrier Air Group, he ended his naval career as Captain of Greenwich. This whole episode was an example of the controversy and bitterness which existed between the heads of the two services over control of naval aviation and from which the Fleet Air Arm had suffered for years.

Buster and I both enjoyed flying Gladiators of which we had two in Naval Air Fighting Development Unit (NAFDU) in April 1941. I had not been trained to fly by the Service and, therefore, had little experience of aerobatics but the 'Glad' was very manoeuvrable with precise controls and between us we worked out a little routine act. Starting in line abreast, about 100 yards apart, we would do a dive followed by a loop, another dive with a pull up and a roll off the top, then a stall turn and a dive followed by an upward roll.

During the first years of the war, my brother Jack was a major in the Gordon Highlanders from which he had retired on joining the Stock Exchange in 1931. Fortunately he was not with them at Singapore, thereby escaping capture by the Japanese. He was in charge of a unit of some sort at Taunton in Somerset, engaged nominally in the supply of equipment and later he was to receive the OBE for administration.

David, meanwhile, had applied to join the navy on his return from Papeete but had been rejected – so he and his artist wife went to the Bahamas where they built a house on one of the outlying islands in which they lived until the end of the war.

CHAPTER 14

Gun Trails at Duxford

From Yeovilton I was posted in June 1941 to the RAF station at Duxford near Cambridge which was the headquarters of the RAF's Air Fighter Development Unit where I joined Lieutenant Commander Brian Kendall RN, Commanding Officer of the Naval Air Fighter Development Unit, the navy's equivalent. I had no fighter experience but our concern was with making our guns work and developing predictor sights and new sighting patterns. The Fleet Air Arm was already becoming dependent on American aircraft and equipment but these sadly lacked any background of operational experience. The Grumman Martlet, for example, just entering service, had two .5 inch machine guns which would fire a few shots and then break their forward attachment mounting on the front wing spars but it did not stop the gun, which would continue to fire through the top skin of the wing. The guns would jam if fired while making a turn at two or three G and they lacked any heating or cooling system.

I liked the big American air-cooled engines with which all their aircraft were fitted, having learned respect for their reliability in commercial flying in Canada, but we soon discovered that one could expect trouble if using full power in a very steep climb or by using high rpm and full boost for any length of time.

Our nearest air firing range was off the north Norfolk coast near Sheringham and we also had the RAF's permission to use Matlask, a satellite aerodrome of Horsham St Faith which was only a grass field convenient for dropping our target flags. The officers' mess was a couple of miles away in a delightful old mill house straddling a stream; it reminded me of one of Constable's famous paintings.

The Admiralty had no reliable information on the speed, rate of climb or range of the American aircraft, including the Martlet. This we did our best to supply although we were not properly equipped or qualified to measure aircraft performance. Lieutenant-Commander Kendall was particularly interested in fighter tactics and thought there was a big future for predictor sights in fighters.

One version had been invented by a professor of mathematics who had been given a laboratory at Exeter airport to develop a practical instrument. This he did and the instrument was ultimately installed in a Hurricane which we had, the trials of which I became involved in. The sighting point was a cross of light which moved ahead of the target on a reflector sight giving the right deflection to allow, provided the range was correct, the range being fed in from a twist grip control on the top of the throttle which lengthened or shortened the cross of light to correspond with the span of the wings of the target aircraft. It was never adopted, however, the old-fashioned method of getting in really close being more effective.

Our naval party fell in with the routine of life on an RAF station, sharing in their duties and entertainments and shortly after our arrival there was a big army defence exercise when we were detailed to defend the aerodrome. There happened to be a main road passing through the station and so it seemed sensible to block this partially with short lengths of railway line lowered into previously prepared holes in the road. A couple of tanks appeared from an easterly direction and tried to squeeze through the gap but it was just too narrow and, after grinding away, showering sparks from their tracks, they reversed clear only to make a rather bad tempered charge. This time they got stuck on top of a spike, their tracks unable to get a grip, so we threw some whizzbang fireworks under them and waited but the bang was almost swamped by the verbal onslaught. We had obstructed the friendly force, not the invaders.

Two captured enemy aircraft, a Fiat CR.42 and a Messerschmitt Bf 109, were being assessed as combat aircraft in comparison with our equivalent. The CR.42 had landed in Essex when Mussolini had sent his big Balbo to help his friend Adolf win the Battle of Britain but, although it had supposedly force-landed with high oil temperature, there was no trace of the problem and it seemed a poor excuse to me.

The CR.42 was a bi-plane with a big air-cooled radial engine rather like a Gladiator but not in the same class to fly, although the Italian pilots were reputed to indulge in all sorts of aerobatics during combat. To start the engine, there was a small motor-mower type engine driving a compressor to pump up the compressed-air bottle first; all very complicated and heavy for a fighter.

The Bf 109 had a Daimler-Benz engine with fuel injection and an electrically operated variable-pitch propeller, the control switch being mounted at the end of the throttle lever. I liked the positive response from the throttle and the negative G capability but the manually operated propeller pitch change required constant attention, especially in any sort of simulated dogfight. The aircraft's handling characteristics, except for very heavy ailerons, were good, particularly in a dive, but not outstanding in other respects. The Spitfire could always out-climb it and turn inside it but, of course, not all engagements developed that way. Our Rolls Royce Merlin engines had conventional carburettors which stopped immediately on pushing the control column forward in a sudden dive leaving the pilot at the mercy of a Messerschmitt on his tail.

The Admiralty was determined to try the effectiveness of various gun alignment patterns, initially focused on a point at 100 yards range; secondly as an ellipse and thirdly as a rectangle. We used a flag target about 30 feet long and 5 feet deep towed behind a Roc or a Skua. The Martlet or Fulmar were loaded with 400 rounds (100 per gun) each and a series of beam attacks was made until the ammunition was exhausted. The flag was then dropped back on the aerodrome and the holes counted.

It was a wonderful opportunity to get some real firing practice in and we made the most of it. Previously I had only used 100 rounds in one gun and then on a circular drogue fired at from astern.

The Martlet's guns were now working well and the average number of strikes varied from 11.5% to 22% but, as with any shooting, one had one's off days. On one occasion, having fired a long burst and finished my ammunition, I was returning to Matlask when suddenly one gun fired a single round; the trigger was on safety but the gun must have jammed and the heat of the breech set off the charge. This was my one and only experience of a 'cook-off' as it is known among the experts.

Towing a target is a thankless task usually reserved for anyone who had recently broken the flying regulations or misbehaved in some other way. It can be dangerous and is very hard work besides being deadly boring. One day when I was in charge of the firing party, the winch operator who was either very stupid or very frightened, failed to tell his pilot that he had not winched in the target flag in preparation for dropping nor had he actually dropped it so when they came in to land they were towing a quarter of a mile of wire cable with the target flag on the end. Apart from nearly stalling the aircraft on approach he had shorted the power line, knocked down telephone wires, frightened the local cows and infuriated the farmer. It was especially embarrassing as we were the guests of the RAF who also took their share of the blast. The naval airman culprit told me that he had forgotten to take his wire cutter, which was standard equipment, with him and when the winch had jammed he had not liked to tell the pilot. After I had had a go at him, Petty Officer Martin gave him the benefit of his 'advice' in no uncertain terms.

Three weeks later the same man was operating the winch in a Skua when the unbelievable happened. This time he did not reeve the cable correctly and failed to notice that the cable was not passing over the sheave where it went through the bottom hatch but was resting on the edge of the hatch itself. He just winched it in regardless, watching the wire cut through the hatch, the fuselage skin and the ribs nearly back to the tail wheel. To saw the aircraft in half must be the nearest thing to cutting off a branch on which one is sitting. I thought Martin was going to have kittens and what made it worse was that he had just completed a major overhaul of the aircraft.

An RAF officer at Duxford had been given the job of installing a big gun in a Blenheim and because of its size, about 40 to 50 mm bore, it had to be mounted externally underneath the fuselage. The aircraft had to be kept serviceable while the bits were made up and a fair exchange was arranged, he to fly the Martlet and I the Blenheim. There was no official permission ever given but these exchanges were often made and I never heard of any accident. I was glad to have a twin-engined aircraft in my log book as up till then I had only flown singles.

In July I received a signal ordering me to report for a deck landing course on HMS *Argus*, an old ship reported to have started life as an Italian liner. She had four screws directly driven by turbines which gave her the necessary speed as an aircraft-carrier but were probably grossly inefficient in fuel consumption. All the upper-works had been removed and replaced by a flat deck without any obstruction, but there was a slight step up in the deck towards the bow which was quite helpful in getting airborne off the short deck. Strangely enough this idea has now been revived to assist the latest jump-jet Harrier to shorten its take-off run and save fuel or to carry a heavier load. HMS *Argus* was based on the Clyde and for convenience used to lie in Lamlash Bay, Isle of Arran, where I completed the required six deck landings in a Fulmar before returning to Duxford to continue the firing trials.

In action, an attacking aircraft's wings and wing mounted guns are usually parallel with those of the enemy, that is in a stern attack. Our target was a flag with the leading edge vertical which meant that all our firing trials were from the beam. To make an attack on the beam meant a deflection shot from a turn with the wings banked at about 80°. In doing this, the convergence of the guns to the aiming pattern would only be correct at a fixed range and, in any case, put a tremendous premium on the pilot's skill in aiming. However, inexplicably, I found that, whereas with the two .5-inch guns of the Martlet I averaged 18% strikes, with the eight .303-inch Browning guns of the Hurricane which we had, I could not do better than 12%. The American .5-inch gun was very high velocity with a streamlined bullet but it had a lower rate of fire and wore out the rifling in the barrel very quickly. After 200 or 300 rounds some of the bullets would become 'tippers', that is, instead of revolving and flying straight they would go end over end! They also lacked enough punch to be able to pierce an aircraft's skin and then go on to knock away any armour plate.

Two twin-engined captured enemy aircraft at Duxford were a Messerschmitt Bf 110 and a Heinkel He 111 bomber. Endless simulated attacks were made on these to try to find their weak points and vulnerable angles of approach. In the Heinkel the pilot sat far back in a kind of streamlined greenhouse and as a result, visibility was bad; it seemed a poor exchange to give away pilot's vision for a small increase in speed due to the streamlining. Fortunately for us the Luftwaffe were largely equipped with 1935 designs, already becoming out of date by 1942, whereas, though we were very late in re-equipping our Air Force with fighters, at least ours were up-to-date.

During my six months stay at Duxford, Ella and I had rented a bungalow in a nearby village but when I received my next orders – in December 1941 – she was unable to accompany me as I was to join HMS *Victorious* at Scapa Flow. Ella decided to spend the first half of 1942 with my sister-in-law at Haslemere before renting a house nearby.

CHAPTER 15

Russian Approaches

O n 7 December 1941, the day of Pearl Harbor, I was ordered to report to Lieutenant Savage RN, Commanding Officer of No. 809 Squadron at Hatston in the Orkneys. This was the second Fulmar squadron to be formed and was earmarked for HMS *Victorious* in the Home Fleet. Savage was keen on flying discipline and we were kept very busy with formation flying and squad drill. It was the equivalent of square bashing in the army in that the four flights of three aircraft had to perfect their own precise formations and, when flying as a squadron, to change position quickly and neatly.

On joining the ship we developed and perfected a technique of taking off from the deck in quick succession. By jinking to port in order to clear our slip-stream for the next aircraft taking off and then proceeding straight ahead for a given number of seconds, depending on the order of take-off, before turning to port, each aircraft was able, by taking a short cut, to join the formation in a very tight sequence. Meantime, the leader, who took off first, had made a rate one turn after going straight ahead for the longest period (one minute, 30 seconds), so that on passing the ship on a reciprocal course, the whole squadron was already in Vee formation. It was quite impressive when well done.

While at Hatston, the American aircraft carrier, *USS Wasp*, in company with the battleship, USS *Washington*, arrived at Scapa Flow and flew off her aircraft, mostly fighters with a few torpedo bombers. The US Navy is dry but this was certainly an occasion for a celebration and we made our visitors welcome. The following day we were invited to their return party, the slight difficulty over the shortage of alcohol being solved by their forethought in tapping off alcohol which was normally used in their torpedoes!

HMS *Victorious* was in Scapa Flow when we landed on her during the afternoon of 24 December 1941. Although, as pilots in the Fleet Air Arm, we had no nautical duties in the ship, it was a stirring experience finding oneself in a new world steeped in tradition and prestige. The ship's routine, the pipes, the discipline and the whole naval atmosphere, particularly while at war, was, I found, intensely interesting and exciting. My first day happened to be Christmas Day and to hear 1500 men assembled in the steel hangar singing 'For Those In Peril On The Sea' was very moving as was the old tradition of the youngest boy in the ship donning the Commander's gold braided cap and solemnly doing the ship's daily round of inspection with his attendant staff. 'The first shall be last and the last first.'

Victorious was a new ship although she had already been involved in the chase and sinking of the *Bismarck*. Like all British Fleet carriers, she had an armoured flight deck. This was 4 inch thick armour steel reputed to have been made in Czechoslovakia by Skoda and shipped out after the war had started. It is interesting to note that although the Americans lost many of their aircraft-carriers which had wooden decks, the Royal Navy never lost one from aerial attack. Even when, later in the war in the Pacific, a Kamikaze pilot made a suicide attack on *Victorious,* he only dented her deck.

While at sea, those with the responsibility for war damage control were distributed throughout the ship, slinging their hammocks in gangways and other odd spaces. The object was to avoid the possibility of losing all the experts in any particular trade. In contrast, the majority of the flying officers had their own cabins close to their aircraft.

Control of fighters from an operations room on board was in its earliest stage of development at that time. As fighters, our prime job was to protect the Home Fleet from aerial attack while at sea, and never to go far afield. It was, I believe, an RNVR officer, Lieutenant-Commander Borthwick, who realised the importance of controlling the fighters and he was given full authority to organise an operations room. By coincidence I already knew Borthwick, a keen dinghy sailor; in fact we were both members of the Itchenor Sailing Club and had been racing Sharpies in competition up at Brancaster the weekend before the war started. He also picked a number of sailing men as Fighter Direction Officers as their racing experience proved very useful in the problems of interception. In some ways a yacht race is also a question of quick decisions and judgement of speeds and angles. Borthwick's nickname was 'Meatball' but it was years after the war before I realised why. His family was the largest in the London meat market!

Most of our early exercises while flying from *Victorious* were devoted to the technique of intercepting an incoming target aircraft simulating an enemy attack on the ship while 809 Squadron was under the control of the Fighter Direction Officer (FDO) in the ship.

In order to give all the Home Fleet's guns an exercise (up to then there had only been a visit by one rather half-hearted German reconnaissance aircraft), we were ordered to simulate an attack with our Fulmars on the Fleet anchored in Scapa Flow. Savage decided to split the squadron into four flights and attack at low level from four directions simultaneously. We worked out a route to all our respective targets as we knew where the big ships were lying in the harbour.

Mine was the battleship *King George V*, the flagship, and our approach was to be over the hill from the south-east and into Scapa Flow. We took off from *Victorious* in the Pentland Firth and each flight made a big sweep round into position well out of sight behind the low hills. At the appropriate moment we all converged and made our attacks, flying very low, the observers firing a red Verey light to indicate that a dummy bomb had been dropped. I do not think there was much aiming done that day as they had not expected that type of approach. In fact, in spite of the expectation of an attack, they were caught with all their big guns pointing at the sky and the short-range weapons unmanned. Our own run into the target went very well but I was shaken when my observer, Sub-Lieutenant Rogers, fired his Verey pistol. The flare bounced across the ship's deck and fell on the edge of a barge moored alongside. It had been hidden during the approach and we had not considered the possibility of the ship loading food or ammunition during the exercise. We heard no more of it but nor were we ever asked to make a raid again.

A few days later we were again exercising in the Pentland Firth. There was little wind but a biggish swell and such wind as there was, was along the swell, just about the worst conditions for operating aircraft off a deck. The ship had to do 25 knots along the swell to get the necessary wind speed and this made her roll. A squadron of Albacore was also exercising and the Commander Flying decided to land them on first. The fifth aircraft made a very heavy landing and had to be craned up and dangled overboard and the next aircraft went into the barrier but after a delay it was dragged forward out of the way while the remainder landed on successfully. Meanwhile our flight of three aircraft, airborne for over three hours, was short of fuel and when the last Albacore landed I had expected to be given the signal to land straight away. Instead the ship turned round with her destroyer escort onto a reciprocal course.

My petrol guage was by now bumping on the empty stop and as we had been forbidden to break wireless silence we were unable to radio the ship. It was too far from land to reach an aerodrome so we flew round the ship in loose open formation at minimum speed to save fuel. I remembered an old trick of Monkey Sherlock's aimed at attracting attention while in flight without radio, which was to switch off one magneto and go into weak mixture so that the engine pops back and misses badly. I did this and they very soon got the message on the bridge but it was a difficult decision for the Captain to take to turn his ship again as he told me later – he had been on one course far too long already and was afraid of a lurking submarine. Although shaken, however, we did save the aircraft from being ditched as it is impossible to land on a deck without power and we were on the point of having to land in the sea.

When HMS *Ark Royal* was torpedoed and sunk in the Mediterranean about this time, we were at Scapa Flow. The Germans had claimed to have sunk *Ark Royal* many times before so, in an effort to confuse them, we in No. 809 Squadron immediately took over her old fighter squadron call sign CAYMAN, which we used in all our exercises in the Orkney area, hoping that our calls were being intercepted by the Germans.

Shortly after the sinking of the *Ark Royal*, *Victorious* was used for stability trials. The *Ark* had been hit in the area of her starboard boiler-room, the side of a carrier on which the 'island' is sited. This extra weight is not balanced by any equivalent structure on the port side but merely with water in the port ballast tanks. It had been reported that on being struck she heeled to an acute angle and water flooded not only the starboard boiler-room but flowed through air intake ducts over the top of the fore and aft compartments, flooding other boilers and leading ultimately to the loss of all auxiliary power and consequently the bilge pumps. In theory the four engines were unitised, i.e. entirely separate power units, but the sinking of HMS *Ark Royal* disclosed this unseen weakness.

While at our moorings and after lashing down all our aircraft very thoroughly, *Victorious* was heeled step by step while measuring the required shift in the water ballast. After reaching an angle of about 30°, she was righted again. Like all warships, she was subdivided into quite small watertight compartments, except for the single large hangar deck with watertight doors and hatches between each. At sea all the doors were kept permanently closed except for a small hatch through which a man could pass and even these were closed in action so, when down below, one might just as well have been in a submarine. There was something to be said for being a pilot.

One soon came to recognise the signs of an impending operation. Black puffs of smoke indicating extra boilers being fired up, the early recall of liberty boats, aircraft to have their daily inspection completed, followed by the series of pipes mustering the sea duty men in preparation for casting off the mooring or raising the anchor. Once the ship was at sea the Captain would speak on the public address system and tell us what the operation was and where we were going. In wartime particularly, a ship's company becomes very much of a team, each man being dependent on others and having respect for the other man's abilities. Beyond that is the knowledge that the ship itself is one's home and its defence is vital in order to survive. This spirit extended to the flying personnel too; we became part of the ship and however far one was from the ship one knew that if you went down in the sea they would come looking for you, no matter what the cost. This feeling of belonging was a great morale boost.

Although Scapa Flow was the normal base for the Home Fleet, we spent more time at Hval Fjord on the west coast of Iceland. On going ashore in Iceland we all wore civilian clothes as it was a neutral country but it had a very left-wing government with leanings towards our new ally, Russia. For political reasons, the United States was sending vast supplies of weapons to Russia and these convoys converged on Hval Fjord before being escorted to Murmansk, their destination.

As the Germans were occupying the whole of Norway, this involved passing close to their fighter and bomber equipped aerodromes in the far north and also within easy striking distance of the Tirpitz, a very powerful ship based near Trondheim. The job of the Home Fleet was to prevent the interception of these convoys by surface ships but not to venture into the area where the Germans had air superiority. Winter provided the cover of darkness but in summer losses in merchant ships were appalling. While waiting, morale among the merchant seamen was very low and we used to invite parties of them over to *Victorious* for hot baths, hot meals, drinks and a cinema show, but little did we know that many of these brave men would shortly be the victims of the ill-fated convoy PQ 17.

While covering the Russian convoys against interception by German warships, our Albacores flew anti-submarine patrols during the daylight hours while the fighters stood by at readiness. Although we knew that sometimes enemy aircraft were shadowing the fleet, we were not allowed to leave the deck. All movements of our aircraft had to be authorised by the Admiral whose flagship was HMS *King George V* and normally all signals were made by lamp or by flag. Why the Admiral chose a battleship for his flagship instead of *Victorious,* which had the necessary accommodation for his staff, was difficult to understand. It was all part of the pre-war thinking of big guns and armour versus the new-fangled aeroplane, a kind of status symbol!

News came through, while we were covering one convoy, of the passage up the Channel of two large German ships. This was a great surprise to the country and a great loss of prestige for the Admiralty and the RAF because the *Scharnhorst* and the *Gneisenau,* which had been in Brest for repairs, had been bombed night after night throughout the winter. They had slipped quietly out of harbour, however, under cover of darkness without being seen and had reached Cap de la Hague before being reported.

Six Swordfish at Lee-on-Solent were immediately loaded with torpedoes and ordered to intercept but before contact was made the two ships had reached the Straits of Dover and the Luftwaffe was out in force protecting them. All six Swordfish were shot down with the loss of their crews, including two friends of mine, Lieutenant-Commander Esmonde VC and Lieutenant North who had been my first flight commander at Lee-on-Solent. At the time *Victorious* was at sea somewhere between the north of Norway and Iceland covering a convoy against interception by *Tirpitz,* Germany's most powerful ship, which was lying in a fjord near Trondheim.

A day or two later, RAF reconnaissance aircraft reported that two warships were proceeding northwards in the fjords up the coast of Norway. Their intention appeared to be to join the *Tirpitz* which would present a most formidable threat both to the Russian convoys and the Home Fleet, so the *Victorious* and three destroyers were immediately detached from the main fleet and proceeded at 28 knots in a southerly direction. Meanwhile, twelve Albacores were ranged on the flight deck, loaded with torpedoes and the crews briefed on the operation. They were to take-off at 1.00am, fly in 50 miles to the Norwegian coast and make a southerly sweep through the fjords with ASV. If the enemy ships were located they were to make a night attack and then fly on to land at Sumburgh in the Shetlands. This hazardous operation was a great deal to ask of crew who had never made a night torpedo attack, barely had the fuel for the distance and did not have the radio frequency of Sumburgh to get direction-finding assistance. *Victorious* could not hang about after flying them off and would be 150 miles away to the north by dawn. Due to the prevailing bad weather, the RAF were unable to confirm the position of the enemy ships and much to the relief of the Albacore crews, the ship *Victorious* turned around shortly after dark with the operation having been called off.

The next day at noon, however, the show was on again so the ship turned to the south once more and at 1.00am the Albacores took off under the command of Lieutenant-Commander Plugge RN. It was snowing but patches of moonlight were visible on a heaving dark sea giving some horizon to fly by. The heavily loaded aircraft went off, slowly gathering speed along the deck and dipping over the bow to gain more speed before disappearing into the night, flames streaming from their exhausts.

The next day we listened anxiously for any news of our aircraft but it was not until the following morning that we changed course for Scapa Flow. It was a lovely day of high wind and bright skies with patches of clear-cut clouds as we slid quietly through the following seas on our way south. A call to action stations on the reported sighting of a torpedo bomber was called off as by this time we were near the Shetlands and a number of RAF Beaufighters had appeared and were circling the fleet.

Before refuelling *Victorious* at Scapa Flow, we were told that the Albacores were going to land on. Three were missing. They had seen nothing of the *Scharnhorst* and *Gneisenau,* two of the Albacores had collided in the darkness, the Commanding Officer, Plugge, was lost while the remainder of the squadron had had to jettison their torpedoes when desperately short of fuel before reaching Sumburgh and landing in darkness. It had been a very expensive, fruitless operation but it was also bad luck as they had, in fact, just missed the German ships by about an hour. I had been in the briefing room with Plugge while he was plotting out his course and he had known then that the operation was extremely hazardous with small hope of success.

The flying training programme continued whenever the ship was able to proceed to sea. Two or three times we were catapulted off in Hval Fjord, flew to Reykjavik and rejoined the ship at sea. Reykjavik was a staging post for the delivery of American aircraft and had a good runway. I once landed my flight of three aircraft in formation on the runway there which did not please the Air Traffic Controller.

By an extraordinary coincidence I was in the Reykjavik airport canteen one day when in walked Lew Parmenter, a Canadian whom I had not seen for ten years. He had been air engineer to Punch Dickins, the famous pilot with Western Canada Airways in the pioneering days of 1929, but now he was chief engineer and was delivering a Boeing B-17 for the US Army Air Forces. He told me that Punch was in overall charge of the whole ferry operation.

It was easy to get back into the routine when I rejoined the convoys at sea. I enjoyed flying over the sea; there were no mountains to hit or power lines which meant I could fly very low. A kind of sixth sense developed giving a hunch for direction and position. An aircraft pointed in one direction travels fast in a moving element, the air, and my point of reference was, of course, a ship which was itself moving along a mean line of advance (a zigzag course) on another moving element, the sea. The sun, the direction of the waves, the tops of distinctive clouds or holes in the clouds, all gave significant information to be stored in my memory but in some ways the best guide of all is the ship's wake which may leave a visible trail for a mile or so and can be seen more easily than the ship itself.

Landing on a deck requires precise flying. After two or three hours in flight one becomes mesmerised by the noise and speed so before landing on it is important to shake off this feeling of lethargy and stiffness and concentrate on being alert. I used to open the hood to let in cold air and bring the aircraft's speed right down to near the stall in order to get the sloppier feel of the response to the controls.

The batsman or deck landing control officer is a great help as he can tell from the relative steadiness of the ship whether the approach is likely to lead to a successful landing. From the deck it is easy to see a crash coming several seconds before it occurs. It is possible even at the last moment for a pilot to avoid the worst, either with a burst of throttle or a twitch of the rudder. I believe the same theory applies to an accident on the road, never give up until the very moment of collision. The smallest gap is softer than the middle of a telegraph pole.

One of our duties was to censor the outgoing mail and return it to the sender if there was any reference to the location of the ship or in fact anything that might remotely help the enemy. One letter which has always stuck in my mind was one from a sailor to his mother thanking her for his birthday cake and asking her, in future, to send him quantity rather than quality! Rather to my surprise we were allowed cameras with which we could photograph life on board, the only restriction being that all films and prints had to be processed by the ship's professional photographer when, of course, the same restrictions regarding censorship applied. Pictures of deep snow on the flight deck with the ship's company clearing it away overboard were unusual, so to me was the order to 'clear the lower deck'. This meant all hands on deck with only those who had duties exempted so one would see pale-faced stokers, tired looking engineers, electricians, armourers and storekeepers appear from the depths of the ship to shovel snow.

In the days of sail, whenever a man was lost or died at sea, his effects were sold or auctioned off 'before the mast' and the money raised, sent to his next of kin. This tradition still survives and often when we returned to harbour the appropriate 'pipe' over the ship's broadcast would be made and a man's kit sold. I bought a collection of Jean Sablon's records which I had heard being played by a brother officer in the cabin next to mine. These frequent pipes were a constant reminder to young flying types of the risks they were running, although not all fatalities were to airmen.

To live cooped up in a steel box in artificial light and with forced air ventilation, sometimes for months on end, was not the most healthy atmosphere and young pilots joining the ship and with only an occasional opportunity to fly, did not find the waiting easy on the nerves.

Most accidents to aircraft were of course due to errors in landing on a deck but the whole operation of handling aircraft in a ship involved hazards to both aircraft and men. On one particular day when the fleet was in usual line astern formation, one of the destroyers sweeping the waters ahead, picked up by asdic a signal indicating an enemy submarine. Instantly the fleet was ordered to make an emergency turn to port which meant the immediate application of full rudder without warning. Cruising at the usual 22 knots, the ship took a 15° list to starboard, causing the chocks of one of our Fulmars to slip and the parked aircraft to run wildly across the deck. The tail wheel was knocked off by the raised edge of the deck and the Fulmar finished up half overboard leaving one more aircraft unserviceable until we reached harbour.

On another occasion when a flight of three aircraft were ranged for take-off, an enemy aircraft was spotted. Our aircraft could not take-off as the fleet was steaming downwind but the ship's 4.5-inch guns were brought to bear. The gun crew, following the various dials in their twin gun turret below deck level, had no view of the aircraft where the crew of one Fulmar, whose engine was running, could only sit helplessly in the cockpit and watch the twin guns in 'Y' turret, swing round, check just above their heads and loose off. The pilot and observer were badly injured by the blast and the Fulmar was more or less written off as the blast from the gun had lifted the top skin of the wing clean off the ribs and spar.

I had a lucky escape when being catapulted off one day. The catapult was a type which had a cylinder and a piston with the air on one side and water on the other. On releasing the water the piston moved forward and through a system of cables accelerated the cradle guided by a slot in the deck. Unfortunately, at the moment of release of the catch holding back the cradle which propels the aircraft, there was a bit of slack in the cable and one of the two legs fell away on the deck leaving me being pushed off with a very big jerk with only one strut. The violent jerk made me black out momentarily and I came to flying over the sea knowing nothing about the mishap until I was told later. If the catapult fails to push at the critical moment of releasing the catch, the aircraft merely trickles forward under its own power and falls off the bow into the sea, more or less perfectly aligned to be chopped up by the ship's propellers.

When flying operationally it was not always possible to park the aircraft in the hangar below in such a way that the serviceable ones were conveniently placed. Sometimes several unserviceable aircraft would have to be ranged on deck in order to get at those required. This caused great annoyance and frustration to those waiting on the flight deck and we used to say 'Uncle Fred has been at it again', which referred to a pre-war music hall comedian Fred Carno. His slapstick act consisted of house decorators carrying ladders, planks and paint in which everything went wrong but somehow the chaotic situation was always saved at the very last moment.

The forward and aft heavy armoured lifts formed part of the flight deck and could be operated at either high or low speed. The higher speed required enormous electrical power and was extremely unpopular with the engineers and so was rarely used – but to save time in No. 809 Squadron, we made a practice of starting up our engines while the lift was rising so as to be able to taxi forward the moment we reached deck level, leaving the spreading of the wings until we were parked. Naval aircraft used Coffman cartridge-type starters which were not too reliable and not infrequently twenty men had to be called upon to push the aircraft clear of the lift.

The flight deck and other aircraft handlers faced continual dangers from revolving propellers, being squashed by folding wings, hit by arrestor wires, falling down lift shafts with everything being done at the double under conditions of noise, sometimes a howling gale and darkness. They had my admiration but it was no wonder that sometimes accidents occurred.

While covering a big convoy in March 1942, the Fleet ran into a severe storm with the wind in the region of 60 knots and mountainous seas causing the ship's speed to be reduced to six knots, the minimum to retain steerage way. In spite of this we were pitching so badly that every now and then we took a green sea over the bow sending a cascade of water sweeping down the flight deck. Eventually the overhanging flare of our bow which was 70 feet above the normal water-line, took an awkward wave and was bent upwards.

Meanwhile down in the hangar we had the aircraft well lashed down but water poured through the catapult rail slot into a trough beneath where it slopped salt water over our aircraft, engines, instruments, guns and ammunition, all of which were fully exposed as the wings were folded.

Looking out from the well protected quarter deck, even the battleship *King George V* was making heavy weather of it; sometimes 50 feet of daylight could be seen back under the bow. The damage to the *Victorious* was severe enough to require immediate attention so the ship was ordered to Rosyth Dockyard in the Firth of Forth for repair. This news was broadcasted throughout the ship and greeted with, I regret to say, cheers from the ship's company as it meant a week's leave.

With just enough time to telephone Ella, I was lucky enough to be able to meet her in London. Both the Savoy and the Berkeley hotels very generously gave special concessionary rates to officers on leave and at 30 shillings a night, including bed, breakfast and dinner, Ella and I made the most of it.

CHAPTER 16

Frustrating Tirpitz

Having spent an enjoyable few days in London with Ella, the return journey north was memorable, though not very pleasant. Three of us from No. 809 Squadron left Euston at 10.30am one morning to rejoin our ship at Scapa Flow. It was an uncomfortable journey as the train had no heat, no restaurant car, not even drinking water. Next morning, when we pulled into Perth, we made a rush for the station restaurant but halfway through bacon and eggs, the train started to move; two of us just made it but one man was left behind. By next morning we had reached Thurso, there to embark in a trawler going to the Orkneys. Crossing the Pentland Firth was miserable as there was no cabin and the only shelter was to stand on deck in the lee of the wheel-house, every now and then being covered with a shower of cold salt spray. We were dropped off at a depot ship only to hear that *Victorious* was in Iceland! An hour or so later we were transferred to a destroyer, HMS *Icarus*, which was taking the mail to the Home Fleet in Hval Fjord. I was as sick as a dog and had to make constant sorties to the deck which was cold, windy and half awash in the rough sea. The crew were dead tired and yet I could not help noticing that in spite of complete informality, in personal relationships they worked to the strictest discipline as a team. On reaching Hval Fjord our first stop was to an oiler to top up tanks and then on to distribute the mail. The navy attached great importance to news from home even, as we saw, by sending a destroyer to Scapa to collect it. Never was I more glad to see *Victorious;* it was almost like arriving home.

While at sea and during daylight hours, an Albacore from the torpedo carrying squadron, loaded with two depth charges, would supplement the destroyer screen searching for submarines. I was having a cup of early morning tea on one occasion when there was a tremendous bang and I thought we had been struck by a torpedo but in fact an Albacore, taking off for a patrol, had swung off line and struck the island with the starboard wing.

The impact had swung the aircraft over the side and on hitting the water the two depth charges were ripped off and the safety pins pulled out. On reaching the set depth they exploded. Fortunately for the ship it happened just as the stern cleared the position. The crew of three were killed.

On our next operation, when we were returning to Iceland, a German aircraft, Junkers

JU88, was shadowing us from about ten miles astern and I could not understand why we had not been allowed to fly off and attack. It had been on our radar all afternoon and by evening, when our position was about due north of Iceland, the pilot's report to his base was intercepted by our radio. He gave our position and added that, as we were obviously returning to Hval Fjord, he was returning home. I then realised that the aircraft had been constantly monitored and our course was a deliberate attempt to mislead the Germans by us acting as a decoy. We had had an Admiralty signal reporting that the *Tirpitz,* with one escorting destroyer, would be at a certain position 50 miles off the Norwegian coast next morning at 8.00am on a certain course and speed. On the departure of the shadowing aircraft we turned round and went east at full speed to be in position to make an attack next morning. During this high-speed dash it became obvious that damage had occurred to the outer starboard propeller when the Albacore had crashed with its depth charges. The vibration in the stern was very bad forcing a reduction of speed to 28 knots. On visiting the heads (in the stern) I noticed that the lead pipes from the overhead cisterns were chaffing on their clips leaving pools of lead powder on the deck. The vibration was so bad that if no action had been taken it would certainly have led to major mechanical trouble. Under the extreme urgency of war, the normal discretion of careful handling of the ship had to go by the board.

Our Captain was sceptical of the Admiralty report and decided to fly off four Albacores with ASV to make a search at dawn but within a few minutes of being airborne they made a radar contact and returned to the ship. Presumably Captain Bovell did not know at that time that we had broken the German naval code and for obvious reasons, of course, it was a very closely guarded secret. However it did seem incomprehensible that the Admiral in command of the Home Fleet should not have been informed. There was a delay while the search aircraft were loaded with their torpedoes but an hour later twelve aircraft took off under the command of Lieutenant Commander Lucas, the new CO who had replaced Plugge. The two other replacement crews had not yet had an opportunity to fly with their squadron. The wind was from the east and to get into position to make an attack the squadron was in full view of the *Tirpitz* for a good half hour. Finally, having reached 10,000 feet, they dived. Unfortunately, not having flown together before and being led into a different method of attack from previous training, there was a misunderstanding and a very ragged attack was made by each flight of three aircraft going in individually instead of simultaneously on the four quarters of the ship. Not one torpedo hit and an Albacore was shot down. It was a poor show with a great opportunity being missed, but the blame for the failure lay at least partly in a combination of unlucky circumstances.

Years after the war, a friend Jeffrey Quill, who was a director of Pan Avia, the consortium of the countries building the latest Tornado Fighter during the 1970s, invited Ella and I to a Christmas lunch in London. The German Air Attaché, who was there with his wife and family, turned out to have been the pilot of the Junkers JU88 that had been shadowing *Victorious* north of Iceland and he told me that he had no idea that he was being watched on radar or that we were intercepting his radio reports! At the time he had been commanding a large Luftwaffe base in Norway. It was strange to meet your late enemy under the circumstances of a Christian festival and to find that you had quite a bit in common besides there being no animosity.

Back at Scapa, No. 809 Squadron returned to training and air firing practice. All our new pilots had to do six deck-landings before being accepted for operational flying but one of them went over the side when, having caught a wire successfully, he began to drift sideways across the deck and, after resting on the edge for a few seconds, went on over. I saw him climb out and swim away a few strokes but by the time the destroyer, stationed just astern of us, had swung round and picked him up, probably in under five minutes, he was dead, presumably from the shock of plunging into icy cold water from a warm cockpit.

In harbour that night it had been decided to bury him at sea but the next day the fleet was ordered to sea at short notice. Being the oldest member of the squadron I was ordered to take the body ashore and be back in time before the ship sailed in four hours time. I had no idea of the routine but a bearer-party of four was organised and a trawler came alongside. The coffin was being lowered by the ship's crane when suddenly the Captain appeared and a bugler played the last post while our party all stood to attention on the trawler's deck. A signal to the hospital at Hoy had requested an ambulance to meet us but on reaching the jetty no ambulance had arrived and eventually we had to go as the ship was about to sail. We staggered up the slippery seaweed covered steps carrying the coffin only to be confronted at the top by a mob of sailors recalled to their ships from an evening shore in the canteen. The sight of our little party sobered them up! The sentry on duty was most reluctant to accept responsibility for the body but the trawler skipper was adamant that we leave at once as the fleet was due to sail and he had orders to return forthwith. The whole episode was painful to all of us in No 809 Squadron as we should have liked him to have had a dignified burial at sea.

We always flew in our ordinary day-to-day naval uniform although there was an issue of a flying suit to those flying open cockpit aircraft such as the Swordfish. The Fulmar had a warm front cockpit as there was a gap in the floor leading to the radiator. However, naval officers' uniform calls for a white shirt and stiff white collar and a black tie (in memory of Admiral Lord Nelson). This was the worst possible rig for swimming in so we made it a rule to slacken off the tie and loosen the collar. In addition, for landing on the deck, the hood would be opened and the Sutton harness locked back to prevent one's face hitting the dashboard in the event of going into the barrier. As a further precaution and to permit a quick exit I used to undo the chin strap of my helmet, release the bayonet fastening of the oxygen pipe and pull out the RT plug lead. This still left the parachute and dinghy attached to one's body and some pilots released these too before landing on.

The best place to watch aircraft operating off the deck is from the protection of the upper deck of the island just abaft the funnel. From this position one can see the approach and is close enough to the point of contact to be able to study the movements of the controls and even the pilot's face. Unless the hook, attached to the bottom of the fuselage, catches one of the eight arrester wires there is no hope of stopping before hitting the barrier. The pilot's main object, therefore, is to catch a wire, not just to make a pretty landing and when this is achieved and the aircraft is snatched out of the air, the tremendous relief is apparent on his face. On being arrested, the aircraft is allowed to run backwards a few yards to release the wire from the hook. In the meantime, the barrier is lowered and the aircraft is taxied forward immediately, using a lot of power, to the forward half of the deck where the wings are folded.

It is not possible to 'strike down' the aircraft on the forward lift as fast as they land on and a traffic jam occurs, hence the barrier to prevent damage to aircraft and accidents to the flight deck crew from over shooting aircraft. A well trained squadron and flight deck crew can, under ideal conditions, land aircraft at twenty second intervals but so many parts of the operation can go wrong that this rarely happens. Nevertheless, to an observer the whole operation is an astonishing scene particularly when the faster and more heavily loaded aircraft land, for it hardly seems possible that they can be stopped in time.

When at sea, the fleet would steam in line astern with an outlying screen of destroyers searching for submarines. To lessen the danger from submarines, a zigzag course was often adopted, all the ships turning to a new course simultaneously at a predetermined time, usually every twenty minutes. As well as a steering wheel on the bridge, a second control position was located several decks below, well protected from damage by enemy fire. One day the Captain happened to be on the bridge when the ship failed to make her regular turn at the appointed moment. The Coxswain was on the lower steering deck at the time and on being asked what was going on he replied in an anxious voice, 'The wheel's come loose in me 'and, Sir.' Control was immediately taken over on the bridge, the rudder having failed to respond to the wheel due to a failure in the operating mechanism. Some of us on the platform thought it funny but the Captain was not amused.

Jason Borthwick, our Fighter Direction Officer and I, were asked to crew the *Victorious'* entry in a sailing race round Scapa Flow, the main base of the Home Fleet because of our pre-war sailing experience. We had noticed the hull of a dinghy hauled up underneath the flight deck out of the way and the Commander gave us permission to get it out. It was about 16 feet long, clinker built but beautifully fitted out and brand new. Launching it from the quarter deck was not easy but with many willing hands helping we lowered it into the water. There was a fair breeze for the race with about a dozen starters. Competition was not too hot so we led the race all the way to within a quarter of a mile of the finish when we were beaten to the post. We both felt it had been a great honour to represent *Victorious* among such an august gathering and everyone was pleased; at least we had not disgraced our ship.

In the late spring of 1942 I received a letter from the Appointments Board at the Admiralty advising me that, with the coming into production of the naval version of the Spitfire, the Seafire, there was an opening for a civilian test pilot with Vickers Armstrong at Eastleigh. Because I had recent experience of deck landing and naval operating conditions, they felt I might fill the position. It was, for me, a very difficult decision; the war at sea was at its height and to take a civilian job looked like opting out. I wanted advice and fortunately decided to request an interview with my Commander, Caspar John. He pointed out that I was 34, had reached the rank of Lieutenant and a steady stream of young fighter pilots were by then completing their training. He reminded me that the Appointments Board were asking me to take the job, adding, 'You cannot do wrong if you do what the Admiralty wants!'

Although Spitfires were designed and built by Supermarine at Southampton, this was a subsidiary company of Vickers Aviation Limited whose headquarters were at Weybridge. I was interviewed there by the chief test pilot, Mutt Summers, and he drove me down to meet Jeffrey Quill at Eastleigh; Jeffrey had the final say and was to be my immediate boss and I was delighted when he accepted me for the post.

Ella and I rented The 'Thatched Cottage' at Burseldon, on the River Hamble, about fifteen miles from Eastleigh, which was quite convenient and in a lovely setting.

CHAPTER 17

Supermarine Test Pilot

S pitfire production at the beginning of the war was based at Supermarine's Woolston factory on the River Itchen at Southampton. The very first enemy night raid on this country, in the spring of 1940, by a single aircraft had been aimed at the factory, probably to test the strength of the defences, but no damage was done. The Southampton area was heavily defended with anti-aircraft guns and a balloon barrage but this did not discourage a second, really determined attack by a squadron of bombers in daylight. This also was a failure as they missed the main factory, their bombs falling half a mile away near the chain ferry by mistake. However, by then, the message had managed to get across to the Ministry that the south coast of England was not a healthy place for the production of our premier fighter with the Luftwaffe only 70 miles away.

Feverish activity on the part of the works engineer, Len Gooch, led to the commandeering of all the large bus depots in the triangle formed by Reading, Salisbury and Southampton and stuffing them with all the production jigs and tools. These were dispersed so that if any one depot was bombed it would not mean the loss of all production of any vital part, such as a wing, tail plane or aileron. Within one week of the departure of the last jig, the Germans attacked for a third time and flattened the place completely. This fortunate dispersal operation was a key factor in our ultimate dominance in the air and those concerned never received the public recognition to which they were entitled as, of course, the whole move was a well-kept secret.

After Mutt Summers had made the first flight in the prototype Spitfire in 1936, he handed over the whole development to Jeffrey Quill. Jeffrey was not only a great test pilot, he also had the ability to explain clearly and in great detail the interaction and subtle effects on an aircraft of every movement of the controls and its response. The third dimension is a new factor in man's experience and, as few can analyse their thoughts and put them into words, the technical team at Supermarine were undoubtedly greatly helped by his reports.

Jeffrey later became one of the very few test pilots to reach a boardroom. In my opinion he should have been promoted to a senior position in Vickers-Supermarine years before but the loss was theirs as on becoming Director of SEPECAT, the Jaguar consortium, in 1965 and later of Panavia based in Munich, his abilities were quickly appreciated. He really knew aeroplanes and their weapons and was very well briefed in the tactical and strategic situation in Europe. He could, and did, lecture to NATO chiefs and has done more than his share in launching the Tornado as the fighting weapon of the future.

I came to know Jeffrey well as we both lived at Bursledon and we usually shared a car to the aerodrome to save petrol. Over the years he has become a great family friend, the sort of friend I can pick up with again even if months have gone by since our last meeting.

The Spitfire was the only first-line, fully operational fighter aircraft in use by the allies from the beginning to the end of the war and the general public had no idea of the technical battle to keep ahead. The aircraft retained the same smooth lines with beautiful elliptical wings and slim body as originally designed by R J Mitchell but its continuing success was largely due to the very close links between Supermarine and Rolls-Royce who worked together hand in hand. The technical story has been told elsewhere but the continuous improvement in performance, in particular its ability to out climb other aircraft, always gave the pilot the advantage of being top dog, able to pounce or dominate in any situation, hence its popularity.

By July 1942, when I joined the company, the principal production of the standard aircraft was at Castle Bromwich near Birmingham where ultimately a peak of 320 aircraft per week was reached, together with another 100 per week from the southern regions. All the experimental and development work as well as some production was controlled from Hursley Park, a large country house near Winchester. The special limited production types were assembled and flight tested at five small grass aerodromes in the southern area, whereas all the experimental aircraft under development were located at the Royal Naval Air Station, Worthy Down. This involved much travelling for the pilots and there was a collection of small, civil aircraft at Eastleigh which we all used. It seemed strange to commute by air but I enjoyed the almost daily flight to Worthy Down, passing over Winchester jail where the unfortunate inmates were often exercising in the yard.

Every Monday there was a weekly meeting at 9.00am which Jeffrey and I attended at Hursley. Joe Smith, the chief designer, presided with Alan Clifton, aerodynamicist, and Mansbridge, the technical officer also being present. Progress on each of the experimental aircraft was discussed and priorities decided. Joe Smith had direct access to Whitehall and the various ministries involved in aircraft production and he would frequently ring up during a meeting and get an immediate reply to some vital change in the development programme.

George Pickering, who had been a Supermarine flying-boat test pilot before the war, was just recovering from an accident when I arrived. He was an amusing character and his description of the occasion when the wings came off his Spitfire and he found himself flying through the air strapped to his seat but without any aeroplane round him, was very funny. He landed by parachute safely after ridding himself of the armoured seat but lost a finger in the process. Unfortunately, a few months later, he was killed when he went for a ride in a Bren-gun carrier which overturned while crossing a bank.

HMS *Victorious* at sea off Spitzbergen 1941.

Part of the Home Fleet looking aft from HMS *Victorious*. Radio masts can be swung out-board to permit aircraft to land on flight deck.

809 Squadron Fulmar catches a wire to land on, short of the barrier.

The Blackburn shark (760hp Armstrong Siddeley Tiger engine) a torpedo bomber used for training at Lee-on-Solent, October 1939.

Spitfire Mark V on floats.
Jeffrey Quill taxis out at
Follands for first take-off
from Southampton water.

Ice in the Arctic covering one of HMS *Victorious*'s starboard forward twin 4.5in gun turrets.

Reindeer Point (Kitigazuit) June 27th 1930 – after a swim in the Arctic Ocean with a Norwegian herdsman.

The Seafire prototype, with folding wings and Rolls Royce Merlin engine.

HMS *King George V,* flagship of the Home Fleet in the North Sea.

The Vickers Supermarine Walrus, an amphibious workhorse of 1920's design which survived into the 1940's, saving the lives of many airmen shot down at sea. Retrieving a Walrus at sea was hazardous.

807 Fulmar Squadron, formed in July 1940. (Note mixture of Royal Naval and Royal Airforce personnel.)

HMS *Victorious,* 809 Fulmer Squadron, May 1942 at action stations off Orkney Islands.

Blackburn Roc with gun turrets and on floats intended for use in the Norwegian campaign. This quick conversion was not a success.

Covering a convoy to Russia in March 1942. All hands on deck to clear the snow off the flight deck – any depth of of snow on the flight deck is destabilising.

A new type of voice pipe.

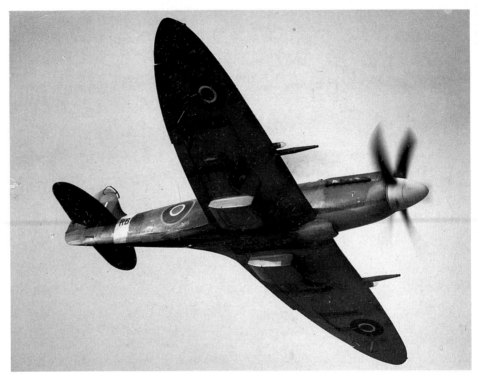

The Spitfire Mark XIV with Griffon engine, the best of the bunch. The propeller thrust just reached the aircraft's weight, giving it an exceptional rate of climb.

One of 809 Squadron's Fulmars nearly goes over the side.

Seafires were just beginning to come off the production line at Chattis Hill, previously a celebrated racing stable near Stockbridge. The early ones were not fitted with folding wings and therefore had limited naval use but by November 1942 the first folding-wing prototype was completed. In the meantime I had been flying other development aircraft at Worthy Down. In the quest for speed, the designer was often looking for quite small increases such as from the effect of different air intake scoops, blanking off air leaks and retractable tail wheels, all details from which a few miles an hour could be squeezed. At other times the whole spectrum of performance from ground level to the ceiling would be covered but in every case accuracy of flying and consistency were important and sometimes this involved half a dozen sorties in a day. The early Spitfire only carried 85 gallons of fuel and this would give time for five or six full throttle level speeds to be measured in a flight of about 50 minutes. Worthy Down was a naval aerodrome and was used primarily for training radio operators flying in Proctors. Coming in to land in a Spitfire, short of fuel, with twenty or more Proctors in the circuit was to be avoided, especially during the hour prior to the bar opening at 12.30pm.

The Photographic Reconnaissance Unit (PRU) at the RAF Station Benson had a special version of the Spitfire which was equipped with cameras and long-range tanks in the wings, but no guns, its survival depending on speed at height. The pilots were engaged in photographing the results of the bombing of the previous night, a hazardous task as the enemy fighters were expecting and waiting for them. The usual technique was to climb until a trail formed behind the aircraft around 30,000 feet and then descend a couple of hundred feet. This was enough to reach a higher air temperature and consequently the aircraft would cease to make a trail. This meant the Spitfire pilots were flying too fast to be intercepted from below and an enemy attacking from above could be seen by its trail. In early 1942 losses started to mount alarmingly for no apparent reason, apart from the fact that those lost had dived to lower heights.

We had one of their PRU aircraft to investigate because it was suspected that the trouble was due to the cold air at 30,000 feet affecting the oil circulation. Heated vents were fitted to the oil tank breathers but the difficulty was to reproduce any failure. I made many long flights at 30,000 feet to simulate the conditions, followed by a dive to sea level at maximum diving speed. It was surprising what a relatively long time it took to lose height and how rapidly the density of the air increased below 10,000 feet so that it felt thick and soupy near the ground. At 400 mph on the AS1 one could feel the air resistance build up. The atmosphere around us is, in fact, a relatively thin skin, only about 1/80th of the earth's diameter.

After several flights without result, we noticed while refuelling one evening that the petrol was blowing back through the filler cap, something it did not normally do. On closer investigation it was found that the flexible fuel tank had collapsed inwards and had kinked the vent pipe which would have eventually stopped the engine through the partial vacuum in the tank causing fuel starvation. The end of the vent pipe itself was in the radiator duct and cut off at an angle of 45°. Unfortunately, the 45° cut off faced aft and not forward as intended so that at very high speed it was sucking on the tank instead of pressurising it. Such small mistakes in assembly are the way aircraft accidents are caused.

The trials involved a period of 30 minutes at about 35,000 feet in order to soak up the cold by the fuel in the petrol tanks which in these particular aircraft were the leading front edge of the wings, and to allow the oil to cool off after climbing. I had already made two earlier flights that day but as there was just time before dark I climbed up again, passing through a thin cloud at 10,000 feet.

While cruising quietly to cool off, the sun was still shining, although the earth was already in darkness, when I noticed that the cloud below me was being lit from beneath by the setting sun which gave a vast sheet of red, like a carpet of fire, whereas the sky above was very dark blue. Down below somewhere people lived out their lives but I was in another world out of reach and out of touch. The beauty of the scene and immensity of the space made me feel very small and insignificant and I realise how privileged I am to have seen such wonders.

Talking one evening to a labourer who was responsible for pushing the aircraft into the hangar at Worthy Down, he told me how much he was looking forward to the end of the war. To my utter surprise he told me that he had had a good job at Porton Down, the Chemical Warfare Establishment, where he was a kind of guinea pig for the testing of mustard gas! He was given an extra week's holiday and £5 for every blister on his skin! Mustard gas had, of course, been used in the First World War with such devastating results that all the countries involved had agreed never to use it again and to the best of my knowledge it was not used in the Second World War.

As was to be expected, naval aircraft only represented a very small proportion of the testing done at Supermarine. Apart from the fitting of a hook, the biggest development was in redesigning the wings for folding. The aircraft behaved in exactly the same way as a fixed wing Spitfire although under heavy G loads there was more wing deflection.

By pushing and pulling on the control column during a high speed dive, the tips of the wings moved about seven inches, an amount quite visible to the eye and about double that of a standard Spitfire. One naturally did these G and diving tests at a reasonable height and approached the maximum figures step by step, making a careful inspection between flights.

Carrier operation of the Spitfire had never been even remotely considered in the original design and understandably the Seafire was not an ideal deck-landing aircraft. The forward view was badly obstructed by the engine and most pilots developed a technique of making their final approach in a gentle turn. Secondly the flaps were on the small side permitting only a touch of power during the approach to the deck. The normal approach to a deck landing is to set the aircraft in the landing attitude (nose well up) and control the angle of descent to the deck by the throttle; with small flaps this is not possible. On other aircraft with large flaps, the extra slipstream from the propeller flowing over the wing root, gives extra lift so that on cutting the power the aircraft drops immediately onto the deck. Finally, the undercarriage had a very limited travel and consequently the springing was stiff and would cause a bounce if the main wheels touched first. A bounce on a grass aerodrome does not matter but on the deck it means that the hook misses the arrester wires and the aircraft floats into the barrier. To overcome this, special hydraulically damped legs were installed in the later designs of Seafire but the leg travel was still inadequate, owing to the restriction of the existing wheel housings in the wings and propeller tip clearance.

Naval aircraft designed for the US Navy all had soft, long-travel undercarriage legs, large flaps and were more robustly built. They also had much longer endurance as it was a requirement in their area of operations, but what they gained in the practical aspects of operational reliability, they partially lost in fighting performance.

Their aircraft carriers had two hangar decks and carried at least twice the number of aircraft that Royal Navy ships could but the Admiralty regarded the ship itself as the vital weapon with the aircraft as rather expensive ammunition. Their argument was that it took six years to build an aircraft-carrier but only three months to build an aircraft. In these respects the requirements of the naval staff of the two countries were quite different.

In order to overcome the increased torque of the more powerful Merlin and Griffon engines which were beginning to come off the production line, the Admiralty were considering contra-rotating propellers for Seafires. While I was at Supermarine I was sent by the Admiralty to fly the Hawker Tornado prototype as a possible answer to the problems of swing at take-off from a deck. This had a complex 24-cylinder Rolls-Royce Vulture engine with contra-rotating propellers. It certainly overcame any take-off difficulties but one wondered what would happen in the event of a heavy landing and the blades getting mixed up. When an aircraft landed heavily on deck the revolving blades usually bent forward, not backwards as happens on an aerodrome. Sometimes it proved possible to fit another propeller without changing the engine by putting a dial gauge on the propeller shaft and, if it was not bent too badly, it was accepted as being serviceable.

An interesting experimental aircraft was the first Spitfire to be fitted with the new Rolls-Royce Griffon engine which Jeffrey Quill first flew in November 1941. This engine was similar in layout to the Merlin but, with an increased capacity of 37 litres, delivered more power at lower rpm. With a two-speed single-stage blower, it delivered 1,735 hp and had been installed in a suitably modified Mark V airframe, DP845. It was a thrill to fly, rather like driving a 3-litre Bentley instead of a buzz box like an MG, and it had a phenomenal performance at low altitudes.

The DP 845, now a legendary aircraft, had a thrust from the engine slightly higher than its own weight so that theoretically it could fly vertically upwards like a rocket. The DP 845 was the prototype of the RAF's Spitfire Mk X11 which was used for low level sweeps over the north French coast, pinpointing and photographing the V-1 flying bomb launching sites. It was faster than the German Focke Wulf 190 and our own Typhoon as Jeffrey demonstrated to the Air Staff.

The naval version was the Seafire Mk XV, the performance of which matched the navy's operational requirements for a low altitude, high performance aircraft to defend the fleet. This was in contrast to the regular Spitfires being used as attack fighters by the RAF and which gave us air superiority in defence of the Fleet.

CHAPTER 18

Stretching The Spitfire

T he original design of the Spitfire was, as in all aircraft, a compromise. Mitchell biased all the options towards performance but he also struck a happy balance, perhaps his finest achievement being the elliptical wing with its curved leading edge and thin wing section. Typically he insisted on extreme accuracy and would not even tolerate any rivet heads forward of the spar. This accuracy was achieved by stretching a single sheet of aluminium over a mould. As a result, a specially prepared aircraft was able to reach, in a dive, a Mach number of .9, far ahead of any other aircraft of its time.

Most people can appreciate that the Spitfire's wing is easy on the eye, almost the work of an artist, but the truth is that the wing *is* the aeroplane – as Mitchell proved so successfully. What the powers that be had also missed was that he boldly designed the whole aircraft using the skin as the load-bearing structure; this meant that the potential for development was vastly increased. As an example, one day after a series of high speed dives, some wrinkles appeared in the rear fuselage just in front of the tailplane. The technical staff were delighted as it showed that their stress calculations were about right and that there was no built-in excess weight; by increasing the skin thickness by one gauge there would be ample strength. The Hawker Hurricane on the other hand received the first big orders but with its steel tube and socket construction, it could not be easily strengthened so was phased out in favour of the Spitfire as our premier fighter. A chief designer's eye for line and the overall concept, in effect, stamps his signature on the aircraft. Mitchell's design of the elliptical tailplane and the curvature of the fin and rudder of the Spitfire followed naturally from the wing and gave it symmetry.

Joe Smith, who took over on Mitchell's death, never altered these particular features except to enlarge their area. The Air Ministry specification for a fighter called for an angle of, I believe, 10° over the nose to permit the pilot to see his target in a turn and allow the correct deflection but Mitchell would have none of this and went for the minimum frontal area. He even persuaded Rolls-Royce to alter the position of the constant speed unit on the Merlin to eliminate the hump it made between the cylinder blocks. Not so the Hurricane, which met the Ministry specification and perhaps, in consequence, received the first large orders.

Absorbing more and more power became an increasing problem on the Spitfire. It started life with a wooden two-blade propeller and went progressively to three-blade variable pitch, four-blade, five-blade and, on the later version of Seafire, the Mk 47, to six-bladed contra-rotating propellers. As the propeller disc area became more dense with blades, so the directional and longitudinal stability decreased. The revolving weight also led to undesirable handling characteristics due to gyroscopic effects. For instance, if at high rpm in a dive the aircraft was yawed from side to side it would pitch quite violently up and down, requiring a considerable stick force to correct. The rotation of the slipstream also affected control. If the aircraft was trimmed for level flight and pulled into a steep climb the change of airflow over the rudder led to a yaw. Any fighter pilot will tell you that it is no good shooting with any yaw showing on the top needle of the turn and bank indicator. The revolving bullet leaving the gun will curve away from the target rather in the way that a spin bowler introduces a curve into a ball's flight, so altering its normal trajectory.

Although from the ground the Spitfire's silhouette did not change throughout the war there were at least five new wings. This was due to changes of armament and to the additional strength required to carry the more powerful engines with their greater weight. The all-up weight increased from 5400 lbs to 12,000 lbs or, as Jeffrey Quill used to put it, from a single-seater to a 32 seater.

There was a very close link between the Supermarine design team and Rolls-Royce who worked hand in hand to such an extent that whenever Rolls-Royce had a new engine, Supermarine had an aircraft in production able to take it. This was achieved by incorporating in any new wing enough extra strength to take more weight than the specification called for. The sequence of new wings was that the Mk V (eight machine-guns) became the VB (four machine-guns and two Hispano 20 mm drum-fed cannons), and the VC (four machine-guns and two Hispano 20mm with ammunition tanks and belt feed) became the Mark IX (two-stage, two-speed inter-cooled Merlin 60 Series). The Mk VIII wing, designed to an RAF requirement to take the advanced but heavier Merlin 60 Series, became the Mk XIV with a two-stage, two-speed inter-cooled Griffon, the final version being the Mk XXI with a completely new, stiffer wing and four cannons. By this process of leap-frogging the Spitfire kept its lead in the battle for performance and this was one of the major factors in the allies' command of the air. From the technical aspect, it was the supreme example of a good original design being developed to the 'nth' degree.

Apart from the handling problems introduced by the large propellers, probably the weakest point was the relatively poor rate of roll. The ailerons had a nose balance but became very heavy at high speed when they also tended to 'float up' or distort upwards. There was no lateral trim control so any tendency to fly one wing low had to be corrected on the ground by reflexing the metal trailing edge of the aileron upwards. Slight variations in manufacture made big differences and a bad aileron would cause so much 'wing low' at take-off that it was wise to land immediately.

Great efforts were made to improve the rate of roll by fitting geared tabs and other methods, but towards the end of the war and, at the request of Fighter Command, the wing-tips were removed. This certainly increased the response but at a small cost in loss of rate of climb and ceiling. Another variation was an aileron with a bulged upper surface which had been thought of by the design staff at Westlands who were also building Spitfires. It certainly improved the lateral control but as Joe Smith did not approve it, the aileron was never fitted to production aircraft. He was probably concerned about the wing strength in torque because if an aileron is very powerful, it can twist the wing in the reverse sense of the direction to that in which the aileron is working; this phenomenon is called aileron reversal, a very dangerous fault. Up to that time the value of a very rapid rate of roll had not been fully appreciated but when flying at a very high speed, it is not possible to make any quick change of direction in the pitching plane due to the build up of G and consequent black-out of the pilot. A quick half roll and dive or an aileron turn in a vertical dive, is a much more effective manoeuvre to throw off an enemy fighter in pursuit.

A great deal of work was done in an attempt to improve the fore and aft stability. Because the aircraft was in mass production, no major alteration, such as a larger area tailplane, could be readily contemplated. A great scare arose when, for unexplained reasons, a number of aircraft, built at the main production factory at Castle Bromwich, lost their wings. Jeffrey flew off to various Spitfire squadrons and immediately hurried back to report that every aircraft being delivered to them was unstable.

He found that the centre of gravity had been allowed to move aft by the unauthorised addition of extra equipment in the tail compartment behind the pilot, the effect of which was to make the aircraft tighten into a turn and thus increasing the G force, a handling characteristic which is quite unacceptable.

There were many of these aircraft already in service and an immediate solution was called for. Within a week 'bob weights' were being made and issued, to attach to the front of the control column and thus apply a forward force on the elevator control during a turn. It was not an ideal solution and was unpopular with certain pilots, but it worked.

At Worthy Down we had experimental aircraft fitted with special long chord elevators, different tailplane incidence and alternative areas of elevator horn balance. Of these, the most effective improvement in stability was obtained with a larger horn balance. This surprised me as increasing the area forward of the hinge line might be expected to do the opposite. The only disadvantage was that, on take-off, particularly on rough ground, there was a certain amount of twitching of the elevator control.

In a fighter, one of the most important characteristics is the stick force required per G force in turns. A difficulty arises in a high-altitude fighter such as a Spitfire because the longitudinal stability decreases at height due to the air being less dense. If the stick forces are reasonable at high altitude they become too heavy low down. Modern aircraft overcome this problem by having powered controls but in the days of reliance on inherent aerodynamic stability this was not possible. The elimination of the elevator and the introduction of the all-moving tailplane, powered by hydraulic ram, paved the way for the swept wing followed by supersonic flight.

The flow of various marks of aircraft from the dispersed southern production units was not a steady stream, as was the case at the main factory at Castle Bromwich, but the pressure from the Ministry of Production for numbers was nevertheless intense with the weekly figures being telephoned to the Ministry every Friday evening at 5.00pm. Jeffrey and I would often help out the local production test pilots on Friday afternoons as there was always a build up of completed but untested aircraft towards the end of the week and bonuses to the men in the factory were geared to results.

A production test flight would commence with a quick circuit and if necessary, a landing to correct aileron trim. For this a man would be waiting at the downwind end of the aerodrome ready to do the reflexing or bending upwards of a small portion of the trailing metal edge of the aileron and, from experience, one could usually estimate the amount required in one flight. Having made this adjustment, a climb to 20,000 feet followed in order to check that the supercharger automatically changed into high gear at the appropriate height, then checks were made of all operational equipment and systems, followed by a level speed and boost check, then a dive to maximum permitted speed watching for upfloat or poor aileron trim and a landing. As zero hour approached I have seen the shop foreman waiting on the tarmac for the thumbs-up signal, indicating acceptance by the pilot before running to the telephone to claim another aircraft completed. In order to meet zero hour I have even seen a propeller changed in twenty minutes which is double quick time for a complicated fitting operation.

The Dowty propellers which were fitted to most Spitfires had blades made of compressed wood and resin but from time to time a bad batch would cause production delays. The Spitfire was very sensitive to small variations in manufacture and, although all the propellers were correctly balanced, sometimes it would vibrate badly on take-off. The motion was relatively slow and caused the nose of the aircraft to move in a circle with a whirling movement. The only cure was to try another propeller, sometimes several, before the aircraft could be accepted. It was thought that the trouble was due to the propeller being out of aerodynamic balance by one blade producing more thrust than another. On take-off a violent vibration would sometimes start on leaving the ground due to the relatively small wheels being out of balance. It was advisable to apply the brakes momentarily to stop them spinning as on entering their housing in the wings, the tyre sometimes fouled the metal sides.

With the developing war in the far east the Chiefs of Staff foresaw a necessity for a high performance fighter capable of operating, not from an airfield, but from lagoons or inside coral reefs. This led to the conversion of a Spitfire to operate on floats.

The Supermarine design team had won the Schneider Trophy in 1931 with their S6B seaplane and in many respects the Spitfire itself was a direct development, or at least was strongly influenced by their previous experience, so that the design and fitting of the floats were no problem to them.

The Folland Aircraft Company at Hamble fitted the floats and, being located on Southampton Water, they also had a convenient slipway. Jeffrey made the first flights and reported that it lacked directional stability but was quite safe to fly. Although highly secret, one could hardly fail to hear it flying round the Hamble area as it made a strange sound like an organ due to the open end of a cross-tube used to locate the axle of a pair of launching wheels.

Under political pressure from the highest level, the urgency of measuring its performance was very great so it was decided to defer the curing of the directional stability until later. We decided to do the performance testing between Southampton and Poole but because this area was only about 80 miles from the German fighter aerodromes and the area was heavily defended, special arrangements had to be made before every flight. This included a two hour warning and a broadcast to every gun site.

During a preliminary handling flight around Hamble, I made several take-offs and landings. It had so much thrust at take-off that the normal seaplane technique was not necessary; it was over the 'hump' almost before the throttle was fully open. In flight, the increased side area of the floats caused a permanent yaw with the rudder trailing slightly out of line although the aircraft could be held straight by continuous corrections with the rudder.

I set off at the appointed time for Poole, flying over Christchurch *en route*, and as the object was to show the aircraft to the gun crews, a height of 1500 feet seemed appropriate. At Poole another Spitfire flew up alongside and after circling around the harbour the pilot waved to me and sheered off. When over the Royal Poole Motor Yacht Club, I suddenly noticed some red tracer shells coming from a Bofors gun emplacement just ahead of me. Having no radio and thinking that perhaps an enemy aircraft was about, I hastened to get out of the way but, to my surprise, other guns opened up, obviously aiming at me! The red tracers seemed to come quite slowly towards me, rather like a catch in the deep field at cricket, but they were travelling fast as they came close. I knew that the aircraft, when pointing in one direction, was moving in another (due to the yaw) and made full use of this. Whenever the shells missed me to port I changed to the other yaw angle and sure enough, they missed to starboard. I was also making violent changes of height and speed but there seemed to be a lot of guns firing and so, at about 100 feet, I tore out of the harbour entrance over the chain ferry and on out to sea. Leaving the harbour I noticed some black puffs in the distance in the direction of the Needles but it hardly seemed possible that they were aimed at me as they were at least two or three miles away. Climbing up to 1500 feet and getting my breath back I thought that the best place to cross the coast was Christchurch where the gun crews could hardly have failed to see the aircraft on the outward flight.

I flew towards the town and to make doubly sure of being recognised, I flew up and down the shore about a mile out and then flew quietly straight over the town. All the local Bofors opened up, however, with a grand firework display of which I took a very poor view. Diving down at full power to tree-top level I then flew inland over the New Forest where I knew I should be too low for them to be able to take aim. It was still a few miles to Southampton Water where I hoped the locals would recognise the familiar aircraft and let me land.

Climbing up to 1000 feet I headed east for Hamble and, keeping a good look out astern, I saw to my horror a squadron of Spitfires coming my way. Pretending not to have seen them, I continued flying steadily east at cruising speed, meanwhile keeping a very careful watch in my rear view mirror. They were in a loose formation but too close to each other to be able to manoeuvre freely. When the leader was about a quarter of a mile astern I suddenly banked 90°, put on full power and pulled about 5G. They immediately sheered off, obviously having seen the distinctive wing shape of a Spitfire, not to mention the RAF roundels.

I reached Southampton Water safely and, not knowing whether the floats had been hit, I landed, keeping well above the hump speed till I approached the slipway. I got out and, seeing no obvious damage, made my way to the nearest telephone to ring the controller to report what had happened. A very high-pitched, excited voice told me, 'Get off the line at once, there's an enemy raid on!' As I was presumably the 'enemy raid', I returned to the aircraft absolutely furious and when a few moments later I had an urgent message to call the controller, I refused to speak to him, sending a message instead telling him what he could do with his 'enemy raids'.

That evening, Ella and I had been invited to a drinks party at the headquarters of the local anti-aircraft regiment in Hamble. We were greeted by the Commanding Officer who said to Ella, 'I bet your husband was scared stiff this afternoon by his unfortunate experience.' Ella replied without a moment's hesitation, 'Not at all. He realised that if your men could not recognise a Spitfire after three years of war, there was little chance of them being very good shots.' That was the end of the conversation but not of the whole incident which was taken to the highest level. I must say it was no joke being fired on by my own people who had fired eight 4.5 inch shells, 90 Bofors and 400 .303-inch bullets.

After some delay, tests were resumed but this time with an RAF escort of two Spitfires from Tangmere. We had no radio communication but arranged the sorties by telephone. While doing the level speeds between 15,000 and 20,000 feet I drew ahead and only saw them on turning round for the next run. Understandably, they were reluctant to use full throttle at maximum revs. In fact their aircraft were theoretically 30 mph faster than the seaplane version. However, in the limited amount of testing we were able to do, we managed to get a good indication of the maximum speed and rate of climb to 20,000 feet. In view of all the local difficulties, it was then decided to move the whole programme up to Beaumaris in Anglesea where some twelve aircraft were due for conversion.

On the personal front this period of the war was a stable one for me when I could return home each evening to my wife and our lovely new daughter, Jane, who had been born on 6 June 1942.

CHAPTER 19

The Quest For Performance

By 1942 the Spitfire had become our premier fighter with all our efforts being concentrated on improving the performance and increasing its speed and rate of climb as well as the handling qualities. It is hard to realise in peace time the pressure that can be put on the development of an aircraft like this. In the spring of that year the latest version of the Spitfire, the Mark 1X, had been wheeled out. It was an outstanding aircraft, having a much higher power to weight ratio and a very lively performance indeed; the civil equivalent of a sports model.

The latest version of the Merlin engine had a two-stage compressor, inter-cooled with two speeds which really gave it the kick of a mule and when it began to lose boost at around 18,000 feet, the second gear clutch engaged and with a shudder the engine came to life again taking the aircraft up to over 40,000 feet. Within Rolls-Royce there was a friendly battle between the Merlin proteges and the Griffon ones as to which could be made to produce the most power and this undoubtedly spurred on the development of the Merlin in spite of its smaller capacity. All the development was concentrated on higher supercharger pressure and not on increasing the rpm.

The higher altitudes achievable with these aircraft led to a requirement for pressurising the cabin so a Mk V aircraft was suitably modified in order to gain experience of the problems likely to be encountered. For military purposes, it was considered that a maximum of two pounds per square inch pressure was enough. On my first flight I heard a loud bang and noticed the sensitive altimeter needle making about one revolution per second, quite a rate of climb! A quick access panel had blown out of the side of the perspex hood but even that sudden pressure drop was quite disconcerting. The hood, which had to be detached completely to enter the cockpit, was held in place with four levers. These were very difficult to reach and the aft ones had to be pushed into place with my elbow. The final seal was made with a rubber tube which encircled the gap in the joint; this was blown up with compressed air.

It was rather like sealing myself into my own coffin and, although I do not suffer from claustrophobia, I did not like it.

There was also the danger of suffocation in the event of the failure of the mechanical pump. On coming down from altitude the interior of the windscreen would mist up and the cockpit became unbearably hot. Most of the development was directed towards trying to improve the ventilation at low altitude with different air scoops and spill valves. Fortunately, after limited production, the Mk V1 project was dropped.

Internal misting of the armoured windscreen had been a nuisance from the very start of Spitfire production. The 2" thick glass became very cold at altitude and retained the coldness on descending to near ground levels, where the atmosphere retains more moisture, and condensation blotted out all forward visibility including the reflector gun sight. Jeffrey had had a small air scoop added on the forward side of the cockpit with a plastic tube to blast cold air over the central sighting position. It worked quite well but the cleared portion was only a streak across the middle. Similarly it was impossible to see backwards as the perspex hood's side panels were flat. An early modification was urgently incorporated to bulge the sliding hood so that the pilot could lean sideways and see backwards.

When Jeffrey, at his request, was released from test work for three months he joined a front line fighter squadron for operational experience and he was also attached to the Fleet Air Arm on a deck-landing course. On his return to Supermarine he badgered Joe Smith, the Chief Designer, to fit a fully transparent sliding hood with a cut down rear fuselage but in spite of every pressure it was not done until the war was almost over. The Fleet Air Arm's other fighter aircraft also suffered badly from this lack of a rear view and we used to buy little cycle-type rear view mirrors from Woolworth which had a rubber sucker and flexible mounting. We used to stick these on to the top inside of the windscreen which gave some backward visibility.

It is difficult to stress strongly enough the importance to a fighter pilot of a view aft. It is like driving on a motorway; one must know at all times what is behind – for a pilot it could mean the difference between life and death.

The Mk XX1 had a two-stage, two-speed, inter-cooled Griffon which made it the fastest and highest flying aircraft under development among all the allied air forces. One day we had a surprise visit from two civilians who turned out to be from MI5. Apparently the Luftwaffe monthly news magazine had not only mentioned the Spitfire Mk XX1 but also its performance. The most recent issue had given its top speed as being 431 mph which was in fact, the very speed that had been calculated by the technical office from figures which I had obtained three weeks before. Obviously there was a serious leak of information and we were questioned in detail on all our methods of operation.

In flight, test figures were jotted down on a pad strapped to my right thigh, the paper or card being held in position with rubber bands and I usually wrote down the headings for the columns of figures required before taking off. For a level speed these would be height, outside air temperature, engine rpm boost pressure, charge temperature and indicated air speed. On landing, the figures were copied out on a form and sent to the technical office at Hursley Park. With special experimental engines such as the Griffon, in which Rolls-Royce were particularly interested at this time, their representative at Worthy Down would telephone the vital figures straight off our pads to his office at Derby. The true airspeed, or the actual speed through the air achieved, had, of course, to be calculated in the Technical Office at Hursley after making allowances for height, outside air temperature, instrument correction and position error; this final figure is not the same as the recorded figure obtained in flight.

After the MI5 visit the whole system was changed. At the end of a landing run and before taxiing in, the test pad record was removed and put into our breast pockets. A motorcyclist with a padlocked box then took this card direct to the technical office. The whole episode made everyone very security conscious; clearly the enemy were very interested in what we were doing at Worthy Down and it came as a shock to hear that we had an informer around.

Much of Spitfire flying involved going above 30,000 feet, sometimes several times a day but we had no radio or navigation aids and the filing of a flight plan was unheard of. Most flights were short in duration, however, due to lack of fuel tank capacity and one developed a kind of homing instinct.

Occasionally Jeffrey and I would have a simulated dogfight at about 35,000 feet in order to assess the handling characteristics of new or different types of Spitfire. In a dogfight one tends to lose one's sense of direction and speed in one's determination to get onto the tail of the other aircraft or to shake it off. One day when Jeffrey managed to get on my tail, I happened to glance at my airspeed indicator while pulling up in a zoom. It showed about 70 mph and, thinking the aircraft was about to stall, I pushed the stick forward. To my surprise the response was a great deal of negative G due to the fact that the needle of the airspeed indicator had already gone round the dial once and my actual speed was about 500 mph! With no sense of gravity, no horizon or location, this was the nearest I ever came to appreciating the third dimension and with the air density only about one quarter of sea level pressure, I was on neat oxygen to breathe enough to stay alive!

Shortly afterwards the engine stopped, and it sounded like lack of petrol although we had only been airborne for 35 minutes. After a long glide I finished up at Blackbush where, although it had a long runway from east to west, there was a strong southerly cross wind. I chose the north-south short runway which crossed the old main London to Southampton road but, coming in off the glide rather fast, I was still doing 30 miles an hour or so as I rolled over it. Fortunately, there was no traffic crossing at the time, although normally this road carried a great deal. It was a dry tank! The petrol gauge was not standard but a new type being tried out and it did not get a good report from me.

As a complete contrast to the Spitfire, Supermarine had also designed a replacement for the old Walrus amphibious flying boat. This was the Sea Otter which, although also a bi-plane, was more sophisticated with a single engine driving a variable-pitch propeller mounted in front of the wings. The Walrus had been demoted from operational use as a shipborne spotter aircraft and was being used, largely by the RAF, for Air-Sea Rescue. Although probably designed in the late 1920s, it was very tough and could be landed in a fairly rough sea, whereas the Sea Otter was more of a fair-weather boat. With an engine and whirling propeller just above one's head it seemed, in many ways, to be a retrograde step; those who have any experience of landing in rough sea will appreciate the tremendous pounding that ensues, the engine and propeller could easily land on your lap!

I did most of the manufacturer's trials and its handling qualities were an improvement over the Walrus but when this same machine later came to Boscombe Down, a brother officer who I had put in charge of the trials there was killed getting out of the pilot's window when he was hit by the propeller which was still turning. No doubt it was his own carelessness as he had been warned, but from a practical point of view it was a weakness in the design.

The retractable wheels and landing gear of an amphibious boat add another hazard to flying, I myself having experienced three incidents. The first was entirely my own fault when I landed on the grass at Lee-on-Solent. There had been a lot of aircraft in the circuit and one in particular had come much too close but, having ignored it, it turned out that he was trying to warn me not to land because my wheels were up. On another occasion a photographer I had picked up at Weymouth harbour could not see how to free one undercarriage leg which had become stuck in the up position when I attempted to lower the wheels for landing at Lee aerodrome. It was frustrating as the spring-loaded plunger of the catch was easily accessible inside the cabin but I was unable to leave the controls and had to land on the sea. The old-fashioned method of a well directed kick immediately freed the offending catch!

Shortly afterwards, when I was a passenger, the pilot asked me to check that the gear on my side was locked up before landing on the sea but he proceeded to land with the wheel on his own side trailing causing the aircraft to slew round to about 45°, throwing up a cloud of spray. We were lucky as with the gear locked fully down, a Walrus would flip upside down on the water. This was a not infrequent event with pilots in training.

The first batch of Spitfires made use of the retractable gear similar to that used on the Walrus but later an engine-driven hydraulic pump replaced the hand-operated one. Although relatively crude by modern standards, the system was simple and light and the somewhat spidery undercarriage proved very reliable in service.

Another unusual aircraft which made its first flight at Worthy Down was the S24/37 or Mayfly as it was known locally; not, I hasten to add, because of doubt that it could fly but because of its low priority in the experimental shop at Hursley. This was built to naval specification and was intended as a torpedo bomber. The unique feature was a variable-incidence monoplane wing, incorporating all the latest high-lift flaps, mounted on top of the fuselage. The wing was arranged to pivot about the centre of lift and interconnect with the flaps to give high lift to allow a low approach speed and good view forward for deck landing.

Jeffrey made the first flight while I watched with a little group consisting of Joe Smith, Clifton and Mansbridge, the design team. The first flight of an entirely new aircraft is still an anxious moment and their evident relief when it landed safely was apparent. The aircraft looked very strange coming in to land as its tail was well up high in the air with the nose pointing at the ground.

Discussing it with Jeffrey afterwards we agreed that from the pilot's point of view it is much better to change the attitude of the whole aircraft in the conventional way during the approach to land and not to change just the wing incidence. The aircraft's nose is in fact a very useful point of reference. In the post war years Supermarine did, however, use the system in a new flying boat where this feature can be exploited to the full to reduce landing speed on the water and to give lift off at a lower speed.

Later I had a go but my own assessment was blurred by events. On taking off, the front edge of the detachable hatch above my head lifted a couple of inches off the windscreen because the forward catch was not fully home, although the aft end was properly located. It created a tremendous draught but for the first few minutes I was busy trimming the aircraft and gaining a safe height. On closer inspection I thought that I could pull the hatch down and fasten it but, on touching it, it flew off taking my hand back which hit the rear edge of the cockpit very hard, cutting one finger to the bone – and so I decided to land.

Jeffrey had had a good grumble about the hand wheel which needed 120 turns to apply the wing incidence and flaps but it only was then that I really took his point. Winding on incidence merely raised the tail as one instinctively kept up a steady approach speed. Before the flaps were reasonably far down for a landing, I was sitting looking at the ground while being held back by my straps to prevent sliding off the seat. Meanwhile in turning the handle I had spread blood all over the place as the injured finger was on that side. As it turned out the cut was deep but not serious although it took a long time to heal probably because of the coldness of the Spitfire's cockpit at height – for I had had a similar experience while flying in winter in northern Canada.

The main production of the standard Spitfire was in a very large factory at Castle Bromwich near Birmingham and I was sent up there to help George Lowdell while Alex Henshaw, who was in charge of the testing, was away attending a funeral. As about 25 aircraft coming off the assembly line daily were waiting to be flight tested, any delay caused a backlog. The weather deteriorated just after my arrival with visibility of about a mile but the whole area was thick with balloons and flying was impossible – or at least I thought so. However the local test pilots were so accustomed to the smoky industrial murk that after a couple of days they decided to try to clear a few aircraft. There was a narrow passage through the balloons in an easterly direction to the big power station at Hams Hall from which point they turned north and went up through it to 20,000 feet, returning on a reciprocal course to complete a dive to maximum air speed. They had no radio for direction finding and navigated by flying accurate courses and using the balloons and smoke from the power station as reference points.

These test pilots made flying in these conditions sound easy but I did not enjoy them and I was very glad when Henshaw returned. They did a tremendous job clearing all those aircraft pouring out of the factory considering it was a tiring, monotonous and highly dangerous task for which they received little thanks.

Back at Eastleigh aerodrome itself, Supermarine did a small amount of production testing of new locally built types of Spitfire. Although there were balloons all round, there was no industrial smoke and the area was familiar. All the ferry hacks were kept there, however, as officially it was our office and, knowing the route from Worthy Down so well, Jeffrey and I would fly in and out regardless of balloons and almost of weather. The railway lines provided the guide and the site of the winches was well known so if we flew at about 150 feet along one side or the other of the railway tracks to allow for sag in the wires according to whichever direction the wind was blowing, we were quite safe. I liked the Hawker Tomtit and the Monospar best as both of them could be turned within the boundaries of the aerodrome to line up for a landing into the wind. They say an old horse can find its way home blindfold and I suppose this procedure was about the flying equivalent.

With the high-flying Spitfires we were running into trouble with both oil overheating and petrol boiling, a strange mixture. The extreme cold at 35,000 to 40,000 feet was causing the oil to congeal on the inner surface of the oil pipes and oil coolers, leaving only a small core for the hot oil to flow through. The symptom was a sudden rise in oil temperature to unacceptable figures while the petrol boiling was simply due to the low pressure of the atmosphere near the ceiling of the Mk 1X and XX1. The engine would start to misfire and on one occasion I had it cut out completely at 38,000 feet but on reaching lower altitude it picked up and behaved normally. The addition of a petrol cooler cured the trouble.

The Spitfire was an interceptor fighter designed to defend the home bases against enemy attack but as the war continued it became apparent that aircraft with a longer range would be required, not only to accompany bombers, but for reinforcement of overseas bases, such as Malta. A programme for the development of long-range tanks was started with slipper tanks of 30, 60 or 90 gallons attached below the fuselage. These tanks could be jettisoned by pulling a lever in the cockpit and were not intended to be used in action. The effect of these on the handling characteristics in normal flight was small but the petrol feed connection was not very reliable and they could not be used for take-off and, not infrequently, failed on the changeover when in flight. A flight test was essential after fitting, although on operations an engine run-up check was acceptable. Later a streamlined pear-drop 90-gallon tank was designed which overcame the feed difficulty experienced with the slipper tanks.

By the early spring of 1943 I put in a request to the Admiralty to rejoin the navy as, by then, the Seafire was in full production and I hoped that I might be given a fighter squadron. On visiting the Appointments Board it was made clear to me that at the age of 35 my experience as a test pilot was of more use than my ability as a fighter pilot and they had arranged for me to be appointed to the Aeroplane and Armament Experimental

Establishment at the Royal Air Force Station, Boscombe Down. I was very disappointed at the time at not getting a squadron.

I remember well one of my last flights before leaving Supermarine. As previously mentioned, the Spitfire Mk 1X had a Merlin with an inter-cooler. We had noticed how difficult it was to obtain a steady indicated air speed when doing level speeds to measure its performance but it was only on adding an inlet charge temperature gauge to the inlet manifold that the reason became obvious. The temperature rose gradually when at full throttle as the water in the inter-cooling system tried to cope with all the extra heat from compressing the charge. As the charge temperature rose, the power fell off and so, of course, did the speed of the aircraft.

I had adopted the habit, between each measurement of speed, of cooling off thoroughly by closing the throttle to about a quarter and putting the propeller pitch into full coarse to reduce the revs. On this occasion, while doing some level speeds, I adopted the usual procedure of selecting fully coarse pitch in order to cool off between each run. On opening up again and fining off pitch, there was no response, the engine just spluttered and would not take more throttle. My first reaction was that there was a lack of fuel or a choked main jet but looking at the slowly revolving propeller it became clear that the blades were feathered and that it was not turning fast enough for the engine-driven oil pump to unfeather it. From 20,000 feet over the Wiltshire Downs I could see some runways in the Swindon direction and made for an unknown aerodrome there. The undercarriage and flaps went down normally and with the engine still idling, I landed safely.

It was, of course, not possible to taxi so I had to wait patiently for help in getting off the runway and eventually a Hillman Minx pick-up arrived but the driver looked blank when I told him that the aircraft could not be taxied and required a tow. He disappeared saying he was going to tell his boss. The aerodrome was Wroughton, a maintenance or supply base under the control of civilians, but after much delay we managed to get the aircraft to a hangar.

It turned out that in the assembly of the propeller someone had forgotten to fit the coarse pitch stop. Whether it was our own fitters' fault or those of the manufacturer, Dowty Rotol, never came to light. In the end no harm came of it and it was a million to one that the combination of events would ever occur again.

My replacement at Supermarine, Lieutenant-Commander Frank Furlong, who as an amateur jockey had won the Grand National on Reynoldstown, kindly came over to Wroughton to pick me up in the Miles Falcon. A year later Furlong was killed at High Post near Salisbury caused, I heard, by a jammed aileron while testing a new Spitfire.

The nine months I had spent with Supermarine had been a very exciting period in my life. To have the opportunity of flying such wonderful aircraft and even to have had a very small part in their development during a crucial period of the war was a great privilege for which I realised I had been very lucky. Aeroplanes and their engines were my great love and I was in the middle of a run of intense activity. Thanks to Jeffrey I had learned what to do and how to do it. A test pilot in a single seater has a lonely job and one needs to discuss the problems with someone who talks the same language.

PART 3

Boscombe Down

CHAPTER 20

Naval Test Pilot

The Royal Air Force Station at Boscombe Down, or, to give it its full name, the Aeroplane and Armament Experimental Establishment (A&AEE), had been moved from Martlesham Heath at the beginning of the war. The new location in the middle of Salisbury Plain was considered to be less vulnerable and, although it frequently had up to 150 aircraft on the aerodrome, most of which were either prototypes of new aircraft or at least developing new weapons, during my time there it was never bombed nor, to my knowledge, was it ever seriously attacked by low-flying aircraft, although the odd single enemy aircraft, unable to find its objective, did unload in the vicinity.

When I arrived at Boscombe Down in April 1943 the war was not going well for us but the country had recovered from the loss of all our equipment at Dunkirk and the mass production of weapons was surging ahead. However, the losses at sea were enormous as were our losses in the very large night bomber raids; the Germans were well dug in and a menace just across the Channel. As for the war in the air, the new Focke-Wulf FW 190 was beginning to appear to challenge our air superiority in the west which we had established while the Germans were fighting in Russia. It was no time for complacency as we expected the renewal of heavy bombing attacks on our cities and factories, these pressures being reflected in the priority and urgency of the trials we were undertaking.

Although it was a Royal Air Force Station, Boscombe Down must have been very difficult to run from the service point of view. There were hundreds of civilians, a large aerodrome without a full perimeter fence, 150 very valuable aircraft dispersed around the perimeter and, over all, a flying programme of enormous variety. It was no wonder that normal service discipline was practically non-existent, with no duties or parades! In addition, there was insufficient housing accommodation and a large number of officers and men lived out as did Ella and I.

As the officers' quarters at Boscombe Down were fully occupied I stayed, during the first few days, at the local hotel in Amesbury. Ella was still at the house we were renting in Bursledon so I started to look for somewhere near the aerodrome. Rather in desperation I took a house at Shrewton, a village about six miles away; it was an old building in a wood and rather gloomy.

I went over to the house on the day Ella and Jane were expected but after a short look around I realised that it was certainly not suitable. It had not been occupied for some time and was bare of furniture, dirty and, furthermore, the landlady had decided to connect two rooms together which had left a large hole in the bedroom wall. It had no door and was completely unfinished. I had hardly completed my inspection of the place when an old van appeared in the drive with all our possessions piled in the back and Ella and Jane perched in the middle of it. My heart sank as I realised the situation but there was no alternative but to camp in the house with its rusty old cooking stove, cobwebs everywhere and no electricity.

The next day Ella set forth and with her usual charm and skill, persuaded someone to let us have a newly built bungalow in Amesbury; an unbelievable bit of luck. It was within walking distance of shops and with the water-meadows along the River Avon at the bottom of a small garden, it was ideal for our old white bull terrier, Pooch. Everything was very small but there were two good rooms, although the kitchen was the size of a cupboard. Nevertheless we were all together and were to live there happily for the next two-and-a-half years.

I had a Lancia Aprilia car with which to get to the aerodrome but unfortunately the local garage put the wrong type of hydraulic fluid in the brake mechanism with the result that the rubber seals swelled up and the pedal failed to return to the 'off' position. There were no spares in the UK so I had to negotiate with the London dealer for another, older Lancia and even then there was more trouble with spares – but at least it was transport.

The best time, and almost the only time, I met other officers and technical staff, was in the mess over a drink before lunch. It was rather like a man's club and in the course of time nearly everyone connected with aviation seemed to find their way there; it was a good place to make contacts and also to get instant decisions.

Boscombe Down was concerned primarily with the testing, reporting on and acceptance of new and modified versions of aircraft for use in the Armed Forces, including the Royal Navy. Later, civilian aircraft were also tested there. Although under the functional control of the Ministry of Aircraft Production, it was administered by the Royal Air Force, No. 23 Group Technical Training Command which ran the station and the flying. The technical office was manned by senior technical officers from the Civil Service who issued the instructions on what tests were to be undertaken and subsequently made the reports to the Ministry in London and so to the Chief of Staff.

I had been sent to Boscombe as a Lieutenant (A) RNVR, seconded from the Fleet Air Arm headquarters at Lee-on-Solent. The only other naval officer there was Lieutenant Commander Torrens-Spence RN, a regular, also on secondment, who had preceded my own arrival in April 1943 by a year.

'TS', as everyone called him, was one of the few experienced officers in the navy who really understood the capabilities and limitations of aircraft, having made a deep study of their application to naval warfare. His interest lay in the tactical and strategic use of this new weapon and with his knowledge I always expected to see him rise to the top. In pre-war days the senior jobs in the navy tended to go to the experts in guns and armour and not the flying side which was still regarded as a backwater where the 'playboys' and other less serious types could be moved sideways! TS was different, although he retired relatively soon after the war.

On arrival at Boscombe Down, I was sent to 'A' Flight Performance Testing Squadron, known as 'A' per T, under Squadron-Leader Sammy Wroath. This was a great piece of luck for me because Sammy had a strong personality, was very popular and already probably the most experienced active test pilot in the RAF. Like Quill, he had a very sharp sense of observation, a gift for explanation in detail besides being a brilliant natural pilot.

Every aircraft that came to Boscombe Down had a programme of trials to assess its suitability for service use and to measure its performance. The organisation was split in halves, performance testing and armament testing, each division having its own officers and personnel. My own flight, 'A' per T, was primarily concerned with fighter and other single-engined aircraft and 'B' Flight dealt with the bombers. Some of the armament trials affected the flying qualities of an aircraft and in that case, we would be called in to make our own reports. The programme for any entirely new type was extensive but under the extreme pressure of war and the practice of laying down a production line before the aircraft had been accepted, we were called upon to produce results in as short a time as possible. We worked a seven-day week taking odd days off when the weather was unsuitable for flying.

There was a graded system of priority with a constant call for interim reports but inevitably a backlog of work accumulated and, although a major portion of the trials resulted in figures to be passed to the technical office, there were also the handling reports to be considered and written. On some days one might fly half a dozen different types or have to make several flights above 30,000 feet; variety, they say, is the spice of life, and I liked it. Sammy was very fair in his doling out of jobs and I was given my share of the 'plums'!

The trials of the new types went, whenever possible, through a logical sequence. On arrival the aircraft would be loaded with full operational equipment, the weight would be measured, the centre of gravity position checked against datum, all the flight instruments removed and replaced by specially calibrated ones and any special instrumentation added. Before any serious flight testing was carried out, the cockpit was checked on the ground and in flight for carbon monoxide contamination. From then on handling at low levels, level speeds, partial climbs, climb to ceiling, dives and all the handling qualities were observed or measured until the whole spectrum of performance had been covered. This could well take three months or more depending on any faults which arose.

Throughout preliminary trials, representatives of the various aircraft and engine manufacturers would be present, partly to advise on maintenance and no doubt partly to advise their companies of progress and the likelihood of acceptability. For the same reason, we received many invitations to visit the various factories and meet the senior people involved. Having been attached to Supermarine for nine months, I knew them all well there but I also came to know Hawkers at Langley, de Havillands at Hatfield and Faireys at Heathrow. The old natural secrecy among different companies went overboard completely during the war and, in fact, all the senior test pilots were welcome to fly any aircraft we had at Boscombe Down and many made a point of flying rivals' latest types.

The permanent test pilots in 'A' per T consisted of Squadron-Leader Sammy Wroath, Flight Lieutenant Brunner, a Polish officer Flight-Lieutenant Kulczyski and myself. This number was supplemented from time to time by other pilots having a 'rest' from operational tours or by borrowing officers from the other flights. Apart from Kulczyski who was also a very knowledgeable expert on missiles, there were a number of Poles at Boscombe Down, all of whom I came to know well. They had escaped when their country was overrun by the Germans, leaving their homes and families behind to survive as best they could. Consequently they had an intense hatred of our mutual enemy and they were waiting and longing to be posted to operational squadrons.

Looking back to 1943 it is interesting to note how the work load shifted to the carrying of external stores (bombs, rockets and other tactical weapons), obviously to support an army in Europe and, later, to modifications to meet the requirements for tropical conditions in the Far East and the Pacific. By 1944 the urgent demand was for longer range by extending the fuel load of our fighters which basically were intended for interception or defence of the United Kingdom rather than in the support of day bombers or advancing armies. Put in another way, it is apparent that the Boscombe establishment was used by the Air Staff to meet their future needs, not only strategically, but also tactically. The Admiralty also had their own requirements so far as aviation was concerned and aircraft such as the Barracuda, Firebrand and the Wyvern, were the result. I was going to say 'the disastrous result' but perhaps the inevitable result would be more appropriate; it was the price the Fleet Air Arm had to pay for the political battles between the wars.

Boscombe Down and the Royal Aircraft Establishment at Farnborough are, in many respects, complementary. The general public are probably more aware of Farnborough as an aircraft testing centre but the work there is of a scientific research nature, concerned with aerodynamics and the future. They are also equipped for testing structures, electronics and other components connected with aviation. If any manufacturer was in trouble with a new type of aircraft they would go to Farnborough for advice. Another division was devoted to naval problems such as catapults and other methods of short take-off and arresting aircraft on the deck. At Boscombe Down we had no facilities for testing these features and we frequently visited Farnborough delivering or collecting an aircraft for some special trial.

As a Service Test Pilot I was, of course, bound by King's Regulations and Admiralty Instructions not to impart information, but there was, in addition, the Official Secrets Act covering Boscombe Down's activities. Inevitably, a great deal of information about existing aircraft, shortcomings in new aircraft, new weapons and other developments, came our way and in our flight we would naturally talk about these things among ourselves.

I soon learned to stick strictly to facts and not to give any opinion unless this was specifically called for in a report. Obviously, a large proportion of the test procedures involved the obtaining of figures, such as speeds, rate of climb, temperatures and so on but in reporting on the handling qualities of an aircraft, great care was needed to describe the response and, wherever possible, to give facts. For instance, one would not write that 'the aircraft was unstable because it tightened up in turns', but ' the aircraft was trimmed in level flight at x miles an hour. On entering a turn to port, the aircraft increased its rate of turn and a forward pressure of 10 lbs on the top of the control column was necessary to prevent the acceleration exceeding 5G'. By describing the aircraft's behaviour in this way the same fact can be checked by others.

One of the reasons for writing a report in this form is that an aircraft which tightens in turns is unacceptable. If it was a new type the Ministry may already have committed itself to a substantial order, a whole factory may be involved in its production with thousands of men and women earning their living working on it and any serious delay could have political implications. As pilots of the aircraft, we had pretty shrewd ideas as to whether it could ever reach operational service but for the civil servants concerned, the decision to cancel was more difficult as it was easier to carry on while calling for modifications. For the manufacturer, the mere thought of the cancellation of an order probably meant the loss of millions of pounds, hence their intense interest in the progress of the acceptance testing.

While aircraft were at Boscombe Down they were maintained by Royal Air Force personnel although in the case of prototypes, the company usually sent their own engineering representative to act in an advisory capacity. The large engine companies, Rolls-Royce, Bristol and Napier had permanent staff as did Dunlop, Dowty and Hamilton propellers. Our own Flight Engineer Officer, Flight Sergeant and airmen were picked men who, having the difficult task of dealing with so many different types, were inevitably under pressure all the time to keep prototypes serviceable.

An entirely separate intensive flying unit was created in 1943. Before any new type of aircraft was issued for squadron service, a sample from the production line came to Boscombe Down where it was flown from morning to night, seven days a week for a period of three months. The engineering staff were responsible for the trial while a complete record was kept of its reliability, maintenance times, spares requirements and all details of any faults which developed, thus providing a source of information which had been sadly lacking in the past and no doubt was extremely valuable.

CHAPTER 21

Fireflies and Other Troubles

The affection which so many pilots had for the Spitfire was, I believe, due to the feeling, on entering the cockpit, of strapping on a pair of wings, sitting behind a powerful and responsive engine and putting the guns to one's shoulder. To me, who never fired the guns in anger, it represented putting on an old glove – it fitted! It responded to the slightest touch, gave an outstanding rate of climb to cheat that old airman's enemy, gravity, but above all, there was the feeling of mastery of the third dimension – climb, dive, quick turns, hanging on the prop. In another mood, one found oneself creeping quietly through the upper sky with a wisp of power or listening to the gentle lapping of the air past the cockpit in a glide, appreciating the beautiful curvature of the wings silhouetted against a cloud or reflecting glints from the sun as one banked and turned. These things to a Spitfire pilot must be what a painter feels when contemplating a work of art, a sculptor the sight of a beautiful figure or a musician listening to music; a sheer *joie de vivre*!

Before being sent to Supermarine I had never flown much higher than 25,000 to 30,000 feet but, while doing development work on various high-flying versions of the Spitfire, I gradually acquired a taste for it. This was partly a kind of competitive urge to get higher and higher but I found there was also a feeling of isolation and solitude at great heights. It was very rare to see another aircraft above 10,000 feet, the sky is so vast and although while climbing one would be concentrating on the test in hand, maintaining the best rate of climb and recording what one was doing, the long slide down to earth was pleasant and relaxing. Similarly, when doing level speeds at altitude intense concentration was required to obtain good figures as the engine power varies with the forward speed due to ram pressure but in a way I was living, at least temporarily, in a world of my own.

During part of my time at Boscombe Down 'A' per T Flight was also responsible for the daily weather flight. This was not done for meteorological or weather forecasting reason's but solely to measure the air temperature at all altitudes for use by the technical office in calculating the true air speeds from figures obtained in performance testing. I enjoyed doing these climbs but rather to my surprise some people did not, although, as none of the aircraft we used for measuring air temperatures was pressurised, it was an effort to go high if one was feeling a bit off colour.

One day, while measuring speed at about 35,000 feet, the Spitfire I was flying started to shake just as if it were a car going over cobblestones or over a bad stretch of road. Although I had not experienced this before, as normally the air at altitude is smooth, others had reported this phenomenon. It was possibly due to the meeting of two horizontal air streams rather similar to the conditions which sometimes occur on the surface of the water when a tidal stream meets the current from a river.

On another occasion I was flying a Spitfire and on completing a climb to altitude, noticed a large thundercloud. I thought it would be interesting to fly through part of it so I headed towards the top. I soon wished I had not as it was extremely turbulent with violent bumps making it difficult to maintain any sort of heading on the instruments. Fine snow was blown through tiny gaps around the perspex hood and at one moment I noticed that the rate of climb was off the clock at over 4,000 feet per minute! One lives and learns and I was glad to shoot out of the far side into clean air but I could not resist clipping round the edge of the enormous and magnificent mountains of cloud!

After the Battle of Britain, the Defence Staff had expected any future attack on the United Kingdom to be from high altitude. The aircraft intended to deal with this expectation were the Spitfire Mk XX1 (later changed from Roman to Arabic figures, ie. 21) and the Westland Welkin, both of which were undergoing trials.

I had already flown quite a bit in the prototype Mark XX1 while attached to Supermarine so it was an old friend but the Welkin, built by Westlands, was rather different. A twin-engined, single-seater with a 70-foot wingspan, it had the two-speed, two-stage intercooled Merlin to give the power at height, a modern pressurised cockpit and electric trimmers. Fortunately, it was an easy aircraft to fly as I had had practically no experience of twins, certainly not of this power but the two engines seemed to give one a sense of security and the cockpit was comfortable compared with other fighters. However, there was a serious failing in its performance, namely a loss of control in a dive at high altitude.

At the time nothing was known about the phenomenon and the words 'compressibility problems' began to be used. There were reports that the American Lockheed Lightning fighter was also in similar trouble. The Welkin would climb up to 40,000 feet at about the same rate as a Spitfire Mk 1X but on putting it into a dive, even of only 15°, it would start to pitch fore and aft and diverge, which could not be checked by use of the elevator control. There was clearly a breakdown or substantial change in the airflow over the wings.

To achieve the high rate of climb and speed at height the designer, Mr Petter, had chosen a very high aspect-ratio wing layout but in order to meet the strength required, he had had to use a thick wing section and it was this which caused the 'compressibility' trouble. It was interesting that, many years later, the same designer was responsible for the Canberra bomber which had a short span and a very thin wing. The Canberra has proved to be one of, if not the most, successful of post war designs, large numbers being built for both the Royal Air Force and the United States Air Force who used it in Vietnam.

Squadron-Leader Brunner, who had recently had to bail out of a Miles Master when the wings came off in a dive and had been badly shaken by his passenger flatly refusing to get out, was shortly afterwards flying the Welkin when an engine caught fire. He soon found he had no lateral control and, in fact, the push pull tube to the aileron had been burnt through allowing the aileron to fly upwards to its maximum travel but, after a series of uncontrollable swoops and stalls, he managed to regain control from the top of one swoop by using full opposite rudder and some power from the good engine. Somehow he then managed to land it at Upavon, really an amazing feat of airmanship; he was very shaken, especially coming so soon after his other recent experience.

One day Philip Lucas, the chief test pilot of Hawkers, asked to fly the Welkin. He turned up in a light check suit looking very smart and while filling him in with details of the aircraft we told him of our new name for it, 'The Japanese Firecracker Model'. This was because, by then, we had had two Welkins catch fire in flight. It was a wet afternoon with low cloud so we were not flying ourselves but making up reports and chatting while he went off. About an hour later a strange car arrived and through the door walked Philip, wet to the skin, mud up to his knees and looking rather pale and shaken, only to be greeted by an unkind roar of laughter! There had been another fire but he had managed to set the aircraft down in a ploughed field without turning it over.

I was detailed off to do the terminal dives of the Welkin at low altitudes. Starting at maximum speed at 10,000 feet, I did a series of dives at increasingly steep angles so that I reached the maximum permitted indicated air speed step by step. On about the fourth dive with an ASI of about 400 mph there was a sudden thump followed by the nose dropping to a steeper angle. It is surprising how quickly one reacts in an emergency and thinking the wings had come off I had instinctively reached for the quick release on the hood in order to bail out when I realised that the hood itself had torn off and that the wings were still there!

It would be interesting to know how much lift the curvature of a hood can give but it certainly made a big difference to the longitudinal trim of the Welkin. A kind spectator of the incident returned the hood to Westlands and I still have a part of it which I use as a ruler on my desk.

By now the aircraft's reputation was not good and rumour had it that as fast as they came off the production line at Yeovil they were flown to Scotland, the two slave engines removed and returned to be reinstalled in the next one at Yeovil. Production continued for some time but I believe no aircraft ever saw active service.

Of all the American fighter aircraft, the various versions of the Mustang were nearest to the British idea of a fighter. It was fast, handled well, carried plenty of fuel and was very well finished – in fact an ideal long-range fighter for daylight bomber support. The Mark V (P-51H) version of the Mustang was almost a new design but the first one did not arrive at Boscombe Down until 1945. Although it made a good impression its arrival was too late to be of operational use. Most of our aerodromes were still grass whereas, I suspect, most of the American air bases were already built with concrete runways. This meant that brakes were more important for a fast-landing aircraft like the Mustang so it was fitted with disc brakes, a very good feature, way before its time.

We also had from the USA a P-40 Kittyhawk and a P-47 Thunderbolt for performance measurement. Both were disappointing and the Kittyhawk, which was a pre-war design, could only be used in secondary operational areas. The Thunderbolt had several big disadvantages for pilots trained on British aircraft, the climb performance was very poor and the big air-cooled engine, a Double Wasp, had a turbo-charger which required an extra lever to control the power.

British engines were fitted with an automatic boost control to prevent the engine being over-boosted at low altitudes; this device automatically opened the throttles to maintain the chosen setting of boost as the aircraft climbed or dived. The turbo-charger of the Thunderbolt had a waste gate which simply opened a valve to release the exhaust to atmosphere in order to prevent overspeeding the supercharger at altitude. In any combat manoeuvre one constantly had to glance at the boost gauge and alter the turbo-charger control lever; in the excitement of the moment some pilots could hardly remember their propeller pitch which controlled the engine rpm let alone the boost pressure. The aircraft was really more suitable as a tactical bomber than as a fighter; like an American car, its sheer weight gave it the comfortable boulevard ride but it lacked the nimbleness of a good sports car.

The Fairey Firefly, the successor to the Naval Fulmar two-seater fighter, arrived at Boscombe early in 1943 but it was in trouble. The company's chief test pilot, Stanilland, had just been killed while doing stability trials. There did not seem to be an explainable reason for the accident, although the spinning trials of a model in the Farnborough vertical wind tunnel indicated a possible reluctance to recover when the flaps were extended. I did endless dives at increasing speeds and it was obvious that the very big change of longitudinal trim with speed was quite unacceptable. If trimmed for level flight, it was not possible to hold it in a dive because, on releasing the stick, recovery produced a great deal of G. Alternatively, if trimmed into the dive, it required about five turns of the trimmer wheel and it then became difficult to pull out as the speed fell off.

Mr Dickenson from the technical office at Boscombe asked for more and more figures and then announced that from an examination of the figures the trouble was caused by an unexplained relationship between coefficient 'A', and coefficient 'B'! This meant in laymen's language that from the figures given to him, there must be a bending of the structure. So it proved, for when an all metal elevator was produced by Faireys, the aircraft behaved normally. The original elevator had been fabric-covered and this must have been distorting at speed. This analysis and cure of the trouble by the 'boffins' was, to me, most interesting as none of them could fly and their deductions were entirely mathematical.

As the Firefly was designed for deck landing it had a special high-lift wing. This was also designed to fold to enable the aircraft to be 'struck down', that is, sent by lift to the lower deck for stowage in the hangar. The Youngman-type flap extended on rails to a position well aft of the trailing edge to increase the wing area and it could then be set at various angles of incidence for extra lift and finally fully down as a powerful flap to increase drag for the approach to landing on the deck. It was very successful and effective but there were doubts about its possible blanking of the tailplane, thus preventing recovery from a spin. Starting gingerly with a forward centre of gravity and one turn only, Sammy Wroath, our CO, gradually covered the whole CG range step by step, both at low and at high altitude. There was no tendency to spin 'flat' or difficulty in recovery, much to everyone's relief.

When the aircraft entered service it was popular but there were requests from the squadrons for a higher rate of roll. By this time spring-tab ailerons, a method of self-powered or servo-assisted control, were being tried on a number of different aircraft and the ailerons of the Firefly were modified accordingly. Rate of roll was measured, relatively crudely, using a stop-watch while the aircraft were rolled through 180°; in other words, one finished the manoeuvre inverted.

When the instructions for doing this trial were received the technical office asked for it to cover the complete speed range. We queried this as it is unusual to roll inverted at maximum diving speed but the instructions were not amended. I did some of the trials and it was clear that the spring tabs were giving considerable improvement. Wing Commander Webster DSO, on loan to us after completing two tours of duty in bombers, undertook the completion of these trials. The aircraft was seen to dive into the ground inverted; whether the wings came off or what went wrong never came to light. This accident was a great shock to all of us at 'A' per T and a sad waste of one of our top bomber pilots. It was a cold bleak day when the little party set off to bury him in the cemetery near Tidworth.

The enquiry into the cause of Wing-Commander Webster's accident was the responsibility of Mr E T Jones, the Chief Technical Officer, and his assistant Mr Scott-Hall. They were both rather distant figures locked away in their backrooms and, although permanent residents at Boscombe, our paths normally never crossed. Having in the past had so many frustrations over obtaining my flying licence from the Air Ministry on my return from Canada, I was prejudiced against civil servants but I came to know, like and respect these two men.

Since I had been the last pilot to fly the aircraft and had given the pre-flight briefing as to how to measure the rate of roll, I was very much involved and was called to give evidence. Accidents in wartime are such frequent occurrences that not much time could be spent investigating them but in this particular case I was satisfied that every possible cause was taken into consideration and that it was not just put down to pilot's error. Somehow it often seems to take an emergency or crisis to break through a person's normal reserve and one can then get a glimpse of the human spirit behind it – and this was proved in my relationship with Jones and Scott-Hall.

CHAPTER 22

High-Speed Passes

K nown to us at Boscombe as the 'blunder bus', the Typhoon came out of the Hawker stable but it did not seem possible that it had come from the drawing board of Sir Sydney Camm, the designer of that elegant line of pre-war bi-plane fighters such as the Fury and the Nimrod. The Typhoon was a low-level, high-speed ground attack aircraft. The very powerful Napier Sabre engine of 2,200 hp had two crankshafts geared together, 24 cylinders and sleeve valves, all of which made it very compact but complicated. The aircraft had a relatively thick wing section and was heavy, making it more suitable for carrying stores (external weapons such as bombs under the wings) than for interception and dog-fighting for which its predecessor, the Hurricane, had been designed. Having been attached to Vickers Supermarine for nine months, I was perhaps prejudiced in favour of Spitfires and could not help but regard the Typhoon as somewhat lacking in finesse as an aircraft, although as a weapon it was an effective blunt instrument backed by brute force.

For dropping stores, bombs or rockets, we had the use of three alternative bombing ranges, Lyme Bay, Crichel Down or Porton. The latter was really for use in experiments in chemical warfare although my first job on a Typhoon was to drop some standard 45-gallon oil drums filled with water there. The drop was to be from 150 feet above ground at a medium speed in order to see if there was any likelihood of them rebounding on hitting the ground and striking the aircraft! They certainly bounced quite high but were well clear of the tail of the aircraft. I am not sure we would have given them such a clean report if we had known that the intention was to use the drums for napalm. Napalm was a sort of petroleum jelly which would stick on whatever it touched and burn with a hot flame when exploded and ignited by a hand grenade which was dropped with it, extracting at the same time the firing pin. Later it was used extensively in Vietnam for destroying villages but at that time we had not even heard of this terrible anti-personnel weapon which, I believe, was never used in Europe.

The Sabre engine was not proving to be reliable in service but we were sent a fully modified version which the makers absolutely guaranteed and which had a special radiator with a mixed matrix. This incorporated an oil cooler behind the water radiator and was intended for use in the tropics as well as for overcoming oil coring problems in extremely cold weather. In order to monitor the oil circulation throughout the system, an automatic recorder was installed in the fuselage behind the cockpit which took photographs every 30 seconds of about twelve thermometer dials mounted in a light-proof box.

On one occasion, intending to do a full power climb to measure the oil temperatures, I started the automatic recorder before take-off and also had prepared my kneepad for other readings. There was a layer of five-tenths cloud at 10,000 feet with a northwesterly wind. My usual practice when flying high was to fly upwind of the aerodrome as, in case of having to bail out, I did not wish to be deposited in the sea but also because navigation was easier as – on taking a reciprocal course for home base – I could recognise any special local features I had previously passed over while still having height in hand.

On reaching 30,000 feet I noticed a faint blue haze near my feet, lit up by a shaft of sunlight from over my shoulder. The oil temperature seemed alright but there was a slight drop in oil pressure both of which I had been recording every 2000 feet. As the oil pressure continued to drop I throttled back and with reducing rpm the pressure dropped abruptly. Turning round to return to base in a long glide I thought that, with luck, there might still be some pressure to allow me to use the engine for landing. However, through a small gap in the high clouds I saw a straight white line indicating an aerodrome runway and decided to glide down there. Unfortunately, there was some more broken cloud at about 3000 feet but from odd glimpses the runway was still there.

The decision to land was made at about 8000 feet when the undercarriage was lowered and locked down. The engine was idling and responded to a touch of throttle but I left the flaps until later. Finally, on breaking through the lower cloud layer in a reasonable position, I selected flaps down but a few seconds later the propeller stopped turning with a thump as the engine seized. By now oil spray was being sucked up onto the inside of the windscreen as I had opened the small side window and from my limited view, I saw that there was a steam roller working on the runway so I should have to land on the grass to one side. The Typhoon, with a dead engine and wheels down, had about the gliding angle of a brick and wanting enough speed to make the flare out, I crossed the boundary at about 160 mph.

The landing hold-off seemed very prolonged and as the aircraft still had flying speed when half way across the aerodrome, I eased it forward onto the wheels and applied the brakes hard. Eventually the tail came down and, having crossed the perimeter track, the aircraft finally came to rest only 50 yards from a wire fence at the edge of a railway cutting! Jumping out and getting clear by 30 yards or so I lay stretched out on my back on the grass. Everything was still and very quiet, the sun had broken through and even the blades of coarse grass looked green. There were some low hills in the distance but the best thing of all was good old Mother Earth; never before had it seemed so solid and peaceful. Glancing up I thought the aircraft looked undamaged although there were brown streaks of oil all along the fuselage which were trickling down vertically to join and form a steady stream along the belly of the aircraft running towards the tail where it dripped off, forming a large pool. At least the aircraft and engine were saved and the investigation would show the cause of the engine failure. I suddenly noticed that the flaps were only 30° down which had obviously lengthened the landing. Then I remembered that the engine had seized up shortly after selecting flaps down and without the hydraulic pump working, the operation had not been completed.

As I lay on my back on the ground exhausted by my efforts to save the aircraft, I had a few brief moments of utter peace. This was shattered by the noise of a fire engine bell and the approach of other vehicles. It appeared that the aerodrome was Defford, a top secret radio and radar experimental establishment which required prior permission to land. It was under repair and notice had been circulated to all RAF stations, etc. I thought the Commanding Officer was going to 'burst a boiler' especially as I was not wearing RAF uniform. In fact I had on naval trousers, a white submariner's sweater, RAF flying boots and over the lot an old brown overall which I used for working on my car in the days before the war; in addition I was looking scruffy as I was covered in oil from head to foot. Although I explained Newton's law on the force of gravity, the Rules and Regulations still had priority! In any event, I was not in the mood to argue and although I was not actually arrested, I was persuaded to wait quietly in the Watch Tower until my story was confirmed. I was not invited to the officers' mess and not even offered a cup of tea. An hour later Brunner arrived in our communication hack, a Miles Mentor, to pick me up.

The Typhoon was dismantled and taken back to Boscombe on a trailer where an investigation showed that one of the special thermometers, installed in the engine oil system for the automatic recorder, had not been properly locked. It had unscrewed with the vibration and all the oil had been pumped out; in other words, it was our own fault and not a true failure in the engine itself!

This forced landing caused me to think very hard. I can truthfully say that the idea of bailing out had never occurred to me, the aeroplane was far too precious, representing the equivalent of many men's lifetime's work as do all prototypes and many other highly technical modern aircraft. To throw it away was unthinkable and while it was able to fly, even without any power, the possibility existed of saving at least part of it to provide evidence of the failure.

There is also the loyalty factor, namely, having been entrusted with such a valuable object you cannot but be aware of your responsibilities. In wartime the aircraft were often ordered straight off the drawing board and put into production before being flight tested. This meant that if the aircraft proved to be unacceptable and was consequently scrapped, the work of thousands of men engaged in building the production craft was wasted. Any serious fault in the prototype had to be brought to light quickly. These thoughts did not pass through my mind at the time, of course, as I was much too busy having to decide a host of problems which multiplied as the ground came nearer. On these occasions the adrenalin flows much faster and speeds up the thinking process so that the reaction time is almost instantaneous

– which is just as well when the ground is only seconds away.

Looking back after many years, I remember that, at the time, the feeling of utter exhaustion was followed by a great feeling of elation and peace of mind as if I had suddenly seen the light of truth.

At the time I knew that this particular mark of Typhoon with its special cooling system, was designed for use in the Pacific as also was the Spitfire on floats, and they had been intended by Churchill to be a political gesture to our American allies in confirmation of our determination to help them after victory in Europe.

All Typhoons suffered from very high-frequency vibration coming from the engine, and in fact the operational squadrons had complained bitterly that it made the pilots impotent! We received a new modified seat with springs set across the frame, like certain types of armchairs, to try on our own aircraft. On this special occasion the technical office only asked for opinions but waived practical tests! History does not record the squadron pilots' reaction.

Boscombe seemed to collect a number of odd aircraft rather like a home for lost dogs. Most had been sent for some specific trial and on completion had been forgotten by the sender. The Commanding Officer's Performance Testing Squadron had a spare Hurricane which could be borrowed for odd jobs and in 'A' per T we had a B-17 and a B-25 Mitchell twin-engined bomber parked on us. It was too good an invitation not to get multi-engined experience so with a little studying we sorted out the taps and flew them. It was, after all, our job to keep the aircraft serviceable!

The B-17, popularly known as the Flying Fortress, was rather like a large four-engined Anson to fly. It was, of course, without any load and so, with a large wing area, it floated round the sky. There was plenty of room in the well upholstered cockpit, chromium-plated switches for all services such as undercarriage and flaps, and all I needed was an airline captain's cap and a large cigar to relax in complete comfort. After I had flown it I was surprised when, on opening the lower hatch, five of our own airmen emerged. They had stowed away in the bomb aimer's compartment and come for the ride without bothering to let me know.

The Mitchell was a different kettle of fish, having a great deal of power, not much wing area and a very complex fuel system. It was also the first aircraft that I flew with a tricycle undercarriage which was not very suitable for the grass aerodrome at Boscombe but very welcome nevertheless. Placing the main wheels carrying the weight behind the centre of gravity, effectively simplified landing and take-off because the aircraft had no inherent tendency to swing or to bounce. Some would say it took the skill out of flying but it was a big safety factor which was soon to be incorporated in the design of all future aircraft.

As very few of the single-seaters under trial at the A & AEE had radios fitted, there was practically no flying control of the aerodrome. One might notify the Watch Tower before doing measured take-offs or before a cross-country flight, but normally, being a grass field, you took your own precautions. There was, however, one particular test which always seemed rather dangerous, namely measuring Position Error (PE). This involved flying an aircraft at a known height, such as the top of a hangar, at a steady speed in a series of passes between its maximum and its minimum. Any other aircraft using the aerodrome, unless familiar with the procedure, might not see the aircraft under test approaching at 50 feet at maximum speed or alternatively, it could be a hazard to the aircraft approaching just above the stall.

The Position Error correction is essential in calculating an aircraft's speed as it measures the error in the Indicated Air Speed instrument as well as that of the altimeter. There is always a difficulty in finding a position on the surface of an aircraft where the true ambient outside atmospheric pressure is not disturbed, otherwise it would give a false reading due to the passing flow of air. Finding a static vent position to give the minimum error involved endless PE flights.

The true height during each pass was found by an observer located on top of a hangar who took a photograph and later analysed the actual flight height against the horizon, measuring in terms of the fuselage above or below the horizon, the depth of the fuselage itself, of course, being a known measurement. At the same time the pilot pressed a switch which took a photograph of a very sensitive altimeter connected to the vent. The resulting figures were of vital importance, both in measuring performance and obtaining the necessary accuracy in bombing and gun sighting.

Before starting this particular exercise we used to inform the Watch Office who would do their best to warn other aircraft and keep them clear. On one particular occasion there was an engineer working on an engine of a Mosquito right in my line of flight; after about a dozen passes at ever increasing speed he finally gave up in evident disgust. He must have thought I was deliberately trying to tip him off his ladder but it did require consistency and extreme accuracy of flight.

One morning in October 1943 while measuring the performance of the Spitfire Mk XX1, I did a level speed at 43,000 feet and, for interest sake, pulled up into a climb until I saw 44,500 feet; not bad with a full load of guns and ammunition. This altitude is getting near the limit for a pilot without a pressure cabin as it is only about 25% of sea-level pressure. I did feel a bit light-headed walking back afterwards to the mess for lunch but otherwise had no ill effects. Plenty of neat oxygen is a help but even so, at low pressures, the lungs are hardly getting enough. When flying high-altitude aircraft an additional emergency supply of oxygen was attached to the parachute harness to sustain life until thicker air was reached during the descent in the event of having to bail out.

A few weeks later I was flying towards the east at about 16,000 feet measuring speeds in level flight. It was still early morning with the low sun reflected by the River Thames winding its way through London to the widening estuary. Trying to maintain an accurate height on the sensitive altimeter and reading the speed, engine rpm, boost pressure and intercooler temperature keeps one busy but, out of the corner of my eye, I thought I saw a fly on the windscreen. The 'fly' turned out to be a squadron of B-17s in formation, gaining altitude presumably for a daylight raid on Germany. They were flying on a reciprocal course to me and I just missed the aircraft on the leader's starboard wing by passing close under him.

Hardly had I had time to realise how lucky I was when I met another squadron, this time slightly lower so that they went underneath me again missing them by about 50 feet. My speed was about 400 mph and their's was probably about 150 mph so that the total converging speed was around 550 miles an hour, not allowing much time to take avoiding action. It was very rare that I ever saw another aircraft above 10,000 feet so I flew in a world of my own but this incident shook me as it was not possible to take accurate readings for test purposes and look where you are going all the time. The B-17 pilots also were probably not looking and in any case, being in close formation, could have taken no action. It was lucky that the second formation was staggered well downwards, obviously avoiding slipstream of the lead squadron.

Occasionally there was a call for an assessment of an aircraft's manoeuvrability in comparison, either with one of our own or an enemy aircraft, although these latter comparisons were usually made by pilots with recent operational experience in, for instance, the RAF Air Fighting Development Unit at Duxford. A Spitfire could turn inside a Mustang in a dogfight, whereas a Firefly could, in a continuous turn, keep its sights on a Spitfire. This was largely a function of wing-loading or, in the case of the Firefly, the high-lift flaps.

During one of these exercises I was flying a Spitfire and Zurakowski*, was flying a Mustang. I should not have liked to have met him in action as he could pull every trick out of the bag and he knew instinctively how to get the maximum out of the aircraft to his own advantage. One of his manoeuvres which completely defeated me was to go into a diving spiral turn at full power pulling a lot of G. As the speed increased the radius of the spiral increased so that the path of the aircraft was like a cone. With 5 to 6 G it was not easy to see where he was as I was on the threshold of blacking out.

Unexpectedly he would turn the diving turn into a steep climbing turn still maintaining high G, this upward spiral finally finishing with a kind of upward flick roll where he had no speed but sufficient control to get round on to your tail!

I have always been amazed how the human body can, without any training or adaptation, suddenly be subjected to all the stresses and strains that occur when flying military aircraft, without coming to any harm. A 5 G turn for instance, means that everything becomes five times its normal weight. The only obvious effect is that the blood is drained from the back of the eyes and vision is lost, ie blackout, but it can easily be recovered by easing the turn. In a simulated dogfight, one can be fully conscious and yet be unable to see the other aircraft which one knows to be 50 yards ahead.

---

*Zurakowski made a name for himself after the war when he demonstrated the twin-engined Meteor at Farnborough. He invented a new aerobatic manoeuvre by turning it into a kind of Catherine Wheel by throttling back one engine in a vertical climb.

In order to reduce the effect of G on a pilot's vision the Spitfire had additional rudder pedals mounted on stalks, about fourteen inches higher than the standard type of rudder pedals. This altered the sitting position so that the pilot's legs were almost horizontal thus raising the level of blood slightly. The Franks suit, named after the person who invented it, was an alternative method of achieving the same result, the pilot being fitted with a special double skinned watertight suit which was not very convenient for normal practical operations. While under G the water in the suit pressed against the pilot's legs which helped keep the blood in the head.

It is also the case that no damage seems to occur to a pilot from a drastic lowering of air pressure and density. At 40,000 feet with the pressure only about a quarter of sea-level pressure, your body does not seem to swell, although I did find it more comfortable to undo my belt and top trouser button. However, there comes a point when lack of oxygen to the lungs through the reduction in density becomes dangerous so that at 40,000 to 45,000 feet, if the oxygen is cut off for any reason, your life expectancy is under one minute. Undoubtedly, the greatest strain is on the nerves. The noise, vibration, cold and anxiety all contribute to this as does the fact that at the back of your mind is always the thought that the fuel and, therefore time, may be running out which will make a landing inevitable. As my friend Monkey Sherlock used to say, 'The worst part of flying is the space between you and the ground.' Those test pilots who had to give up testing were referred to as 'having seen the red light' or 'he decided there was no future in it'.

The officer commanding the Performance Testing Squadron was Group Captain 'Bruin' Purvis, popular throughout the RAF and probably the oldest and most experienced test pilot in the service. I was detailed to fly one mark of Spitfire while he flew another with the object of comparing their manoeuvrability at 35,000 feet. We went up together and having no radio I kept in close formation until we started our dogfight. After a hectic tear round the sky, he throttled back and seemed to lose interest and, thinking that he was satisfied with the trial, I attempted to take up formation on his port wing but overshot hopelessly. Thinking it was the altitude affecting my speed as we were above 30,000 feet, I made another attempt, coming in slowly and carefully; again a bad overshoot. The third time I was determined to make it so I came in throttled right back and very low so as to be able to pull up and lose even more speed. Finally I made it successfully only to be greeted by Purvis waving me away. My first thought was that I had made a serious error but it turned out that he had burst his engine and was making a forced landing.

Bruin Purvis was the most calm and collected pilot, completely at home and at ease in the air. When going on a cross-country flight with him he took no map and it was rather like going for a country walk with any point of interest *en route*, such as a cricket match or a picnic party, being worthy of a diversion to have a look.

CHAPTER 23

Firebrands and Rockets

oscombe Down's armament squadron had its own pilots but in some ways our
trials overlapped, for instance, the equipment of fighter aircraft with rocket
projectiles (RPs) involved measuring the attitude of the aircraft or wing incidence
at different speeds, because the flight of the rocket would not be true if it was fired with
any 'skid'. This new weapon was extremely important to the Allies as it would knock out
a well-armoured tank much more effectively than any fighter bomber.

Firing a rocket projectile takes time to perfect as its trajectory is quite different from
that of a shell from a gun which leaves the barrel at its maximum velocity. The rocket
continually gains speed in flight but leaves the aircraft relatively slowly. To get accuracy
with the RP it was necessary to fly the aircraft at a pre-determined speed, to dive on the
target at a fixed angle and, of course, to fire the rocket at the correct range. All this required
great skill on the part of the pilot. In order to broaden the chance of a hit, a number of RPs
were carried on metal rails under the wings along which the rocket would slide. Some rails
carried two rockets, one above the second below and known as duplex rockets; they were
entirely separate. A Typhoon was equipped with eight duplex RP, ie sixteen rockets, which
could be fired singly, in pairs simultaneously, in a trickle by a timing device known as a
Mickey Mouse or, finally, as a salvo.

Having carried out much of the measurement of attitudes at varying speeds in level flight
in the Typhoon, I was given the job of assessing the handling characteristics and in
particular to determine the maximum speed for release in a dive. Our bombing range for
this type of trial was Lyme Bay off the Dorset coast and after a search round for any fishing
boats I climbed up to 10,000 and dived, reaching a speed of 380 mph. On firing the salvo
of sixteen RPs there was a fine firework display around the aircraft followed by flames
which disappeared into the distance with a number of splashes appearing in the sea roughly
in a circle of about 100 feet diameter. The aircraft had been trimmed into the dive and after
releasing the load, recovered normally.

Talking to the armament experts afterwards they told me that the salvo was the equivalent
of a broadside from a cruiser. In fact, the RP head was a 60 lb 4.5" diameter naval shell
with a tube attached carrying a solid propellant. There is a streak in human nature which

makes us like to play with fire, and guns have the same attraction. Some people are even prepared to spend their life perfecting them and their use. I had not recognised this until the war but firing a salvo of rockets was, I must admit, very satisfying! It was rather like having a Guy Fawkes party all on your own.

Some 45 years after the end of the war I was invited by a society of Typhoon ex-pilots to go on a visit to Normandy. They were all from the RAF Typhoon squadrons who had flown rocket equipped aircraft in the early stages of the landing in France in 1944. I hesitated about joining in the party which numbered 80, as I was the odd man out, not having seen any fighting there. My experience, however, as a test pilot at the Aeroplane and Armament Experimental Establishment at Boscombe Down had included a considerable amount of the development of this aircraft and the firing of the rockets which had not been fitted to any aircraft before, so I was very honoured to have been included in this reunion.

There was a fair spread of nationalities in the party when we gathered in Portsmouth before sailing for France – Australian, New Zealand, American, Canadian as well as Polish. The Free French joined in at Caen where we stayed two nights and where the Mayor of Caen met us, showing us round the Town Hall, the only building left undamaged after the terrible pounding the city had taken. There had been a special request to the allies by the French for it not to be attacked as it was to be used as a refuge for the civilian population. The next day a couple of buses took us around the old battlefield the first port of call being a small village about fifteen miles west of Caen.

The whole village turned out and, the police having closed all the approach roads, we formed up in the street headed by the equivalent of the girl guides, the boy scouts and the village band as we marched about 300 yards to the Memorial Hall. There, all the flags were flying and after various speeches of welcome we assembled in a circle around an old Napier Sabre engine, complete but somewhat damaged. A local farmer had dug it up from twenty feet underground and because of the location and date it was recognised by one of the Canadian pilots as probably having come from his aeroplane when he bailed out in 1944. The village mayor then presented it to the Canadians as a momento and I expect it finished up in a museum. Afterwards we all drank champagne and had a buffet lunch. These Typhoon pilots represented the release of the French from all the years of occupation by the Germans and they were showing their appreciation to them but even so the warmth of the reception from the French was astounding. For me, as an outsider, it was very moving.

From the village we went westward into more open country where, at various crossroads and odd woods, we stopped to speak to little groups of men. These were farmers from the grass fields which had been our forward airfields during the war, now returned of course to full cultivation. It was a meeting, in some cases, of old friends who had something in common, in others it was simply a nostalgic memory of where they had fought in their youth. The next day we visited two large cemeteries and had lunch in another tiny village, sitting down about 12.00 noon in what I suspect, was the school building. After nine courses and many drinks served by the local girls, a series of speeches finished off a delightful meal. The calvados flowed freely and everyone was feeling very happy. As we rejoined our buses some of the party wandered off down the village street where an old lady, standing on her doorstep in her apron, shook hands and spoke to some of them. The last wanderer gave her a kiss and she burst into tears; it was a moving sight, obviously a feeling of thanks felt from the heart and for me, an unforgettable occasion.

The same evening we went on to a crossroad at Tilly, the scene of some fierce battles but where a museum has now been built. This, among other war relics, contained a large number of broken bits of Typhoons, parts which were only just recognisable as such. The French invited everyone to help themselves to souvenirs which many of the pilots did but I felt uncomfortable about it – somehow it seemed like robbing a grave. Perhaps it is not sensible to feel this way about a mechanical or material object.

These rocket equipped aircraft really came into their own when, in August 1944, the Seventh German Army of about 100,000 men tried to retreat out of the pocket south of Falaise. Air power alone could not seal off the gap but the Typhoons caused havoc in creating the enormous traffic jams which ultimately left about half the army trapped and taken prisoner – but only after the most appalling bloodshed.

Another weapon-proving trial which required the use of Lyme Bay involved the guns of the Spitfire and all the other fighters. Starting with a full load of ammunition the object was to investigate any stoppages while firing under heavy G in a turn. Again it was up to the pilot to ensure that the firing area was clear. Having climbed to 10,000 feet and while maintaining a steady 4G in a full-power turn, all guns were fired and kept firing until they stopped or the ammunition ran out. On returning to Boscombe the reason for any stoppage was investigated. The belts of .303 cartridges lay on top of each other so that when subjected to 'G' the upper layer of cartridges dropped into the gaps of the lower layer causing an added resistance to their movement and so to the breech blocks feeding the machine-guns. The Browning could usually cope with this but the 20 mm Hispano cannon often stopped until someone invented a spring-loaded sprocket feed which overcame the difficulty. Spraying out bullets and shells like this while circling seemed hazardous to me but I was assured that the lateral distance never exceeded a mile before all the energy had been dissipated and they fell harmlessly under the force of gravity.

Boscombe Down had no concrete runway until the end of 1944 so that for trials involving bombs, we flew over to Thruxton to load up for take-off on the long runway there. The bombs were always dummies and merely represented the true shape and weight. These were dropped on the range at Crichel Down, a place which received some political notoriety after the war when the Ministry proposed selling the commandeered property to a new buyer rather than to the previous owner! These bombs were mounted on external racks under the wings and our trials consisted of releasing them at increasing speeds in dives. Occasionally a bomb would be deflected by the airflow and knock its detachable tail fin off on the underside of a wing, sometimes causing damage. It would then 'tumble' end over end and undershoot the target.

Another difficulty could be a 'hang-up' or, in other words, a failure to release. This could be embarrassing, as on fighters the bombs are hidden by the wings while in flight, and one did not know whether it was a mechanical fault, in which case it might fall off at any moment, or whether it was only electrical trouble. In order to assess the handling characteristics we had to drop one of two 1000-lb bombs off the wing. We then had to decide whether, with the subsequent imbalance, the pilot should bail out or attempt a landing, in the event of a failure in the release mechanism which would cause one bomb only to be dropped.

Another armament trial which 'A' per T Flight was involved in was a comparison of the effectiveness of a ground attack on dispersed aircraft with fighter aircraft guns, as compared with low-flying aircraft carrying bombs. About 25 different types of aircraft, which were serviceable but becoming obsolete, were parked haphazardly around Stoney Cross aerodrome in the New Forest and our orders were to make a live ammunition attack from a low level, thereby simulating an attack by the enemy. All the pilots concerned went over by road to inspect the site after being briefed on the direction of attack and where the spectators were to be.

It seemed a pity to ruin so many good aircraft and I am slightly ashamed to say that some of the hard to get spares and instruments mysteriously disappeared *before* our onslaught! After every attack a party of engineers searched each aircraft for damage to vital parts such as the electrics, the hydraulics, the fuel system and marked each bullet hole with a different coloured paint so that the damage inflicted in each attack could be assessed. We never saw the final report but it was an expensive trial much enjoyed by all! A brother officer in No 807 Squadron capped it though when he told us about the time he put a torpedo into the French battleship *Richelieu* in Dakar harbour when the Vichy French refused to join our side. She sank alongside the quay. He reckoned he had done a few million pounds worth of damage that afternoon.

The same aerodrome was also used for the trials of the 'Dambusters' weapon which, at the time, was highly secret. Another secret weapon tested there was the Grand Slam. This was a 22,000 lb bomb in a streamlined casing with four tail-fins set to make it rotate in flight like a bullet from a rifle. Several of us, not directly concerned, went over to witness the first release which was to be dropped from a Lancaster at 18,000 feet, calculated to allow it to gain supersonic speed. The top brass having assembled, the Lancaster began its dummy run dropping a 12-lb marker to check the allowance for wind. A loudspeaker had been installed so that the bomb aimer's instructions to the pilot could be heard on the ground. In the briefing we had been warned that there would be a delay of about 25 seconds while the bomb fell with an eight second delayed fuse in the bomb itself.

The big moment arrived: 'Left, left, right, steady, steady, steady, bomb away.' There was a hushed silence and considerable tension as everyone waited for what was thought to be the biggest explosion ever. As we waited a firework was let off just behind us and we nearly jumped out of our skins. Practical jokers can be a menace sometimes and this time the culprit was someone from 'B' Squadron.

We continued watching as a splash of earth was thrown up at the designated target followed shortly afterwards by a supersonic bang and what seemed to be an interminable delay. Suddenly there was a deep thud and chunks of earth half as big as a railway carriage flew up into the air to several hundred feet and fell pitter patter for seconds afterwards leaving a crater about 60 feet across. These bombs subsequently penetrated six feet of concrete covering the submarine pens at Brest.

Two new, purely naval aircraft, designed to meet Admiralty requirements, came to Boscombe Down for trials: the Firebrand, a large single-seater able to carry a torpedo or a variety of stores under its wings produced by Blackburns of Brough, and the Fairey Barracuda, a two-seater with a similar capability. Both of these aircraft had many technical and handling troubles. The Firebrand even reached the Mark V version before reaching training squadrons but was too late for operational service and the Barracuda, although reaching squadrons in 1944, was not exactly a popular aircraft. About the same time a flood of different US Navy aircraft also arrived for assessment, including the Corsair, Wildcat, Avenger, Hellcat, Dauntless and a big twin-engined fighter, the Tiger Cat. All these were built to a different set of requirements, presumably with the Pacific in mind where long-range and tropical conditions prevailed. Fundamentally they were good aircraft adapted to carry weapons into action whereas ours were weapons which needed an aircraft to carry them into action.

The Firebrand was a well-engineered aircraft, that is to say the systems, electrical, hydraulic, air pressure and fuel were easily accessible and servicing was simple. The troubles lay in its aerodynamic qualities, basically those of the wing, which could be folded. It was a high-lift wing with big flaps but when the flaps were extended for deck landing there was a serious nose down change of trim. This was checked by an equally large up movement of the elevator so that perhaps half the extra lift from the high-lift wing was countered by a large downward force on the tail.

The Marks 1 and 11 had a Napier Sabre engine but as more and more power was required for the take-off from a deck, a Bristol Centaurus was fitted to the Mark 1V. The torque of this could not then be held on the rudder at take-off power and this had to be increased, producing the Mark V. All these difficulties arose while the production line was rolling and some fairly heated meetings took place; the navy urgently wanted the aircraft and contracts worth millions of pounds were involved. It is on such occasions as this that a test pilot must base all his reports on fact which can, of course, be verified by being repeated. The personal opinion of the test pilot must not be given and this applies particularly to permanent Service officers who naturally have to consider their future. The wartime-only officers were in some respects able to be more outspoken, rather like a non-executive director of a company.

I had an unfortunate experience taxiing out a Firebrand one day when, a couple of hundred yards from the tarmac, the undercarriage started to collapse, the legs splaying apart like a giraffe lying down. Those who saw the accident said they thought I was trying to lay an egg. Fortunately the torpedo had just been removed or the remarks might have been ruder.

The Barracuda met all their Lordship's requirements. It had a hook, folding wings, retractable undercarriage, dive brakes, high lift flaps, catapulting hooks, tropical radiator and a cabin for the observer and was equipped to carry a torpedo, bombs, RPs, radar and, of course, radio with even a coffin-like container under each wing from which special agents could be dropped by parachute! In fact it was a versatile aircraft, all singing, all dancing! The difficulty arose over getting all this weight off the deck and again, as with the Firebrand, more and more power was required. The final mark had a low altitude rated Griffon but this reduced the range and consequently the aircraft's usefulness.

The American Corsair became, during the latter part of the war, the main fighter for the Royal Navy. It was a tough, no-nonsense aircraft which did yeoman service. Our trials at Boscombe were not extensive but were confined to measuring carbon monoxide contamination, lengthening the control column to British standards and measuring flame damping and take-off distance with varying loads. The aircraft, in common with all American fighters had an enormous cockpit by our standards. If one dropped something like a pencil it would disappear into the depths and require a proper expedition to find it. American seat-belts were lap straps only and their requirement was for the instrument panel to be clear of the pilot's head when leaning fully forward. On one occasion, during the flame tests at night, I inadvertently switched off the cockpit instruments. These were lit by 'black' light which illuminated the instruments only but I could not find the variable resistance knob which was almost out of reach and in total darkness. To add to my troubles the wind changed and the glim lights marking the landing strip took some time to be repositioned. In the blackout with no horizon I was powerfully worried, especially as my experience at night was virtually nil. At least I never flew again at night without a hand torch!

There were two naval aircraft which, in their different ways, were outstanding; both were conversions of Royal Air Force fighters. The Seafire Mk XV had a Rolls-Royce Griffon engine rated to give maximum power at low altitude which gave it an exceptional rate and angle of climb; in fact, although few realised it, the thrust from the propeller was about equal to its all-up weight and theoretically it could have climbed vertically like a rocket without wings thus beating the 'Flying Bedstead' by many years. In fact, of course, vertical flight was not feasible for many reasons connected with control and engine lubrication but it was quite an aircraft with its power or thrust to weight ratio of one to one.

When Sir Sidney Camm, the chief designer of the Hawker Aircraft Company, replaced the Typhoon, he chose a laminar flow wing with the thickest part about half way back on the chord for the F2/43. Called the Tempest, the Mark 1, which did not enter service, and the Marks V and V1, which gave excellent operational service, had the Napier Sabre like the Typhoon. However the last production model, confusingly designated Mark II, had the Centaurus, which with a new fuselage but the same wing, became the Fury for the RAF but also did not enter service in any quantity. The naval version of the Fury, the Sea Fury, had a redesigned fuselage with a raised cockpit to improve the view over the nose for deck landing. Although the aircraft had a high wing loading and stalled at about 90 knots, it was easy to land on deck. The propeller diameter was large and the slipstream covered a fair proportion of the wing so that on cutting the throttle it just fell out of the sky on to the deck without any 'float'.

Compared with the Seafire Mk XV, the Sea Fury was rather underpowered, although it handled very well, being just positively stable in all axis with light, crisp and powerful controls. It also had a very high cruising speed and plenty of fuel. Although it did not reach the squadrons until after the war, I personally felt at the time that at last the navy was going to get the fighter it deserved. Ultimately it did see active service in the Korean war when its outstanding qualities were appreciated. It was the last piston-engined fighter before the arrival of jets. In spite of its early handling troubles, the Firefly had, by the end of the war, been well developed, establishing itself as a tough, reliable, long range, highly manoeuvrable aircraft. With its formidable armament of four 20 mm Hispano cannons and carrying rockets or 1000 lb bombs it was highly regarded by the US Navy. Although they did not use it in combat, the US Navy Test Establishment, which had been sent one, liked the aircraft and its versatility.

To the best of my knowledge when flying in the Pacific from the three aircraft carriers, including HMS *Indefatigable*, which were part of the American Fleet, the Firefly was the first all-British aircraft to fly over the mainland of Japan followed closely by a group of four Seafire squadrons who attacked Tokyo. Later I learned that a brother officer from 807 Fulmar Squadron, Commander 'Buster' Hallett DSC, a regular naval officer who later commanded a wing of three Seafire squadrons in the Pacific, had also made a sweep over the mainland of Japan. These Seafires were brought home to Lee-on-Solent to act as spotters for the big guns of the battleships deployed in the Normandy landings in 1944. They obliterated the very heavy gun emplacements overlooking the beaches on which our troops landed. These aircraft had cover provided by two layers of fighters from the RAF and US Air Force and operated from Lee-on-Solent and although these squadrons had many casualties they were never mentioned in any despatches. Buster Hallett who had a very checkered career in his youth finished up his service in the navy as Captain of Greenwich.

CHAPTER 24

Rogues and Failures

Most accidents to aircraft are fatal and test flying then adds a fraction of extra risk as a great deal of the testing involves using full power. I had six total engine failures or at least six landings without power. During wartime life is necessarily cheap but somehow I always expected it to be the other man although, if one knows the person concerned, particularly if it is someone in your own flight or squadron, it is much more of a shock. On two occasions I had to attend a brother officer's funeral and somehow I felt the loss of those friends even deeper.

The routine measurement of performance called for full engine power both in the climb and during level speeds. In normal use full power is, of course, used at take-off but rarely at other times, so occasional engine failures were understandable in test flying. Having made a forced landing in a Typhoon following an engine failure and knowing the reputation of the Napier Sabre engine, from that time onwards, when flying any Sabre-engined aircraft, I made a habit of doing all level speeds above the aerodrome or at least upwind and within gliding distance. Although the previous failure had not been due to any engine fault, within weeks I experienced a genuine one when, with a bang and a gush of steam and oil, a cylinder head came off, quickly followed by a complete stop. From 10,000 feet I could see Boscombe Down lying conveniently on my port bow so I was able to glide down and make a normal landing.

With a sleeve-valve engine the sleeve slides up into an annular slot in the cylinder head and it was suspected that oil trapped in this slot had caused an hydraulic lock. Whatever it was, this failure did not increase my faith in the Sabre. The Bristol engine company had put their faith and reputation into backing and developing the sleeve valve, producing a string of successful engines based on that principle. In earlier days many great engineers had also pursued the same valve mechanism in motor cars; it was smooth and silent as well as being totally enclosed and the famous Daimlers used by the Royal Family all had sleeve valves.

Unfortunately, the lubricating oil of the period lacked present day qualities and every sleeve-valve engine's exhaust left a trail of blue smoke. In addition there was also much viscous drag from the sleeves and in the case of the 24-cylinder Napier Sabre, this became excessive in cold weather. During the months before D-Day, we received orders to warm up all Sabre-engined aircraft every four hours throughout the day so as to ensure an easy and certain start. It had been found that, even with the correct mixture, they became almost impossible to start from cold if parked in the open as the engine would fire correctly but each single cylinder lacked the power to overcome the viscous drag and it would gradually peter out. What this order entailed in increased maintenance and ignition troubles can be imagined but it did mean that the aircraft were at immediate readiness for the landing of our armies in France.

Another serious failure occurred with a Rolls-Royce Griffon in a Spitfire Mk XIV while doing partial climbs which involved climbing at full power at different indicated air speeds. At low forward speed the angle of climb of the Mark XIV was very steep, probably about 45° from the horizontal, and the first sign of trouble was a puff of blue smoke from the exhaust followed by a stream from the radiator breather. The engine was still alive but I dared not use any power so I crept back and landed where I discovered that the forward piston had failed.

About a week later, repeating the trial with a new engine, exactly the same symptoms developed followed immediately by total failure. I had taken off from Boscombe Down and was near Warminster about ten miles away at 10,000 feet in a clear sky except for a line of nine-tenths cloud lying over Boscombe Down hiding the aerodrome from sight. I could see Stonehenge, however, and knowing the area well, I decided to go for a landing with wheels down, approaching through the 500 feet layer of cloud. Using Stonehenge as a point of reference my navigation proved about right as on breaking cloud the aerodrome was within comfortable gliding distance.

It seemed clear to me that there was some shortcoming in the Griffon's lubrication or cooling system which would not cope with high power when running at a steep angle but Rolls-Royce, as was their habit, insisted that it was due to incorrect installation or mishandling and not their engine! For making a successful landing in difficult circumstances my Commanding Officer, Air Commodore Sir John Boothman, gave me a green endorsement in my log book, a kind of Brownie point!

The acceptance of new fighter aircraft involved spins, both at low altitude and near its ceiling. These tests were about the last to be undertaken just in case the aircraft should fail to come out, although new types always had tail parachutes to assist recovery in the event of the spin becoming 'flat'. The requirement was to complete three turns in both directions before taking recovery action and whatever action one takes with stick and throttle, full opposite rudder must never be taken off. The main warning of danger is when the spin becomes flat and quiet; the more the aircraft pitches the better.

Jeffrey Quill had a nasty experience with an anti-spin parachute. Later versions of Seafire had what became known as a 'sting' type hook instead of the more usual A-frame type which retracted into a recess in the bottom of the aft fuselage. The sting type projected beyond the rudder and was attached to the rudder post which meant that the bottom of the rudder was cut back, losing a small amount of area. More or less as a formality to cover the regulations, he decided to do a check spin but the aircraft failed to recover so Jeffrey pulled the plug to release the parachute. The parachute's cable somehow wound round the outside of the rudder which was fully over, flicking the rudder and rudder pedals over so violently that it broke Jeffrey's ankle but it did stop the spin and he landed the aircraft safely. This was the second incident Jeffrey had had as when doing the spinning trials on the Vickers Wellsley in pre-war days, the aircraft refused to respond to the controls and he had bailed out, landing successfully in the driveway of a house in Weybridge, much to the surprise of the lady who lived there.

It fell to my lot to do the spinning of the Sabre-engined version of the Tempest Mk I which was a relatively heavy aircraft with a laminar flow wing, a new development at that time. At 30,000 feet it behaved impeccably, rather to my surprise and relief, but on the recovery I noticed blue smoke coming from exhaust stubs. On the next spin I glanced at the engine revs which indicated 4,200 rpm with the throttle fully closed! The maximum permitted at full power was only 3,600 rpm. It was clear that the propeller pitch and constant speed control mechanism could not cope with the rapid increase of windmilling speed during the spin recovery. The over-speeding of a big engine like the Sabre, particularly with closed throttle, meant an engine change.

The Centaurus-engined Tempest Mk II completed its trials almost without fault although the Mk I had run into the problem of a change of trim in a dive with high G on recovery. There was, in fact, some doubt about its acceptability for service use but what I found interesting was the report from the technical office for the Ministry in London. The cautious civil service approach, not wishing to upset the powerful Hawker Aircraft Company by turning their product down, stated that the Tempest Mk I was 'not unacceptable'. This double negative meant to imply that they did not like to accept it as it did not quite meet the requirements laid down in the rule book but that it was a marginal case and under the exigencies of war they would accept it. To them, a double negative had a subtly different meaning to a positive!

As a light relief we had two very unusual aircraft sent to us in 1943 at 'A' per T, one being the Boulton and Paul P92, a light twin Gipsy-engined aircraft with a large saucer-shaped centre section. It was a half-scale model of a project, the purpose of which was top secret. We thought at the time that it was a flying radar scanner but we found out later it was for mounting a 40mm gun in a revolving turret. Its flying characteristics were very good, the back to back saucer-shaped housing for the gun producing considerable lift.

The second unusual aircraft was a half-scale model of the four-engined Short Stirling bomber fitted with four Pobjoy radial engines. Well before the war, Short Brothers of Rochester were in full production of the Sunderland flying boat with the wings and tail well proved and by designing a suitable fuselage and undercarriage it was hoped to build a heavy bomber with the minimum expenditure of time and money. How successful Stirlings were in service I do not know but a re-hash of something built for a different purpose is a doubtful policy to follow. The half-scale Stirling was another type for my log book but left no lasting impression. The actual prototype of the Stirling had a lengthy retractable undercarriage which, owing to a structural miscalculation in its design, unfortunately collapsed on the first landing.

Apart from the designer's own stamp on the actual design of any aircraft, the manufacturer used to put a family image on his product. This characteristic up to 1939, and which has now faded out, was a survival from the early days of aviation when the pioneers were not only the designers and test pilots but were even responsible for the formation, finance and running of their own company. The names of Sopwith, Hawker, de Havilland, Blackburn come to mind but there were also other companies such as Bristol, Fairey, Gloster, Handley Page, Armstrong Whitworth, Westland, Vickers and a number of others which came into existence during World War I which had their own characteristics. Nowadays all modern aircraft are, of course, the design of a team of specialists in aerodynamics, engine installation, landing gears, electronics etc, with stresses and structures being calculated by computer; it is no longer a personal inspiration!

All the companies mentioned above were deliberately kept in business before the war by the government of the day so as to have an industry which, if called upon, could be rapidly expanded in the event of another war.

The respective design teams were kept busy and endless prototypes appeared but the factories were kept alive by sharing out orders for limited numbers of the best aircraft in their particular range whether designed by them or not. This policy gave great flexibility of choice to the Air Staff and incidentally led to the Supermarine Company designing the Spitfire, although it could be argued that it left the country in a vulnerable position at the time of Munich in 1938 as our factories were not capable of mass production.

If an older pilot had been placed in a cockpit not knowing which aircraft it was, it would often have been possible to tell the manufacturer by its construction methods and cockpit layout. Supermarines could be recognised by their use of stressed skin construction and cocks and pumps made by their parent company, Vickers, while Hawkers had their tube-and-socket-type structure. Faireys were different from other aircraft in that the various controls were made in their own factory, the naval connection being apparent by the strange boxes, switches and other gadgets. Blackburns were more formal in their cockpit layout, everything neat and tidy with all the pipes and wires clipped in parallel lines, the controls logically laid out and marked, rather like a robot, not untidy like a Spitfire which had had so many additions over the years, that it felt rather like a well-loved home. American aircraft were always recognisable as they had extremely large cockpits by our standards. This was partly because of the specification called for by their Service Chiefs but I suspect that, as they had no powerful in-line water-cooled engines, the natural streamline behind their large radial air-cooled engines, designed for civil aircraft, led to a fat teardrop shape.

As they used electricity for operating their auxiliary services such as undercarriage, flaps and cooling gills, the appropriate switches were arranged conveniently in neat rows, often

THE AEROPLANE AND ARMAMENT EXPERIMENTAL ESTABLISHMENT, ROYAL AIR FORCE STATION, BOSCOMBE DOWN, NOVEMBER, 1944

The Aeroplane and Armament Experimental Establishment, Boscombe Down, November 1944. The author is standing at the extreme right, in Naval uniform. Commander Torrens-Spence 6th from the left sitting.

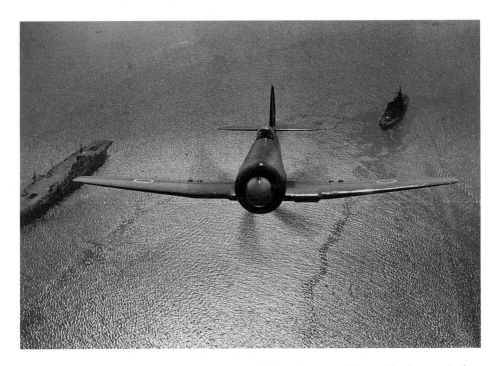

The Hawker Sea Fury, the last piston-engined fighter from a celebrated background of world beaters, was a real aristocrat with the sort of performance, handling and formidable weaponry expected from over thirty years' experience of building fighters.

Westland Welkin, Boscombe down, April 1943. Developed as a high altitude fighter with pressure cabin, it was in serious trouble from compressibility, or the sound barrier. (Photo: Charles E Brown.)

The Author, his wife, Ella and his father outside Buckingham Palace in 1945 when awarded the Air Force Cross.

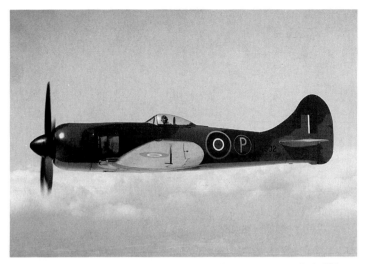

The author flying the Hawker Tempest Mk II prototype, LA 602 (Bristol Centaurus), Boscombe Down, 3 May 1944. Intended to replace the Typhoon, the Tempest had a greatly improved laminar flow wing. Relatively free of development problems, it had great potential as a weapon carrier.

The American Grumman F74 Tigercat was the equivalent of the de Havilland Sea Hornet. It was the first fighter with a powered control, the rudder.

Richard Muspratt riding a Mustang, not a wild horse, but an American thoroughbred. It carries two duplex rockets under each wing which proved a devastating weapon against tanks.

The US Navy gave the Chance Vought F45 Corsair second choice but the Royal Navy liked it and found it a tough and reliable fighter.

Part of the Home Fleet in the North Sea.

The Vickers Supermarine Spiteful prototype at Boscombe Down in 1945. The new Laminar Flow wing was fitted to a Spitfire fuselage which went 30mph faster but ultimately the new wing was incorporated in Supermarine's first naval jet aircraft, the Attacker.

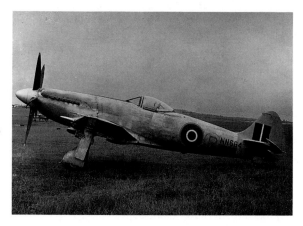

The Author flew a friend's Hirtenberg HS9A (DH Gipsy) G-AGAK in the 1950 Daily Express Challenge Trophy, finding it pleasant to fly with unobstructed view.

A de Havilland Hornet F Mk I (Merlin 130/131 engines) at Boscombe Down in March 1945. A lot of power for one man (4600hp) but with controls to match its performance, the Hornet was the ultimate in piston-engined aircraft. The author nearly wrote off this aircraft on his first flight in it.

Some type F7 Meteors had a second tandem seat for training. The Gloster Meteor was the first jet aircraft to fly operationally and obtained the world's speed record of 606 mph in 1949 with a special Rolls Royce engine.

The Fairey Barracuda met all the naval requirements for a general purpose torpedo spotter and reconnaissance aircraft. The trailing edge outrigger flaps gave both lift for landing and drag (as shown) for torpedo attack (Photo: Charles E Brown).

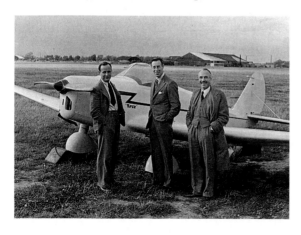

Fairey Tipsy at Heston in 1946. Left to right: Dixon, Fairey's Chief Test Pilot, the author and McLaren, Dowty's undercarriage designer.

The author in the Hawker Sea Fury making the first take-off from the light Fleet Carrier HMS *Ocean* (Captain Casper John, RN) on 10 August 1945. Interestingly, this Sea Fury is in standard RAF daylight camouflage.

Vice Admiral Sir Denis Boyd KCB, CBE, DSC, our greatly respected Commander of the Mediterranean Fleet, prepares for a flight to his headquarters at Lee-on-solent in a Meteor.

Competing in a Moth Minor at an efficiency competition at Panshanger, the author won a prize for achieving 28 miles per gallon.

Bill Humble, Hawker test pilot.

The prototype de Havilland Vampire (code name Spider Crab) at Boscombe Down. For the author – it gave a totally new experience and foresight of the future for gas turbines.

on a shelf beside the pilot. On their fighters the control column was much lower than on our aircraft and the firing button, and safety catch were mounted in a straight moulded plastic handle on the top. Our own guns were fired pneumatically and the firing button with its safety lock, was incorporated in a circular ring type handle which in some cases was hinged at knee height to allow unobstructed movement of the lateral control. One reason for short control column was because the pilot only had a lap strap and the specification called for the pilot's head to clear the instrument panel when fully stretched forward as may occur in a crash.

British aircraft still retained one vestigial relic of the early days. The dual ignition switches were still an aircraft version of the ordinary domestic light switch which is pressed down to turn a light on but in an aircraft it switches the engine off. The down position earths the contact breaker of the magneto and prevents a spark; how many men have been killed or injured by not understanding this will never be known. The Americans, however, were more sensible as all their aircraft were fitted with a swinging lever switch with the various positions unmistakably marked.

One day a signal arrived at Boscombe for me to report to Air-Commodore Jones at the Ministry of Aircraft Production at Millbank. Intrigued, I flew up to Fairey's private grass aerodrome at Heathrow and parked my Firefly there. Dixon, the Chief Test Pilot, kindly drove me as far as Osterley Park to catch the tube into London. On reporting to the Air Commodore we immediately, without explanation, set off by car for Heston where I used to fly in pre-war days. To my astonishment he then asked me if I considered the grass aerodrome there as being large enough for use by naval aircraft, which it obviously was.

It was only later that it became known that Fairey's Heathrow aerodrome had been commandeered under wartime legislation for conversion into a 'bomber' station! My little visit had been a yard-arm clearing operation in case the navy objected to Fairey's, the chief contractor of naval aircraft, being moved out. As is well known, Faireys fought for fifteen years or so for compensation, finally receiving a pitiful sum for their valuable land. Vast sums were involved in turning the grass field into the present international airport, including the cost of filling a very large gravel pit where the approach tunnel from the motorway now is.

While we were standing on the tarmac at Heston a US Army B-17, obviously lost and exhausted, taxied in, returning from a daylight raid on Germany. I remember in particular one young gunner who could not have been more than about nineteen, coming up to our little party so excited that he had to tell us all about it. He said he saw the enemy fighter coming in to the attack over and over again. He could see it firing, actually aiming at him, he was sure, because it came so close he could see the pilot who was trying to kill him! It was his first time in action. I went over to look at the aircraft which was riddled with bullet holes and the side gunner's blister had certainly seen some use; the bottom of the fuselage was six inches deep in empty .5 inch shell cases.

From time to time 'rogue' aircraft were reported as being unacceptable by squadrons. For various reasons these particular aircraft misbehaved, or at least had a bad name for handling qualities, and whenever possible they were quietly or unofficially returned, either to the main maintenance depot or passed on to another squadron which was not popular with higher authority.

A scheme was put in hand by which independent assessors flew these aircraft and if possible put them right on the spot, the result of which meant that I was sent up to Castletown on the north coast of Sunderland to deal with a rogue Spitfire. For this sort of journey a Firefly provided ideal transport as it was reasonably fast, had plenty of fuel and would land in a short space if required.

On my arrival at Castletown the local RAF fighter squadron was, I think, a little surprised to see someone in naval uniform appear but they could not have been more polite and made me very welcome in their mess. It happened to be the week of Christmas, 1943. The offending Spitfire was flying very right wing low and the wing could not be held up in a dive, a not unusual fault on a new aircraft coming off the production line but which certainly should have been rectified before being issued to the squadron. It may well have had a damaged aileron replaced while in a maintenance unit but had not been subsequently test flown. They changed the starboard aileron which made a big improvement and with a bit of reflexing of the trailing edge, it flew well and was accepted by the Commanding Officer.

Returning south via the Western Highlands and Machrihanish on the Mull of Kintyre I had a superb view of this lovely mountainous country. It was a change from flying over the southern half of England with which I had become very familiar. Although occasionally a radio was fitted, frequently it was not, and as a great deal of our flying was at altitude, quick recognition of our locality was important. On breaking cloud, often only a glance was sufficient to identify my whereabouts such as the plains to the north of Salisbury, the flat area of Somerset with its drainage dykes, the Cotswolds with yellow limestone houses and the sandy pine tree area around Aldershot. Strangely enough I found it was often more difficult to recognise my position when flying low. Below 1000 feet, the contours of hills and other landmarks appear different to the view from above. In a way the sky became my habitat, I lived in it and became part of it.

During 1944, Air Commodore Boothman (later Sir John Boothman, KCB, KBE, DFC, AFC) took command of Boscombe Down. He was well known as the outright winner of the Schneider Trophy in 1931 and was a popular commanding officer, much liked throughout the air force. He and his wife entertained a good bit, giving a number of small dinner parties and Ella and I came to know them well, Ella got on particularly well with Mrs Boothman who used to drop in to our small bungalow quite often, enjoying, I believe, not having to be formal as she had to be with regular RAF wives.

Sammy Wroath had left 'A' per T in the spring of 1943 to set up and command the Empire Test Pilots School (ETPS) whose main object was to train test pilots for the future and to raise the standard. Whereas in the past pilots had been picked for these jobs largely for their skill in flying, now, with the latest aircraft, the testing was becoming more sophisticated and much more technical. A greater knowledge of engineering and science in all its aspects was of far greater value than an ability to give a good demonstration of aerobatics. The ETPS was set up to emphasise this and was a turning point in the type of pilot specialising in test work, candidates coming not only from the Empire but also from America, Canada and eventually they were to include men from the armed services of nearly every country in the world. It had the intended effect of standardising performance measurement, handling and all other aspects of an aircraft's behaviour world-wide and unquestionably raised immensely the professional test pilots' status in the aviation industry.

Group Captain McKenna took over the second course at the ETPS in 1944 but as he had not flown a Mustang, he came over to 'A' per T one afternoon to borrow one of ours, a standard Mark IV in which I had been measuring the stick forces in turns. On my last flight I had noticed that a panel over the ammunition tank on the starboard wing had started to lift at the aft edge when pulling about 4 G.

On landing to investigate, it appeared to be fastened down normally but it was reported to the engineering staff who examined it and were satisfied that it was fastened securely. The quick release fastenings were an American type with two sets of slots for a screwdriver, the alignment of which confirmed that it was locked down properly. I showed McKenna the taps and off he went but half an hour later an aircraft was reported to have crashed somewhere near Salisbury. It had been seen in a steep, high speed dive when it rolled over and dived straight into the ground. One can only assume that the loose panel had lifted with a subsequent loss of control. McKenna's death was a great loss as he was one of our older and most respected test pilots. His name lives on as the much sought after McKenna Trophy is presented each year to the test pilot who has done best in the course.

This incident was followed by a spate of other accidents. 'B' Squadron were investigating a series of losses in Halifax squadrons which, I was told, were occurring during take-offs at night. Take-off conditions were being simulated at 10,000 feet when the aircraft under investigation was seen to spin and crash, killing the whole crew; this particular trial entailed switching off one of the outer engines as if an engine had failed. The final investigation showed that the pilot had no positive indication of which engine had failed as the offending engine was still showing some boost and rpm because it was being turned over by the windmilling propeller which had of course not been feathered. Attempting to hold the aircraft straight while in the climb led to a fully stalled fin and rudder followed by a spin. As a result of these trials some multi-engined aircraft were fitted with torquemeters which gave a positive and immediate indication of which engine was failing or had failed.

Another Halifax accident, which had a happier ending, occurred one evening when we in 'A' per T had finished for the day and were walking back to the officers' mess along the perimeter road. There is a big dip in the road in front of the mess and we saw, on the other side of the aerodrome, a Halifax approaching to land. The sun was low and the aircraft dipped out of sight to make the touch down. To our surprise instead of the aircraft appearing over the brow, the first thing to appear was a very large rubber tyred wheel which came bounding over the hill in our direction. It turned out that it was being flown by Al Truran, a very popular Canadian Wing-Commander. An armament expert, this was his first flight in a four-engined bomber which he had borrowed from 'B' Squadron. He and his crew were unhurt but in spite of much talk about 'sun in his eyes' he had his leg well pulled and was not allowed to forget it in a hurry!

One terrible accident which should never have occurred involved a Liberator that took off with locked controls, killing everyone on board. American aircraft had a different method of operating the brakes from the British system. On our own aircraft the differential use of the brakes for manoeuvering on the ground, was controlled by movement of the rudder bar and the application of the amount of braking by a hand-lever on the control column. The Liberator had hinged pedals on the rudder control, their brakes being activated by pivoting your foot from the ankle using the ball of the foot to apply the appropriate brake. It was not easy to apply heavy pressure as in a turn your leg was nearly fully extended so it was easier to taxi with the rudders locked central. I never heard the result of the final investigation of this accident but confusion could well have been the cause.

One afternoon when we were grounded by low cloud and unable to do any test flying, a friend of Wing Commander Peter Lamb's, who was then commanding the flight, flew over to see him from an operational Spitfire squadron in Southern England. We sat around chatting and after a cup of tea he decided the weather was just passable and that it was time for him to return to his base.

Peter and I helped strap him in and pulled an accumulator trolley over, plugged in and he got a start. As he taxied to the far end of the aerodrome and we set off on foot for the officers' mess, we glanced up in time to see him immediately make a left-hand climbing turn. This became a vertical bank and it was clear that he was evidently stalling out of control. The aircraft hit the ground with full power and burst into flames amid a cloud of black smoke; there was nothing we could do. The accident was like a bad dream and my mind went over it again and again rather like a slow motion action replay. After a sleepless night, the next day broke dry and clear and fortunately, with a backlog of work, we were all kept busy and I was able to put my fears behind me. There are many men alive today due to the fact that the Spitfire, especially near the stall, was a very forgiving aircraft but there was a limit to what it could take.

With a little mental arithmetic one could work out one's life expectancy which, while at sea in wartime as a pilot in an aircraft-carrier, was not very long – so understandably there were some who could not stand the nervous strain. The test pilot on the other hand had the advantage of a house and privacy, possibly a wife, but there were no tours of duty with regular breaks. No-one liked flying more than me but it became a regular job, a great deal of hard work and inevitably it was the wives who took the strain. Day after day one said farewell leaving one's wife to wait with dread a ring at the door by a uniformed officer coming unexpectedly bringing bad news, these feelings remaining until we returned safely at night. My Ella had Jane to look after but even she started to smoke and drink to ease the constant strain.

CHAPTER 25

The Coming
of the Jets

March 15, 1944 was a red letter day for me; one to be remembered. Brunner and I were ordered to fly to the Gloster Aircraft Company's aerodrome, which had a very long single runway, at Moreton Valence in the valley of the River Severn. All we knew was that the aeroplane we were to fly was top 'A' star secret and that the aircraft had problems of directional stability.

It was called the F9/40 which was the number of the requirement specification and later became known as the Gloster Meteor. At the time we knew nothing of the existence of gas turbines and were therefore astonished to find the aircraft was fitted with two jet engines as they were called. Unknown to us, an aeroplane, the single-seater Gloster E28/39 had flown secretly on 15 May 1941, fitted with the original Whittle W1 gas turbine engine of only 800 lbs thrust. The new aircraft, the F9/40 Meteor, was designed as a single-seater fighter for the Royal Air Force and had two of the Whittle WIIb engines designed to give 1600 lbs of thrust each or double the thrust of the original W1. These had been de-rated to 1350 lbs each in the F9/40 to ensure good reliability.

Gloster's senior test pilot, Crosby Warren, took us up to his office and explained on a single sheet of foolscap how the engine worked, roughly illustrating the layout. It sucked in large quantities of air through the intake at the front of the engine cowling, compressed it in a large centrifugal air compressor and from there was distributed to ten separate combustion chambers where, on the injection of paraffin fuel, it was ignited and the very hot gas was directed through a turbine giving enough power to drive the compressor. On leaving the turbine, the air was still compressed and so expanded rapidly out of the jet pipe at a greatly increased speed, being several times the volume of that required for combustion. Crosby Warren warned us that the take-off would be prolonged and the climb away, shallow. The aircraft had a tricycle undercarriage so it was possible to fly the aeroplane very easily off the smooth runway, having gained plenty of speed.

He described the starting procedure in some detail for it was possible to burn out the turbine with any coarse movement of the throttle. First the low-pressure cock was turned on to pressurise the fuel line to the engine, followed by the electric starting motor which cranked up the engine to give a good air flow through the engine and then, and not before, by opening the high-pressure cock, the spray of fuel would ignite, firing up the engine. With the electric motor still running, the rpm would be increased until the turbine/compressor was self-sustaining at which time the electricity could be turned off.

Sometimes the fuel failed to burn if it was not properly atomised in which case solid drops of burning fuel would be blown out of the jet pipe for 20 feet or so, quite an alarming sight. This was called a 'wet' start and the engine had to be shut down immediately. To simplify this procedure the sequence of the various switches was operated by a 'black box' and there were also protection devices to prevent the turbine exceeding the 17,000 rpm maximum and also if the jet pipe temperature exceeded the limit.

As a further precaution to avoid any sudden movement of the throttles and so cause a possible burn out through overheating, the turbine blades, the two controls, were mounted on two long slides. By twisting ones wrist in the lateral plane it was possible to use one knob as a pivoting point to move the other knob, thus avoiding any sudden opening of the throttle. The temperature response in a gas turbine is instantaneous, not delayed as in a conventional piston engine. The throttle (still called throttle) was really a spill valve to divert surplus fuel to the tank by releasing the fuel pressure to the burners and the engine fuel pump was of the gear type as no variable delivery pump was available at the time. The pump only had a life of five hours so was constantly being changed.

This explanation I found to be very interesting as, back in 1926 when an apprentice with Armstrong Siddeley, I had helped to build the first superchargers for the Jaguar radial engine for the Siskin, the first-line fighter for the Royal Air Force and in the Second World War, I had been with Vickers Supermarine during the introduction of the two-stage, two-speed intercooled Merlin and Griffon engines from Rolls-Royce.

At the time of my visit to Gloster's I must admit, as a pilot, that I did not like the low thrust of the new engine and I could not really understand how it would perform. Like other people, I thought in terms of horse power instead of thrust, thinking that the thrust came from the jet pushing on the air behind it! It was only later that someone told me that that had nothing to do with it but that it is all explained by Newton's law of 'action and reaction are equal and opposite', like the recoil of a gun when it fires a shell. Every ton of air that is passed through the engine is accelerated in the exhaust pipe to very great speed but of course as a continuous stream like a river, not by a series of explosions and blank periods as in a four-stroke piston engine. Sir Frank Whittle's invention was a tremendous advance as it simplified the whole concept of thrust for propelling an aeroplane without the complication of a petrol engine with pistons, connecting rods, crankshaft, reduction gears and a variable pitch propeller.

The object of our visit from Boscombe Down was to assess the handling qualities of the Gloster F9/40 and comment on its capabilities as a gun platform for a fighter, but not on its engines. Brunner went off first and I heard for the first time the whining sound of a jet aircraft in flight. When my turn came I was, in spite of the warning, quite surprised at the extremely long take-off but once at 5000 feet I found it an exceptionally easy aircraft to fly and fast in a shallow dive but at any speed above 250 miles an hour it developed a strange motion described by many as a 'snaking' path.

It yawed from side to side at an ever-greater rate as the speed of the aircraft increased so that it was yawing and rolling about 20°, at a rate which could not be countered by use of the rudder. The reflector sight could not be kept on a steady target and this made it unacceptable.

A series of modifications, including the elimination of friction in the rudder circuit, skinning the rudder with metal instead of fabric, reducing the fin area and thickening the trailing edge of the rudder, finally overcame the snaking. What had not been appreciated at the time of the Meteor's original design was the big gyroscopic damping effect a normal propeller has on directional stability as the usual parameters of fin and rudder area in relation to the wing did not apply to a jet aircraft. As an aircraft it was a delight to fly, the impression being that of a glider with power. The cockpit was quiet, roomy, pressurised and, since there was no engine in front, had good forward visibility. It was, with the WIIb, badly underpowered but as the first British fighter with a tricycle undercarriage, very easy to fly. With a jet, the aircraft has, of course, no slip-stream from a propeller and manoeuvrability on the ground becomes dependent on the differential brakes, or in the case of a twin-engined aircraft, by using the thrust of the one engine only. There are other major advantages to a tricycle landing gear as with the centre of gravity ahead of the main wheels, touching the ground, on landing the nose of the aircraft, tends to drop and the reduction of lift prevents a bounce or any tendency to swing off line followed by a dangerous uncontrolled swerve. These features reduce the requirement of skill by the pilot and consequently increase safety.

Another Meteor was delivered to Boscombe Down but this was fitted with two WIIb engines now at 1600 lbs thrust. This was followed shortly by the arrival of Geoffrey de Havilland with the E6/41 code name Spider Crab, later to be known as the Vampire with a single Halford lb or Goblin gas-turbine engine.

Part of our hangar was screened off and other pilots from our own flight were not even allowed in. Security guards maintained a 24-hour patrol while Brunner and I were forbidden to mention the aircraft in the mess.

The inhabitants of Amesbury must have been aware of these strange aircraft because they made a totally different noise and obviously had no propellers but even so we were very surprised when, one day within a couple of months, every newspapers' front page was plastered with the news of this new British invention. Apparently the explanation for this sudden disclosure was that the Americans, to whom we had sent a couple of gas-turbine engines for evaluation, were just about to announce their existence so Churchill pre-empted them by giving his consent to have the news released in the UK first.

The Vampire had considerably better performance than the early Meteor and was comparable with contemporary fighters, largely due to the Halford engine which gave the aircraft a high thrust-to-weight ratio. The combustion chambers pointed aft and converged on the turbine whereas the Whittle combustion chambers reversed the air-flow, thereby losing a lot of energy in the process. These early gas-turbines were mechanically quite reliable, thanks largely to the simple centrifugal compressors and low compression. Our main worry centred around fuel-pumps which were of the gear type and had to be overhauled every five hours, the more sophisticated variable-output pumps coming as a later development.

The other weakness was a tendency to get a 'wet' start. On the twin-engined Meteor this did not matter much as the tail was well clear but the Vampire with its single engine, had twin booms carrying the rudders and the raised tailplane was only just out of the line of fire. When sitting in the pilot's seat and starting up a Vampire, the only indication of a 'wet' start was a look of horror on the faces of bystanders as orange flames at least 20 feet long shot out.

Soon after his first flight in the Vampire, Brunner had a wet start and shut off the high-pressure cock immediately but when he had restarted and taxied out to take-off we noticed a wisp of smoke coming from the rear cone of the fuselage. Having no radio to warn him we rushed out onto the aerodrome with Verey pistols shooting off any cartridges which came to hand. Fortunately he saw them and landed immediately, rather irritated at being brought back until he could see that the bottom of the fuselage had already been partly burned away and was still burning. Obviously liquid paraffin had collected behind the ribs of the engine nacelle (streamlined engine cowling) and had been set alight by the heat of the jet pipe. Following this experience we always tipped the aircraft back on its tricycle undercarriage to drain any surplus fuel away after a wet start.

De Havilland urgently wanted the aircraft back so our early trials were limited to measuring speed and climb. A performance climb to altitude was normally preceded by partial climbs at varying speeds and altitudes to obtain the best climbing speed but I was sent off to use my own judgement as to the best speed. The early jet engines had a fail safe overspeed governor which cut-off the fuel above the maximum rpm and another safety cut out device, activated by the jet pipe temperature, protected the turbine blades against excessive temperature. There was, however, no automatic control to maintain a constant rpm for a fixed throttle setting and the pilot constantly had to close the throttle as altitude was gained because the rpm increased as the air became less dense. To my surprise at high altitude the position of the throttle was only about one-third open and on throttling back the fire would sometimes go out. I was told that this was due to the burners not spraying the limited quantity of fuel passing but that they merely dribbled. Whatever it was, the maintenance at high altitude of any steady rpm was most difficult, requiring constant attention.

I set off from Boscombe one evening in April in a northwesterly direction, the sun already low in the west shining on the waters of the Bristol Channel with the outline of both the Welsh and North Devon coastlines showing clearly, providing a good navigational fix. The Vampire seemed uncannily smooth and quiet and I flew on and on in the rather dreamlike world, concentrating on recording what I hoped were some good figures and getting as high as possible. The climb above 35,000 feet was very flat but by keeping a good forward speed the engine, which had been running out of breath by then, seemed to take on new life and finally 40,000 feet came up. It was time to turn for home which was back down there somewhere in the murk while I cruised along in my own world in a strange way enjoying the sun and crystal clear atmosphere. Riding the quiet, ripple free air in an aircraft whose engine was so smooth that the only indication of its turning was the rev counter, was a new experience for me and very thrilling. I realised at that moment that the advent of this new invention would be by far the greatest advance in aviation during my lifetime.

The return to Boscombe was only a question of pointing in the right direction helped by the Bristol Channel and 30,000 odd feet of altitude but I was short of fuel and it was important to hit the right spot and not have to search around in the dusk because a jet engine uses a lot of fuel low down. All was well and the de Havilland engineers were glad to see their baby safely back after such a relatively long flight. Three weeks later, after the completion of the preliminary trials, I flew the aircraft back to Hatfield.

In June 1944 the first production line Meteor arrived at Boscombe Down. The main difference from the prototype was the installation of Rolls-Royce B37 engines. This engine had more thrust than the WIIb and the combustion chambers converged on the turbine like those of the Halford engine in the Vampire, thus improving the internal air-flow. One of the new engines gave trouble after a few hours due to a bearing failure.

The early gas-turbines had ball-bearings throughout and these were lubricated on a 'total loss' system rather similar to early motor-cars with drip feed! Our new engines had a plain white metal bearing between the compressor and the turbine with a full oil circulation system which presumably was intended to dissipate some of the internal heat, but instead the heat melted the white metal of the bearing. This fault was soon rectified but even the best engineers made mistakes sometimes! Eventually this basic engine used as a gas generator to drive a turbo-prop and known as the Dart, powered most of the early gas turbine-driven civil airliners, achieving a life of 5000 hours between overhauls – a very big step forward.

Apart from the 'snaking' troubles, the Meteor as an aircraft was very free of vices and, although not a great fighter, it was an excellent introduction for the Royal Air Force to this new form of propulsion. As the first gas-turbine aircraft to undergo full performance and handling trials at the A & AEE, the Meteor required new methods of measurement and techniques. Performance was more affected by the aircraft's weight and the ambient air temperature compared with a conventional piston-engined aircraft. On measuring speeds, for instance, instead of flying at 2000 feet intervals at decreasing altitudes, the exact reverse was adopted. With the heavy fuel consumption this practice compensated in some measure for the decrease in weight due to the consumption of fuel. We were aware of the effects of high ground temperature on the take-off performance of the new jets but with only a grass aerodrome at Boscombe Down (a new runway was being built at that time) the increased resistance of grass over smooth concrete and, of course, in the normal UK temperate climate, we were unable to measure the effect on take off performance in high temperatures. These trials were not carried out until after the war in Europe was over as it meant taking special equipment to Khartoum.

One of the troubles encountered with gas-turbines was a phenomenon known as 'surge'. The symptom occurred particularly when climbing at full power and consisted of a series of thuds or hesitations in the engine, very similar in feel to driving a car when the engine is cold and spits back into the carburettor. On throttling back a little it would stop but the cause was not fully understood and was believed to be a stall in the compressor. No failures ever occurred on this account but even a momentary hesitation in the main air flow through the combustion chambers was enough to enrich the fuel-to-air mixture and raise the temperature of the blades of the turbine. Jet pipe temperatures respond instantly to the fuel flow as opposed to the relatively slow rises in the oil and water temperature of a piston engine.

On the introduction of jet-propelled aircraft, with their characteristic whine, it was interesting to note how quickly a new language or jargon came into use. Instead of 'start up' the new phrase became 'light up' or 'fire up'. 'Did you have a good flight?' became 'Did you have a good squirt?' or alternatively, 'Did you enjoy a bit of curving?' Perhaps one reason for these new descriptions of flying a jet aircraft was that the usual practice of making a circuit of the aerodrome before landing was made at a much higher speed. In losing height, the aircraft, which had no air brakes, gained a lot of speed and, in addition, there was a considerable residual thrust from the engine even with the throttle fully closed so that, in order to check on whether other aircraft were circling to land, it was best to enter the circuit below 1000 feet, use a lot of G in the turns and ultimately pull up to lose more momentum and speed before lowering the undercarriage. To be baulked on the approach to land was quite a serious matter as opening up and going round again might easily take 25 gallons, a margin which was not always available.

Another characteristic which I noticed was the much greater height required to recover from a loop. On going over the top at what would normally be a reasonable speed, the aircraft would gain speed from the inverted position very rapidly indeed making the pull out prolonged. The residual thrust when throttled back, together with the lack of resistance of a propeller, were obviously the cause but it was disconcerting to the pilot and later resulted in some fatal crashes before it was realised what was happening.

Geoffrey de Havilland used to give a spectacular demonstration of the Vampire using a special technique of his own. On take-off he would go into an extremely low turn maintaining full throttle while circling the aerodrome and so build up to a high speed before using the momentum to make a vertical climb to about 5000 feet. To a pilot, high speed at ground level or plenty of altitude is like money in the bank, a comfortable feeling.

After the war we learned that the Germans had also secretly been flying a jet aircraft at about the same time as our E28/39 but they had favoured a multi-stage axial compressor. We knew that an axial was more efficient but deliberately avoided them because we knew they sometimes surged badly and we already had a great deal of experience with the centrifugal superchargers as used on the Merlin and Griffon engines.

The Halford HIb had the combustion chambers straight through to converge on the turbine thus avoiding the reversal of flow in the Whittle engine, but all later designs of Rolls-Royce incorporated this feature. I remembered Major Halford from years before the war when he had successfully raced his own design of car at Brooklands, the engine of which ran at exceptionally high rpm.

CHAPTER 26

A Love of Engines

E arly in June 1944 it had become evident that something was about to happen. The traffic through our local village of Amesbury built up to a crescendo of grinding and creaking tanks, all moving west by day and by night, making walking along our narrow pavements highly dangerous. Even the air became crowded. There happened to be heavy overcast skies with a base at about 1500 feet forcing all the air traffic into a narrow band. Many squadrons, spread out in ragged formation, were criss-crossing Salisbury Plain, their leaders map-reading to try to find strange airfields. Every type of combat aircraft seemed to be airborne and on the move.

After news of the invasion of Normandy and the difficulties of landing supplies on the exposed beachheads, the armies seemed to get bogged down as the Germans brought up their powerful mobile reserves. It was with relief that we heard of the American breakout and sweeping movement round to the south and east.

The RP-equipped Typhoons then came into their own. The German Panzer's escape route through the Falaise gap, flanked by the British to the north and the Americans to the south, turned into an enormous traffic jam of tanks, head to tail, over miles of typical French *routes nationales*, that is to say, dead straight roads. A more perfect target for the new rockets would be hard to imagine – with enfilading fire, if the rocket missed one tank, it clobbered the next in line. Furthermore, the armour of tanks was designed for deflecting a horizontal attack, not one coming at 30° from above, with the result that the rocket heads went clean through like a hot knife through butter. According to eye witnesses, the shambling, bloody chaos had to be seen to be believed. With the teeth of their army knocked out, enemy resistance crumbled, allowing the allied armies to make a wild dash forward to Paris and as far as the Rhine, by-passing the Germans bottled up in the Channel ports where they had expected the invasion to be. Those rocket Typhoons were surely the right weapons at the right place at the right time.

Ever since I was a child, I have had a great love of engines, starting with the working model steamboat and then from aged fourteen onwards, a series of motorbikes. My first was a 1914 model Royal Enfield followed by an AJS (A J Stephens won the TT race in the Isle of Man for three consecutive years) and a Red Indian which was an American design with a V twin engine and belt drive but with no gears, just a clutch. Starting was by pushing and jumping on then a very advanced design called an ABC with two cylinders horizontally opposed across the frame with a combined crankcase and gearbox. It was years in advance of its time but never properly developed. I believe it was designed after the First World War by an aircraft company struggling to find a market for a civil project. These and many others were all a source of interest to me by taking them apart and tuning them.

While learning to fly at Brooklands in 1928 I saw many of the racing cars of the day being prepared by Thomson & Taylor – Delage, Talbot, Sunbeam, Bugatti and the supercharged Alfa Romeo. Later I found the big aero engines even more exciting, the air-cooled Jaguar, American engines like the Pratt & Whitney Wasp and the Wright Whirlwind. These were followed by the Rolls-Royce Merlin and Griffon which were wonderful pieces of engineering, built to technical perfection regardless of cost. Other engines such as the Bristol sleeve-valve family and the Napier Sabre had their admirers but for me the gradual development of more and more power was always of intense interest.

An engine is one of the few material objects which becomes 'alive'. To fly a single-seater de Havilland Hornet with 4600 horsepower was to experience this eager animal, power, to the 'nth' degree. The gentlest pressure of the palm of your hand was all that was required to release a burst of noise, a surge of thrust, a whole explosion of activity propelling you onwards and upwards into the sky. The jockey on a racehorse must experience the same sort of sensation at the start of a race. The thrill it gives a human being is not to be despised even if, as in my case, it is given by an engine.

I always enjoy seeing the engine of any ship in which I travel be it paddle steamer or trans-Atlantic liner. The robust and ornate construction of some of the machinery of the Victorian engineers is greatly to be admired as are the massive cylinders, crankshaft and turbo-chargers of the modern big ship diesels. All these engines give me a thrill when seen in action or even when stationary. An engine is to an engineer what a sculpture is to an artist – every line, every curve and every shaft is suitably proportioned to take the load to which it is subjected; the good designer moulds the many functions into a three-dimensional whole.

My job, as described earlier, was to investigate the flying characteristics of the Meteor and had nothing to do with the engines although, with my early background of engineering training and love of engines, I found it fascinating and rather hogged the hours enjoying every minute of it. Every single operation on these new engines, whether starting up, taxiing, climbing or measuring speed, required a different technique and, still being in the experimental stage, at least sympathetic handling and a watchful eye.

For me the change from piston engines to gas turbines was a transformation. Almost for the first time in my life I felt relatively safe flying. I shall always feel eternally grateful to whoever it was that sent me to fly those first jets and the more I thought about the future course of aviation, the more convinced I became that it lay in the application of the gas-turbine. The conventional piston engine had more or less reached its limit of power and size of cylinder and suddenly we were presented with the answer; it was unbelievable and made civil aviation on the grand scale possible.

New engines were produced exceptionally quickly by many designers. The Nene came from Rolls-Royce giving 5000 lbs of thrust, having been produced in seven months – an incredibly short time. This was followed later by the Bristol Engine Company's mighty Olympus, a big two spool, 10,000 lb engine with axial compressors in tandem, giving far greater efficiency and fuel consumption for civil airliners. It was eventually to engine our supersonic Concorde and warships, not to mention its use as a generator to some of our main suppliers of electrical power fuelled by our surplus gas from the North Sea oil fields.

We have many outstanding engineers in this country but the concept and design of an entirely new engine for jet propulsion required a technical understanding of thermo-dynamics, fluid dynamics and gas combustion not available in text books and it was thanks to the mathematical brains of Sir Frank Whittle and later Sir Stanley Hooker that brought the whole engine to a successful conclusion. Needless to say there were many frustrations and difficulties, both financial and practical, to be overcome, not to mention a highly sceptical political atmosphere, before success was achieved and everyone tried to jump on the bandwagon.

Many years later when I became an outside director of Royal Doulton and Co. Ltd, the big ceramic manufacturers, I learned that Bristol Engines and later Rolls-Royce were trying to produce a ceramic core for making hollow gas-turbine blades. The object was to raise the engine compression ratio in order to improve the thermal efficiency but this meant higher turbine blade temperatures which would not stand the heat, hence the proposal of hollow blades passing cooling air. After much development work on the ceramic material, Doulton Research Company produced a core around which the mould of the blade was mounted.

It had to withstand the heat shock of molten steel at $1700°$ C without cracking or warping and when the turbine blade became frozen, to be extracted leaving a hollow core. This was done by leaching the ceramic core with acid under supersonic vibration until not a grain was left behind. This permitted a very considerable increase in power to be extracted from the turbine which in turn gave Concorde the endurance to be able to fly non-stop from Heathrow to Washington with a full load of passengers and meet all the requirements for reserves of fuel.

This and other developments for aviation were carried out by Mr Norris, the Head of Research for Doulton, at their Chertsey Basil Green Laboratory. Again the costs, frustration and lack of orders nearly led to the removal of cores from the Directors' Agenda. Afterwards the Chairman was one of the first to take a supersonic flight to New York, the main US Headquarters of Royal Doulton.

Nevertheless, the fact that even the Meteor was an unknown quantity was brought home to me in an abrupt and very unpleasant fashion. One morning Squadron Leader Majergik, a Polish officer, took off to carry out the first spins but he did not appear for lunch in the mess and later in the day we heard that an eyewitness had seen the Meteor spin into the ground. It was, to my knowledge, the first time a jet had been spun and it caused much concern. It was presumed that there had been insufficient response from the rudder as it had not been appreciated that the lack of slipstream from a propeller in a jet might prove disastrous in spin recovery. Majergik's wife who had been left behind in Poland, had spent the whole war in the Austwich concentration camp but had somehow survived until she was released by the advancing allies in 1945. She had only been reunited with her husband a week before this terrible accident occurred making it even more tragic. It was an unbelievably cruel blow to her.

It took me many years to learn how conservative and slow people are in accepting any invention or new idea. I had seen how slow the Admiralty was in adopting the then highly secret airborne radar in 1940 and the Air Ministry's resistance to monoplanes, variable-pitch propellers and retractable undercarriages in the 1930s – and so it was with the jet engine. To my surprise very few of the fighter pilots or squadron commanders who flew these aircraft liked the early Meteors as their fighting methods were not suited to these new jet engines. The jet has little thrust at low speed compared with a propeller and mixing it in a dog-fight showed the jet at its worst. There was little acceptance of the fact that this was something different, the first effort in a new field. Sir Charles Parsons had found the same with his steam-turbine-powered 'Turbinia' years before.

Geoffrey de Havilland produced another interesting aircraft in the spring of 1945 – the twin-engined Hornet. It had two of the latest versions of the Merlin 66 which, using 150-grade fuel, were boosted to 25 lbs per square inch manifold pressure. The wing area was just adequate but was increased for landing by large extending flaps and also helped by the slipstream from two large diameter four-bladed propellers. The two propellers rotated in opposite direction to counter torque which led to some longitudinal instability until the respective directions of rotation were reversed when, with the change in the slipstream over the tail, the trouble disappeared. With 4600 horsepower, the performance was staggering and it had the handling qualities to match. With the war in Europe drawing to a close, the Hornet was being considered for the Fleet Air Arm for operation in the Pacific. When it first came to us the hook for deck-landing had already been fitted.

On arrival at Boscombe Down for a brief preliminary assessment, Geoffrey brought the prototype over. He explained that the aircraft had a thermostat in the coolant system which operated a ram to the rear, variable area, exit flap from the radiator duct so that the volume of air was controlled, maintaining the water at an optimum temperature, also reducing cooling drag to a minimum. He also warned us that lowering the wing flaps gave a big nose down change of trim and that full flap could not be used. He had stuck a piece of white tape on the flap position indicator and marked with a pen the maximum to be used.

Brunner flew the aircraft first and I took over while the engines were kept running. I noticed that the water temperature of the starboard engine was over 100° so I hurried to take off and get a good airflow through the underwing radiators. On crossing the boundary of the aerodrome I saw what appeared to be grey smoke pouring from the front of the bank of exhaust pipes on my side of the starboard engine. I thought it was about to burst into flames and throttled the engine back while still climbing away in a left hand turn on the port engine intending to land as soon as I was downwind of the aerodrome. Not being familiar with the layout of the cockpit and in a great hurry to get down, I could not see the fire button immediately and did not feather the propeller as the engine was still idling and it could have been of use in the approach to land. Having lined up for the landing I dropped the undercarriage and selected flaps down forgetting about the limit on flap angle. The flaps went down all right but so did the nose. In fact, to hold any sort of reasonable approach angle of descent, took most of the nose up travel of the elevator but, worse still, reducing power made the approach angle even steeper. Eventually I managed to fly parallel with the ground and by throttling back on the good engine and easing the stick forward, touched the ground at about 130 miles an hour. The fuselage felt as if it was about horizontal, if anything nose down, but the flaps were creating a big ground effect.

The wind was from the northeast and the ground fortunately sloped slightly uphill so gradually the speed fell off and the tail dropped down out of my control. Immediately, the aircraft leapt into the air about six feet and landed on three points with a bump. By now I had about reached the perimeter road coming finally to rest on some rough ground near the outer fence and it was only then that I realised that it was steam and not smoke pouring from the engine!

Subsequent investigation showed that the 'inching' device on the radiator flap had an electrical fault, the effect of which was to close the outlet completely so that no cooling air could pass. The operation of vital controls by an electronic system had been unheard of up to that time and a fail safe system or stop had not been incorporated in the design. All the rest was entirely my own fault and it taught me a number of lessons; I was just glad not to have wrecked the aircraft, an extremely valuable prototype. The combination of circumstances was never likely to occur again but the introduction of overriding electronic controls has not, even now, been made as fully reliable as a human brain as is shown by the accidents to the 'fly by wire' of the Airbus.

As the intention was to operate the Hornet from aircraft-carriers, Lieutenant-Commander Brown, a very experienced test pilot from the Royal Aircraft Establishment, Farnborough, and I were sent to Hatfield, de Havilland's private aerodrome, to assess it for deck-landing qualities. The two big propellers sweeping their slipstream over the wing gave the necessary control over the lift at low speed and my only criticism was of the throttles. They were fitted with large, clumsy knobs and the mechanism had a lot of friction and backlash. Considering the importance for deck landing of delicate control near the stall and the rapid response from the fuel-injected engines, there was room for improvement. In the event, 'Winkle' Brown did the actual deck land trials on HMS *Ocean* at the same time as I was doing them with the Sea Fury.

The 150 grade fuel used in the Merlins of the Hornet was something special. Even before the Schneider Trophy days a great deal of research and development had been carried out in this field. Although the Merlin had not changed in its basic design, being 27 litres capacity, the power was increased from about 1000 to 2340 horsepower and yet the maximum rpm of 3000 was never altered. Rolls-Royce worked in collaboration with the fuel specialists and so was able constantly to increase the supercharge or boost pressure and obtain the power without increasing the piston speed, a wonderful achievement by both engine manufacturer and fuel chemists.

The problem of the so-called 'sound barrier' began to be of some importance towards the end of the war. The Royal Aircraft Establishment, Farnborough had been investigating this for some time but the A & AEE was also interested. A pilot at RAE was reputed to have reached a Mach number of .9, or 90% of the speed of sound in a specially cleaned up version of a PR (Photographic Reconnaissance) Spitfire which carried no guns and whose wings had no bulges or other excrescences to upset the airflow. Although the tips of the propeller are, of course, moving supersonically or at a much higher speed in relation to the air than the main body of the aircraft, they produce virtually no thrust travelling at Mach .9. We were advised to use full engine rpm, however, as the ejector-type exhausts give considerable thrust at high engine speed, particular at high altitude, in fact, a minor form of jet propulsion.

Flying our Welkin and a Spitfire Mk XXI, we started an investigation into compressibility with a series of high dives at increasing speeds. The Welkin was almost in trouble in level flight at 40,000 feet but the Spitfire could be dived at very steep angles without showing signs of loss of control.

The procedure was to reach maximum speed at 40,000 feet in level flight and then dive at an angle of 30° until a terminal speed was reached. Gradually the angle was increased to about 80° which feels very steep but I lacked the courage to invert the aircraft and dive vertically. The highest speed I recorded was Mach 8. One thing which I did notice was that buffeting occurred in the pull out under G and the higher the speed, the lower the figure of G which could be pulled before buffeting occurred. By plotting the figure of G against speed it was fairly clear at what speed the buffeting or onset of compressibility would occur in steady flight, ie. 1G. One of the biggest mistakes made by our technical authorities was not to pursue these investigations post-war. Instead of continuing with manned flight experiments, presumably because it was thought to be too dangerous, it was decided to use models. The jet engine was making rapid development in terms of the thrust available so that those compressibility trials could have been made in level flight. Clearly, if one could have achieved supersonic speed in a climb, as later became possible, any breakdown in control would have solved itself by the immediate loss of speed and resumption of subsonic flight on closing the throttle.

The relatively poor take-off characteristics of jet-propelled aircraft was an area which could not be properly investigated at Boscombe Down as no concrete runway was yet in use although one was being built. Our Commanding Officer, Air-Commodore Boothman, made a case for an extension of the A & AEE technical facilities by arranging for tests to be carried out in a hot climate. Whereas a propeller-driven aircraft can be pulled off the ground and into the air with insufficient flying speed, this is not so with a jet-propelled one. The drag of a wing at a big angle of incidence may exceed the thrust of the jet and the aircraft will then lose flying speed and perhaps never take off. This tendency is increased in hot weather when the engine thrust is decreased and the wing lift lowered so that a higher forward speed is required to lift off.

We set off on 16 April 1945, in a Liberator, for Khartoum which is supposed to be one of the hottest places on earth. With due respect to my Commanding Officer, I think his experience of four-engined bombers was little more than mine which was practically nil. After a nine-hour flight we landed at Castel Benito, Tripoli and the following day flew to Cairo West where we were delayed overnight by engine trouble. Disembarking at Khartoum, the temperature was 110° F and with the wind blowing through the hot engine nacelles, it was so hot that I instinctively put an arm up to shield my face from the searing heat. Having no previous experience and no-one to turn to for advice, my own problem was deciding what a naval officer should wear in the tropics, 1000 miles from the sea. I could not bring myself to wear white shorts so I compromised on some light khaki trousers, a white shirt with epaulettes and my naval cap with a white cover. I doubt if their Lordships would have approved even if they had known where I was.

An unusual feature of the Liberator was the flexibility of the big span wings. From the cockpit the wing-tips were out of sight when taxiing but in flight they appeared to be at least a couple of feet above the engine cowlings. Having completed the arrangements for tropical trials to be undertaken there, we set out for home.

We landed at Cairo West again for petrol but were delayed a day while a magneto was changed. At least it gave me a chance to visit Mena House, the Pyramids and to buy my daughter, Jane, a toy leather camel and a bunch of bananas, the latter being a rare sight during the war years. Jane, however, was not impressed by this great wartime treat, and spat her first bite out in disgust. We landed at Luqa in Malta the next evening but although we touched down in good time and were immediately busy with the brakes, backed up with full auxiliary brake power – I thought the runway was very short for a Liberator.

On the way to England we passed over the Channel Islands which were still occupied by the Germans although the allied armies had already advanced almost to the Rhine. In spite of all the freedom of flying and of landing wherever we chose outside the UK we still had to clear customs at Lyneham before returning to Boscombe.

Back at Boscombe Down the pressure to get results was easing off as the war in Europe was clearly drawing to a close. We became engaged on odd jobs such as the dropping of 'window'. This was the secret weapon consisting of stranded metal foil intended to confuse the enemy radar by causing an almost unlimited number of 'blips' on the screen. By releasing the 'window' in a kind of paper chase the enemy could sometimes be misled into believing an alternative target to the true one was about to be attacked. For other trials we fitted fighters with containers carrying 900 lb of incendiaries, which had previously always been dropped at night by the heavy bombers; other alternatives were extra external fuel tanks of every description, slipper, streamline, underwing, all intended to give longer range and to be dropped before combat. In this connection I did many measurements of longitudinal stability in a Spitfire, taking the centre of gravity well aft of the acceptable range approved by Supermarine. It was intended to extend the range by adding extra internal fuel tanks so that the aircraft could be used for long distance day bombing escort purposes.

The delicate balance between accepting an unstable aircraft for a limited purpose, against the peace of mind of the pilot in having fully adequate fuel to return to base, was a matter of opinion and very difficult to assess. It could be perfectly safe at take-off when flown by an experienced pilot in good flying weather but for an inexperienced pilot on a misty autumn day with a low sun, it was an entirely different matter as it was highly dangerous to fly such an unstable aircraft on instruments.

On flying back from Farnborough one day in a Tempest Mk II, which had a Centaurus with fuel injection, the engine suddenly cut out at about 500 feet. However, on throttling back it picked up again and continued to run so long as the throttle was not opened beyond about one third which gave just enough power to maintain height. It seemed a long drag back to Boscombe watching out for each possible landing field, rather like a game of musical chairs but fortunately it kept going and I was able to go straight in to a landing. Fuel injection was just being introduced on the latest engines, the mixture being controlled by a black box or computer which measured the engine rpm, the manifold pressure and temperature and metered the correct amount of fuel. In the past all the vital functions of flight had been mechanically controlled by the pilot but the introduction of electronics seemed to have introduced a new element of risk; I was particularly conscious of this after the recent near shave with the Hornet in which one engine overheated. Both of these incidents shook my confidence even more than total engine failure as they gave no prior warning or feedback of information.

Every new type or even variation of an existing type of aircraft that came to Boscombe was photographed for recognition purposes by the Observer Corps. Most people like to have their photograph taken and as the aircraft was invariably another new type to be added to our log book these sorties were much sought after. The rear gunner's turret had been removed from a Handley Page Hampden bomber in order to give the photographer a good all round view to take the standard set of pictures of astern, quarter, abreast, ahead on the quarter, taken from above, level and from below. If possible these were taken just above the clouds so that the reflected light shone on the lower surfaces and gave a good silhouette.

At the time this routine exercise seemed of very minor importance as the Observer Corp was manned by a devoted band of older men who were well able to recognise British aircraft at a glance, but the official historical record may have been of considerable interest to later generations. Sadly, many of these historic photographs were destroyed while stored in a basement which flooded at Boscombe Down after the war.

My previous association with Supermarines meant that the arrival of their new Spiteful was of great interest to me. Carrying on their policy of only making one alteration at a time, the prototype Spiteful had a new laminar-flow, low-drag wing but retained the Spitfire fuselage. The wing section was built to an accuracy of five thousandths of an inch and was very free of any roughness, such as rivet heads, to give it the desired airflow characteristics; even dust was supposed to degrade its performance. For the same power the top speed increased by about 30 mph over the equivalent Spitfire but so also did the landing speed. Later the same wing was incorporated in another fuselage fitted with a Rolls-Royce Nene gas-turbine; this was in use by the Royal Navy for many years and was called the Attacker.

In early June 1945 I received an envelope from Buckingham Palace which, to my surprise, contained a request to attend a reception at Buckingham Palace on 4 July to receive the Air Force Cross which I had been awarded. It was a great honour and naturally I was delighted, especially as the Royal Navy has no award for flying, the DSC being for sea-going officers only and therefore not appropriate – but I had been under the control of the Royal Air Force as a test pilot of both naval and RAF aircraft for a period of over two and a half years and at 37 years of age had become one of their longest serving active test pilots. On 2 July 1945 I flew up to Heston and left my Firefly there before joining Ella and my father who had also been invited. I, of course, wore naval uniform and King George VI asked me how I had obtained a Royal Air Force award! There was still work to be done at Boscombe, however, so I flew back there the next day after a night of celebration.

CHAPTER 27

Last Days at Boscombe

At Boscombe Down we were fortunately spared visits from VIPs as nearly everything there was top secret, but after the Germans had been driven back out of France in the summer of 1945, we did welcome a party of senior officers from the French Air Force and later from the Russian Air Force, none of whom had seen a jet aircraft. The latter were treated to a fine display of aerobatics by Zurakowski in a Spitfire but to his embarrassment, in making a show of its low speed manoeuvrability, he then landed a few yards in front of the party and knocked the tail wheel off.

General Smuts, our old enemy of the Boer War but now highly respected, and of course our ally, was given a great reception, and for the first time in the two and a half years I had been at Boscombe Down, everyone turned out on parade. The General was a great believer in an independent air force and the effectiveness of the strategic heavy bomber. He was obviously surprised to see a naval officer on a Royal Air Force station as he stopped on seeing Torrens-Spence and asked him questions. He could not have chosen a better man to state the Fleet Air Arm's case.

One visitor to Boscombe Down whom I came to know was MacLaren, employed by Dowty Rotol on retractable undercarriage design. He had invented a kind of swivelling undercarriage which allowed an aircraft with the usual three-point undercarriage to land with drift on. The object was to avoid building expensive runways by making use of a single strip only and landing in a cross wind with drift on, something normally to be avoided as the aircraft will tend to swerve off the runway or possibly damage the undercarriage. This idea was not adopted, but years later the US Air Force used the same principle on the tricycle multi-wheeled landing gear of their very big Globemaster. On a heavy freight-carrying aircraft in a cross wind, the wheels must be aligned with the flight path as, on touching down, the tyres and gear would not stand the side load.

As a different but good example of the spin off from aviation technology, Maclaren's knowledge was applied to children's pushchairs. His pushchairs are very light, fold up simply without trapping fingers, and look like a two handled walking stick which can easily be carried onto a bus. Even the paired wheels are designed like aircraft tail wheels to eliminate shimmy.

Another interesting visitor was Geoffrey Tyson, Chief Test Pilot of Shorts, builder of the highly successful Sunderland flying boat. In his younger days he had been a great aerobatic pilot and used to tour the country with Cobham's Flying Circus, giving demonstrations of inverted flying at no height just to liven up the crowd. He was a very keen character who took his test flying very seriously. He borrowed several aircraft from us and on each occasion came back with his pad covered with figures and notes. In one single flight he would have taken the measure of its performance and handling qualities, a useful independent report to supplement our own assessment.

George Bulman, the highly respected Chief Test Pilot of Hawkers up to the launch and production of the Hurricane (on his retirement he was superseded by Philip Lucas) was the doyen of the test pilots' world and represented their interests at the highest level. He had been responsible for the development and handling qualities of the much loved family of pre-war biplanes of which the Fury was the last of the line. By the middle of the war when I first met Philip Lucas, he had picked up the torch, carrying on the tradition of Hawkers for building great fighters. The latest, the new Fury (and Sea Fury) was a real pilot's aeroplane and the last to be powered by a piston engine. By then other test pilots were taking over including Bill Humble and Richard Muspratt from 'A' per T.

Bill, always immaculately turned out, would step into a Tempest or a Fury and give a demonstration which really shook those watching, squeezing every ounce of performance out of the aircraft and showing off its manoeuvrability to the spectacular limit. Taxiing in afterwards and throwing back the hood he would emerge smiling without a hair out of place!

On the entry of the United States into the war, any qualified American test pilot was given official clearance to fly any of our aircraft and some of them made the most of the opportunity. I remember particularly one who used to like doing aerobatics in the Typhoon, hurtling it round the sky. He thought it was terrific but I thought it was he and not the aeroplane that was impressive as it was no boy's toy and not everyone's choice, weighing as it did about as much as a double decker bus.

On 1 June 1945 a new division was formed at the Aeroplane and Armament Experimental Establishment, 'C' Squadron. This was the first naval test squadron and became responsible for the testing of naval aircraft only. For administrative purposes it came under HMS *Daedalus* at Lee-on-Solent but was subject to the discipline of the Royal Air Force at Boscombe Down, our hosts. By this time I had had nearly three years test-flying experience but I lacked experience in naval administration or discipline. In spite of this, however, I was appointed to command the new squadron with the acting rank of Commander (A) RNVR. We were allotted some wooden huts near the officers' mess as our headquarters and dispersed our aircraft on the slope below the control tower. This was very convenient but it was, at times, very noisy. Just below our site there was a firing range for testing guns and beyond that, in a slight dip, was an open-air wind tunnel which had been used for investigating the behaviour of jettisoned hoods, tanks and other external stores.

In their advance across northern France, the army had captured some V-l sites and these included some serviceable flying bombs. One at least found its way to Boscombe Down and was set up near us in the blast from the wind tunnel where measurements of the engine thrust, consumption and other data were collected. There was considerable excitement when the engine started for the first time but interest quickly died away due to the noise generated. It was unbelievable and literally shook your whole body. The people living in London took a different view of this noise as they just prayed that the engines would keep going until it had passed over their own heads before cutting out at which time the bomb would drop. The engine's operating cycle was based on resonance and depended on a large number of light metal flaps which acted as a form of inlet valve in a very similar manner to the inlet valve of some outboard motors. Fortunately, the trials only lasted a couple of months after which we in 'C' Squadron were able to settle down to a relatively peaceful routine.

Shortly after Paris was relieved by the US Army, Group-Captain Wroath, my old flight commander but now returned to A & AEE as Officer Commanding Flying Wing, was asked to pick up a Fieseler Storch from Paris. I flew him over to Le Bourget together with an engineering officer in a Stinson Reliant, a six-seater American civilian aircraft which somehow had come our way. The Storch was not at Le Bourget as we had expected but at a very small grass aerodrome near the centre of Paris. It was too small for a Stinson Reliant to land in so we spent the night in the city. Apparently the Storch had been built by the French and assembled at this aerodrome where the Germans had realised it would be safe from Allied bombers. Because of its very short take-off and landing characteristics, the Storch was an excellent aircraft and very easy to fly but our own Auster fulfilled much the same role at a fraction of the cost.

Returning to England we flew in company following the twisting course of the Seine to Le Havre where we had to land for fuel. Camped out round the aerodrome were hundreds of German prisoners most of whom looked very young to me, only about sixteen to eighteen. They were being guarded by French Colonial troops who did not look the types with whom to argue, their guns at the ready and fingers on the trigger. Even our little party were rather nervous as, of course, one of our aircraft was German! I fear our combined effort to explain ourselves in French was not very convincing and it was a relief to depart for home without incident.

In the early days after the war there was, of course, no civilian authority in control of aviation, one simply took off to fly wherever one wished. At Boscombe Down practically all of the experimental aircraft had no radio although some of the larger military aircraft had radio with RAF frequencies. On the two flights I made to Paris and to Khartoum we just arrived and landed, no permission, papers, customs or passports, just my uniform. The enemy had been conquered and we were the victors; it was a strange feeling of freedom but it was not to last long. The RAF made all aircraft from overseas land at Lyneham for clearance when it was realised that aircraft were being used for all sorts of illicit purposes.

In the early autumn of 1945 Vice Admiral Boyd, KCB, CBE, DSC, the head of the Fleet Air Arm, decided to come over to Boscombe Down on an official visit of inspection of the naval Test 'C' Squadron of which I had been in command for three months and which had settled down well on what was basically a Royal Air Force station. Admiral Boyd, although not a pilot himself, was known and held in very high esteem by all the Armed Services as the victor over the Italian fleet. He had commanded HMS *Illustrious* and planned the night attack on the Italians at Taranto harbour and also defeated the remainder of their fleet at Matapan.

The Taranto operations were carried out by Swordfish with torpedoes and virtually eliminated the Italian fleet in the Mediterranean. The night attack was brilliantly executed with three aircraft dropping flares to the south of the anchored fleet while the main force approached low down from the north. The attack came as a complete surprise to the enemy who fired wildly at the flare-dropping aircraft while the main attack met little resistance, finding the ships to be clearly silhouetted against the light.

Wartime parades and inspections were not exactly up to the Guards standard but we put on the best show we could and gave the Admiral lunch when he also met all the senior boffins from the Technical Office. He had planned to return to his headquarters at Lee-on-Solent in his official car in the afternoon but when I suggested that he should fly back in a two-seater Meteor he jumped at the idea; jet aircraft were very rare in 1945 and there was only one which had a passenger seat. For certain trials an observer was required and the ammunition tank and guns had been removed from the compartment immediately behind the pilot's cockpit. It was not pressurised, visibility through the perspex roof was very poor, there was no proper ventilation or heating but as I expected, he was keen to have a go. To give him some impression of the speed I dived down to about 200 feet along the West Solent, the ASI showing about 450 mph, and approached Lee still travelling fairly fast. I knew the aerodrome well but I made two circuits to lose speed and to ensure that other slower aircraft were clear of the approach.

On landing and taxiing back to the Watch Tower we found a small delegation there to meet us. I assumed them to be meeting the Admiral although I was surprised at their presence because I had forgotten to send a signal notifying them of the Admiral's change of plan. I helped the Admiral out but to avoid the complication of having to restart the engines, I kept them running and shortly afterwards made my departure.

Later I learned that the group of people by the Watch Tower were there to arrest me as I had broken several aerodrome rules! I had landed without proper notification, flown high speed in the circuit and landed without a green light as well as other crimes. I was fortunate that when the Admiral appeared from the aircraft all was quickly forgiven. I also heard a rumour that the biggest ticking off was received by the Admiral himself from his wife who said he had no right to go tearing round in jet aircraft at his age. As Flag Officer commanding the Fleet Air Arm he was, I believe, the first head of any flying service to fly in a jet aircraft.

The end of the war in Europe, VE Day, 8 May 1945 was, of course, a day to celebrate and a day of relief, all flying ceasing for three days. It seemed, at first, hard to believe that at last after six years it was over. Ella and I tried to explain to Jane, aged three, what an important day it was but she was too young to understand.

There was great rejoicing in the officers' mess with Mr Noble, the chief steward and major-domo, at his very best and drink flowed all day. 'B' Squadron celebrated by firing their ornamental brass cannon at odd moments which added to the general excitement. The following evening all the officers and men, together with their wives and families, were invited to an enormous bonfire and firework party. An effigy of Hitler was put on the top of the bonfire as well as a captured German flag which was attached to a wire strung between two tall poles. It was a clear, dark night when Air-Commodore Boothman put a match to the bonfire which blazed quickly, the Hitler dummy disappearing in the flames but much to everyone's surprise the swastika did not. The cloth was obviously made of some special asbestos material which would not burn so nearby aircraft were raided for their Verey pistols and cartridges, the firing of which produced a fine coloured display. Despite shooting through the flag, however, it was only brought down by cutting the guy wire off the poles.

Life slowed down considerably after VE Day. On 10 August 1945 I was sent to do the first deck landing trials of the Sea Fury on HMS *Ocean*, a light fleet carrier. I flew it up to Prestwick from Boscombe where I met 'Winkle' Brown who was carrying out similar trials on the Sea Hornet. Waiting to join the ship I was doing practice deck landings on the aerodrome when, while in flight, a pressure gauge in the cockpit burst and a jet of hot hydraulic fluid squirted into my face. Instinctively I put my hand over the gauge and small chips of glass were driven into my hand. The stream of oil soon stopped and fortunately the undercarriage had already locked down. Overnight, the Hawker engineer blanked off the pipe and I continued flying the next day; the hydraulic gauge had been installed in the prototype for test purposes only.

Eventually Winkle and I were ordered to rendezvous with the ship off the Mull of Kintyre. HMS *Ocean* was doing sea trials when we reached her so we circled round watching her. She was going full speed astern and then applying full rudder, no mean test of a rudder! Finally, she headed into wind and with a wind speed of 30 knots over the deck, I was given the 'Land on' signal. I caught a wire, landing safely and, after shutting down, I made my way to the bridge to report to Captain Caspar John, the son of the celebrated painter. I found the whole ship in an uproar of excitement as it had just been announced that after the atom bomb had been dropped on Japan, the Japanese had that day asked for an armistice. The war was over.

The night was spent at Lamlash Bay but no-one had much sleep and the next morning Winkle and I continued with the trials. By the time we had completed the scheduled six landings we were beginning to feel the effects of the previous night's celebrations!

About three o'clock in the afternoon we had finished and I flew off as the ship made her way back to the Clyde. I had just one thought, to get home to my family so I poured on the power and headed south. An hour and five minutes later I landed at Boscombe and was soon home with Ella and Jane, an emotional moment in my life.

CHAPTER 28

Return To Reality

A s I had a job in the family firm of Wedd Jefferson in the City to which I could return after the war, my demobilisation papers came through very quickly. Returning my revolver and other service equipment to the Fleet Air Arm Headquarters at Lee-on-Solent and having said my farewells to the friends I had known at Boscombe Down for the last three years, I collected my free civilian suit from a grateful government at a garage in Portsmouth.

By December 1945 I was my own master again but Ella and I had no home to return to so we began house hunting. It had to be within range of the City but otherwise we had no particular ties except for our bull-terrier, Pooch, who had to have her walks. We finally settled for a country house with four bedrooms at Kingswood about twenty miles south of London near Walton Heath and within walking distance of a railway station. Like every house we looked at it was in a poor state. A flying bomb had fallen 100 yards away so the garage was just a damaged roof on a skeleton framework with no walls while the leaded diamond windows of the house were shattered and the garden of one and a half acres was hopelessly overgrown, although it did have a magnificent oak tree of great age. Relatives and friends helped us out by giving and lending us furniture as all our belongings had been lost in the blitz while in storage.

After seventeen moves during the war it was wonderful to have a permanent home at last even if everything was a bit tatty. We employed some German prisoners-of-war from the local prison camp who tidied up the garden and grew some vegetables but the shops were very bare; furnishings, carpets and food being on strict rationing of course. We gave our prisoners, all of whom were about eighteen, herring and corn on the cob, something they did not eat in Germany! Some busybody from the local council had reported us for rebuilding the garage without permission but they were disappointed to find we had used only blackout paper and a few nails! The eagle eye of bureaucracy was already in full swing. We were lucky enough to find an excellent small private school for Jane nearby and Ella made many new friends.

Shortly after moving in and having had no real holiday I started commuting again. It was a bad mistake as the contrast was too sudden and made worse by the fact that the other young partners had not yet returned from overseas. Another partner had taken over as Senior Partner when the popular George Wilkins had died but, although the size of the market had increased by about five times, Wedd Jefferson, as one of the biggest dealers pre-war, had slipped badly. My brother David had had a great dislike of our new head and had retired from the firm in 1931 as a result of his attitude which had caused him to suffer a nervous breakdown. My brother Jack was demobilised early and had returned to the Stock Exchange to take over the corporation stocks by the time of my own return.

I joined young Dick Wilkins, George Wilkins's son, who had recently been made a partner dealing in the main British Government stocks, just as I had done as a very junior dealer before the war, but I too took an instant dislike to the Senior Partner who I found to be insensitive and very difficult to deal with. I had grown up during the five-and-a-half years of war changing from a nervous, shy junior very conscious of being the poor relation and lacking in self-confidence, to a man with self-assured maturity. One morning after about three months of trying to 'get on' with our new leader, he arrived late due to his train being delayed through fog. Dick Wilkins and I had gone ahead and opened the market, a task we felt quite competent to do, but the head was furious when he came into the Stock Exchange, losing his temper and telling us to 'get off his pitch' and 'now you have had your fun go down and get some work done'. We were both furious, me especially, as I threw my jobbing book down on the seat and walked out of the Stock Exchange in a rage. That evening I called for a Partners Meeting and although I had calmed down a little by then I informed my partners that I could no longer work with this man and that I wished to resign.

It was a painful affair because Wedd Jefferson was a family firm, my great grandfather having been Harry Jefferson, and telling Ella that evening was a shattering moment. Having endured the war years Ella, naturally, was looking forward to a life of peace, security and stability, but I had made this very big decision without even consulting her first, and yet she never condemned me. It also meant, of course, that our financial future from then onwards would be very bleak, to put it mildly.

I had never been very interested in making vast sums of money but I had had my fingers on the very pulse of the nation's economy while working in the financial world and, at times, it could be a thrilling experience; I had, however, thrown the opportunity away and had to face the consequences of my decision.

With what little money we had we started to look around for something else and finally decided to start a little company with Dick Wilkins, hoping to exploit some inventions of a friend of his connected with automatic clutches for cars. I took an Austin fitted with one of our clutches over to Detroit but nothing came of my visit although later the Chairman of Royal Doulton's china, who I had met on board the *Mauritania,* offered me a directorship in his company. After some early interest in the invention when we made prototypes for various manufacturers including Morris Motors and R A Lister, it became clear that no British car manufacturer would rely on electricity for the main transmission. That really finished the company and we ran out of money but fortunately we were able to sell the company for its losses for tax purposes which in those days was possible.

While I had been endeavouring to exploit these inventions my partners in the City had also come to the same conclusion as I had concerning the Senior Partner at Wedd Jefferson and had somehow 'persuaded' him to resign at which point they invited me to rejoin the firm in 1950; I accepted with great relief. My brother, Jack, then became Senior Partner and the firm flourished especially from the efforts of Dick who became, perhaps, the best known and certainly the most successful jobber in the market.

I had not completely given up flying in post-war years, although I realised that I should never fly a service aircraft again, and as there were many surplus aircraft for sale in the spring of 1946 I bought a Fairey Tipsy which had been built by the Belgian subsidiary company before the war. Richard Muspratt, a friend from 'A' per T, who was still a test pilot with Hawkers, and I entered the Tipsy for a race at Lympne and although we came nowhere in the race, we had a good day, meeting friends and doing some low flying. In many ways it was a delightful aircraft of very light construction but the 60 hp of the Walter Mikron engine was not really powerful enough to make it a practical machine so I sold it buying a Percival Proctor as a replacement.

The Proctor was nearly new, similar to those used by the Fleet Air Arm at Worthy Down to train wireless operators, and for which I paid the vast sum of £1000. I never liked it, selling it shortly afterwards but not before Ella and I flew to Deauville when the French Aero Club very kindly invited members of the Royal Aero Club to a weekend rally. We stayed at the Hotel Royale which had been Goering's headquarters during the Battle of Britain but the receptions on both evenings were held in the restaurant of the Casino, Les Ambassadeurs. We were astonished to find such luxury after the war years; the dinners were real gourmets' dreams, seven courses with appropriate wines while the women were wearing the most lovely clothes, obviously the latest Paris models, and laden with jewels. We were still very heavily rationed for clothes, in fact everything, so we just stared and wondered. Ella, of course, had no suitable clothes so she had adapted an old blackout curtain and added a few frills. I am afraid it was no fun for her but she did at least win the Landing Competition which was for the most apt remark on landing in France. Ella came up with 'I came, I saw, I *was* conquered'. Robert Perfect from Westlands had come over in his new Vanguard car and six of us had a mad, hilarious drive in a haze of Pernod, to see the Bayeux Tapestry. One of our party had previously taken the bridge over the river to Trouville in his army tank giving us quite a vivid description of the action.

In 1950 a friend of mine, Jack Davis, loaned me his Hirtenberg to compete in the Daily Express Challenge Trophy, a race round the south coast. Jack had been the representative for Bristol Aero Engines in Europe which had given him the opportunity to visit many aerodromes and meet many personalities in the aviation world in the year just before the war. The aircraft had, I believe, been built in Austria and was an open two-seater, high wing, braced monoplane but built more as a military trainer than as a private aircraft, a pleasant aircraft to fly but slightly underpowered with the 120 hp Gipsy Major. Having had my appetite whetted again I found and bought a Moth Minor for £160.

The de Havilland Company had built the Moth Minor in 1939 when the government had commandeered all private aircraft at the outbreak of war. De Havillands had intended phasing out the Tiger Moth, a fifteen-year-old bi-plane design and were concentrating on this new monoplane as a trainer. The start of the war, however, led to an immediate demand for large numbers of trainers and as the Moth Minor was still in an early stage of development and also fitted with the Gipsy Minor, an entirely new 90 hp engine, it was decided to concentrate on the Tiger Moth of which thousands were ultimately built. I liked the Moth Minor and kept it for nine years. It was a simple clean design, economical to run with a cruising speed of about 100 mph. As it was normally flown from the front seat, the cockpit was relatively free of draught and quiet.

I entered several Air Races during 1953 and 1954. By making a number of minor modifications to the standard Moth Minor and by preparing the engine carefully, I obtained an increase in speed of the order of 4 or 5 mph. Unfortunately these modifications were noticed by the handicappers who promptly altered my starting time after estimating that the aircraft would be 7 or 8 mph faster.

The following year I removed all the visible alterations but left in place a non-standard bulkhead between the cockpits and another at the front of the engine cowling which gave about an extra 3 mph by sealing off air leaks. The result was that I won the Grosvenor Challenger Cup Race and was third in the King's Cup being passed by two aircraft between the aerodrome hedge and the finishing post.

Another form of competition for private aircraft was an economy and navigation exercise which seemed, in many ways, more sensible than air racing and certainly it had a more practical application for the private owner. I took a great deal of trouble and enjoyed preparing the Moth Minor for an event of this kind which took place at Panshanger. I gave the engine a top overhaul during the winter taking the cylinder heads home to my workshop for polishing, completing the final tuning of the carburettor by fitting short exhaust stubs and running it at night to get the right mixture for economy from the colour of the flames from the exhaust. Over the course, which extended to about 160 miles, the aircraft averaged 28 miles to a gallon which was good enough to win the first prize of £100. Its most economic cruising speed was, however, only about 70 mph.

One evening in the summer of 1955 I was flying from Redhill to take part in another navigation competition at Cranfield. At about 2000 feet over Great Missenden and cruising along quietly, the engine suddenly lost power. The engine ran alright at a fast idle speed but coughed and spluttered on opening the throttle. There was a fair sized field to the east of the village but the crop had recently been harvested and it was covered haphazardly with bales of straw. I thought I could see a straight line through these but unfortunately the field sloped slightly downhill and at the end of my run the port wing trailing edge hit a bale.

I suspected a choked main jet which in fact it proved to be, but I had hardly opened the engine cowling when three people appeared offering help. They introduced themselves as Roald Dahl, an ex-fighter pilot, his wife Patricia Neal and Sir Matthew Smith. At the time their names meant little to me but it is not often that one can drop out of the sky, so to speak, to be greeted by a well-known author, a glamourous film star and a celebrated painter!

As they had a car, they very kindly drove me into Missenden to the local cobbler where I bought some thick thread and a needle to repair the wing fabric and then on to the local farmer for me to apologise for landing in his field. On arrival the door was opened by a butler who greeted me with the news that the host was changing and would be down in a few minutes but in the meantime would I like a drink. It turned out that there was to be a party that night and the butler had mistaken me for a guest. Altogether it was a forced landing to be remembered.

I had kept the Moth Minor at Redhill but it was a wooden aircraft which had been glued with cassein glue which hardens with age and becomes brittle. Although it still had a full Certificate of Airworthiness I thought it was time to sell it. As a member of the Redhill Tiger Club, I continued to fly their aircraft enabling me to keep my licence up to date. In 1970, however, my licence finally lapsed when high blood pressure put an end to my flying at the age of 62. I was disappointed but I had had a good run as I had had 42 years of active flying and more than my share of luck and excitement.

EPILOGUE

L ooking back I realise how very fortunate I have been. My decision to go to Canada after learning to fly was just a hopeful leap in the dark but it had a profound effect on my life and character. The urge to fly had been very strong, unbelievably strong, so that I disregarded my parents' advice, giving up any advanced education, even leaving the country for an unknown future. Thanks to many older pilots' experience and help I learned about life the hard way. The Far North and the Arctic taught me the elements of survival and an appreciation of the wide open spaces where a man stands on his own two feet and is judged by his ability. Looking back it was an astonishing effort to establish one of the first air lines in the world and under conditions of which most people have no concept.

It was a great moment to be accepted by the Royal Navy in 1939, to fly service aircraft and finally serve as a fighter pilot at sea in the Home Fleet. As a peacetime civilian pilot, to land on board and be accepted by the Regulars, was the greatest honour. One soon learned the ropes but it took a little time to become accustomed to the centuries old traditions and customs. As a member of the crew of a carrier, one became part of the ship's company and knew that if one was forced down into the sea the ship, if possible, would come to look for you. This was a definition of fellowship which embraces the old saying of 'one for all and all for one'; it certainly gave a boost to my morale.

To be sent by the Admiralty to help in seeing the Seafire developed for naval service was another turning point in my life. Jeffrey Quill, the senior test pilot of Supermarines, became my best friend and most able teacher. The designer of the Spitfire had never considered its use on the deck of a carrier and although the Seafire version had an unmatched performance in flight, the well known short-comings on the deck caused many accidents. I was fortunate in being involved in all the current marks of developing Spitfires which ultimately went into first line service in the Royal Air Force.

For the last two-and-a-half years of the war at the Aeroplane and Armament Experimental Establishment I was sent to 'A' Flight Performance Testing Squadron ('A' per T), the fighter and single engined aircraft testing flight. I was lucky to find myself testing the fastest and highest flying aircraft of the Allies. I could not help feeling that I had at last disproved the doctor's original assessment of me as being an unsuitable recruit for the RAF which had hurt me so much in my youth.

Undoubtedly the high point in my life came on 15 March 1944 when I was sent to Gloster to fly the F9/40 or prototype Meteor with the first W11b Whittle engines, the first jet fighter and the first gas turbines to fly in this country. The turbine engine was then unknown but its merits for aircraft were quickly appreciated, and were finally to dominate all aircraft including, in particular, all civil passenger aircraft.

One evening in 1983 I was walking in the grounds of the Royal Hospital, Chelsea, when I heard a roar of engines and saw Concorde for the first time. The long white pencil body and delta shaped wing was the most beautiful sight in the evening sun. When an old pensioner, bursting with pride, came up to me, a total stranger, and said, 'That's Concorde.' I was overcome with emotion and could not speak. It was truly the culmination of man's effort in my lifetime.

APPENDIX

AIRCRAFT TYPES FLOWN

Date	Aircraft	Engine	Comments

1928 Henderson School of Flying - Brooklands

Date	Aircraft	Engine	Comments
09.08.28	Avro 504	Renault 80	Air Cooled V8
09.08.28	Avro 504	Anzani	10 Cyl. Radial

30.09.28 International Airways of Canada Montreal

Date	Aircraft	Engine	Comments
06.12.28	DH Moth	Cirrus	
17.07.29	Fairchild FC1	Wright Whirlwind	Engineer
02.08.29	Vickers Vedett		Dual
24.08.29	Fairchild FC2-WC2	P & W Wasp	Engineer
06.09.29	Curtiss HS2L Liberty	Photographer	
10.10.29	Ireland Amphibian		Dual

05.12.29 Commercial Airways Limited - Edmonton

Date	Aircraft	Engine	Comments
08.12.29	Lockheed Vega	P & W Wasp	Engineer
06.01.30	Bellanca CH300	Wright Whirlwind	Skis
08.02.30	Bellanca Pacemaker	Wright Whirlwind	Skis
13.05.30	Bellanca Pacemaker	Wright Whirlwind	Floats

(30.04.31 Company taken over by Western Canada Airways)

1934-39 Private and Club Flying

Date	Aircraft	Engine	Comments
09.06.34	Klemm	Salmson	
06.07.34	Desouter	DH Cirrus	
10.09.35	'Cierva C.19	AS Mongoose	Autogiro
25.07.36	DH Hornet Moth	DH Gipsy	
18.02.39	DH Tiger Moth	DH Gipsy	
28.08.39	DH Moth Minor	DH Gipsy Minor	

Sept.1939 Royal Navy Fleet Air Arm

Date	Aircraft	Engine	Comments
20.09.39	Miles Magister	DH Gipsy	
25.09.39	Hawker Osprey	Kestrel	
28.09.39	Fairey Seal	AS Panther	
03.10.39	Hawker Nimrod	RR Kestrel	
04.10.39	Percival Vega Gull	DH Gipsy 6	
11.10.39	Blackburn Shark	AS Tiger	
11.01.40	Fairey Sea Fox	Napier Dagger	Floatplane
19.10.40	Percival Proctor	DH Gipsy 6	
20.01.40	Fairey Swordfish	Bristol Pegasus	
22.01.40	Blackburn Skua	Bristol Perseus	

Date	Aircraft	Engine	Comments
08.02.40	Supermarine Walrus	Bristol Pegasus	Amphibian
09.03.40	Fairey Albacore	Bristol Taurus	
11.04.40	Blackburn Roc	Bristol Perseus	
06.05.40	Blackburn Roc	Bristol Perseus	Floatplane
21.05.40	Fairey Fulmar	RR Merlin	
24.06.40	Gloster Gladiator	Bristol Pegasus	
15.08.40	V-S Spitfire	Merlin Mks.IA,IIB,VA, VB,VI,VII,VIII, VIIIC,IX,IXC	
01.08.40	DH Leopard Moth	DH Gipsy	
12.12.40	Fairey Battle	RR Merlin	
26.02.41	Hawker Hurricane	RR Merlin	
28.02.41	Grumman Martlet	Wright Cyclone	US Navy F4F Wildcat
26.06.41	Curtiss Mohawk	Wright Cyclone	USAF P-36
17.08.41	Fiat CR 42	Fiat	
05.09.41	Bristol Blenheim	Bristol Mercury	
22.11.41	Messerschmitt Bf 109E-3	Daimler-Benz DB-601	

July 1942 Vickers Supermarine - Eastleigh

Date	Aircraft	Engine	Comments
08.07.42	Miles Falcon	DH Gipsy	
08.07.42	Hawker Tomtit	AS Mongoose	
09.07.42	Monospar	Pobjoy	
20.07.42	V-S Seafire	RR Merlin	Mks.IB,IIC,III
20.07.42	V-S Seafire	RR Griffon	Mks.XV,XVII
06.08.42	V-S Spitfire	RR Merlin	Pressure Cabin, Mk VI
02.09.42	V-S Spitfire	RR Griffon	Mks.XIV,X IX,X XI
06.09.42	Airspeed Oxford	AS Cheetah	
19.09.42	NA Mustang	RR Merlin	USAF P-51
13.10.42	V-S Spitfire	RR Merlin	Floatplane
17.10.42	Hawker Tornado	Rr Vulture	Contra-Propeller
22.11.42	V-S Spitfire	RR Merlin	Mks.PRs X,XI
23.11.42	V-S Sea Otter	Bristol Mercury	Amphibian
15.03.43	Supermarine S24/37	RR Merlin	

Apr. 1943 Royal Navy Fleet Air Arm - 'A' Flight Performance Testing Squadron, Boscombe Down

Aeroplane and Armament Experimental Establishment

Date	Aircraft	Engine	Comments
28.04.43	Hawker Typhoon	Napier Sabre	
28.04.43	Fairey Firefly	RR Griffon	
30.04.43	Westland Welkin	RR Merlin	
04.05.43	Miles Mentor	DH Gipsy 6	
05.05.43	Curtiss Kittyhawk	Allison	USAF P-40
11.05.43	Republic Thunderbolt	P&W Double Wasp	USAF P-47
01.06.43	Fairey Barracuda	RR Merlin 32	
13.06.43	Boeing B-17	Wright Cyclone	Flying Fortress

Date	Aircraft	Engine	Comments
14.06.43	Handley Page-Halifax	RR Merlin	
15.06.43	Curtiss Seamew	Ranger	
27.06.43	Avro Anson	AS Cheetah	
05.07.43	Boulton Paul P 92	DH Gipsy	Turret Gun (½-scale)
05.07.43	Grumman Hellcat	Wright Cyclone	US Navy F6F
28.07.43	Stinson Reliant	Lycoming	
05.08.43	Blackburn Firebrand	Napier Sabre III	Mk I
07.08.43	Vought Corsair	P&W Double Wasp	US Navy F4U Mk.I
27.10.43	Hawker Tempest	Bristol Centaurus	Mk.II
12.12.43	Short Stirling	Pobjoy	Half-scale Model
01.01.44	Auster	Lycoming	
08.01.44	DH Mosquito	RR Merlin 72	Mk.IX
09.03.44	Blackburn Firebrand	Bristol Centaurus	Mk.III
15.03.44	Gloster F.9/40	Whittle WIIb	Meteor
26.03.44	Harvard	P&W Wasp	
26.03.44	Handley Page-Hampden	Bristol Pegasus	
22.04.44	DH E6/41	DH Halford HIb	Vampire
06.06.44	Gloster Meteor	Rr B/37	Mk.III
05.07.44	Miles M17	Gipsy	
06.07.44	Beechcraft	P&W Wasp	
15.08.44	Douglas Dauntless	Wright Cyclone	US Navy SBD
27.08.44	NA Mustang Mk.V	Packard Merlin	USAF P-51
14.09.44	Miles Monarch	DH Gipsy Major	
23.10.44	Hawker F2/43	Bristol Centaurus	Fury
30.10.44	Bristol Beaufighter	Bristol Hercules	
19.01.45	Douglas Boston	Wright Cyclone	Mk.IIIA
20.01.45	Beech Traveller	P&W Wasp	Staggerwing
27.02.45	Miles Messenger	DH Gipsy	
28.02.45	Grumman Tiger Cat	P&W Double Wasp	US Navy F7F
01.03.45	DH Hornet	RR Merlin	
03.03.45	Douglas Skymaster	P&W Double Wasp	
20.03.45	Lockheed Hudson	P&W Wasp	
01.05.45	CAL Cygnet	Cirrus	
17.05.45	Fieseler Storch	Argus Fi-156	
25.05.45	Hawker Sea Fury	Bristol Centaurus	
12.06.45	V-S Spiteful	RR Griffon	
21.06.45	Grumman Wildcat	P&W Double Wasp	US Navy F4F
20.07.45	Fairey Barracuda	RR Griffon Mk.V	
27.08.45	Grumman Avenger	Wright Cyclone	US Navy TBF
20.09.45	Consolidated B-24	P&W Wasp	Liberator
29.09.45	DH Dominie	DH Gipsy 6	

April 1946   Private and Club

Date	Aircraft	Engine	Comments
04.04.46	Fairey Tipsy	Walter Micron	
21.08.50	Hirtenberg HS9A	DH Gipsy	
11.07.62	Jodel 1050	Continental	
06.03.63	DH Puss Moth	DH Gipsy	
10.07.63	Condor	DH Gipsy	
12.10.63	Turbulent	Volkswagen	
27.10.63	Super Cub	Lycoming	
29.05.64	Jodel 150 Muscadet	Continental	
01.06.66	Britten Norman Islander	Lycoming	
09.02.69	PiperTripacer	Lycoming	

INDEX